MADHAVI MENON is professor of English at Ashoka University, and writes on desire and queer theory. She is the author of *Wanton Words: Rhetoric and Sexuality in English Renaissance Drama*; *Unhistorical Shakespeare: Queer Theory in Shakespearean Literature and Film*; and *Indifference to Difference: On Queer Universalism*. She is also the editor of *Shakesqueer: A Queer Companion to the Complete Works of Shakespeare*.

INFINITE VARIETY

A History of Desire in India

MADHAVI MENON

SPEAKING
TIGER

SPEAKING TIGER PUBLISHING PVT. LTD
4381/4, Ansari Road, Daryaganj
New Delhi-110002

First published in India by Speaking Tiger 2018

Copyright © Madhavi Menon 2018

ISBN: 978-93-87693-28-9
eISBN: 978-93-87693-24-1

10 9 8 7 6 5 4 3 2 1

Typeset in Garamond Minion Pro by SÜRYA, New Delhi
Printed at Naveen Printers, Okhla, New Delhi

There are so many ways of doing everything, all over India, that descriptions quickly fade into falsehood.

—E.M. Forster, *Abinger Harvest* (1935)

If not him, there is his brother—
Mir, are there any restrictions in love?

—Mir Taqi Mir (1723-1810)

Like a silkworm weaving
her house with love from her marrow,
and dying in her body's threads winding tight,
round and round,
I burn desiring what the heart desires.

—Mahadeviyakka (12th century CE)

Passion knows no order.

—Vatsyayana, *Kamasutra* (3rd century CE)

Contents

INTRODUCTION

A History of Impurity

Two women sip wine as they caress one another. All around them is beauty and light. They enjoy the revels with abandon, their jewels sparkling, and look straight at the artist who is putting up their image for posterity. People from around the world will see this image and wonder at its sensuality.

An Instagram photo taken in one of the metropolises of the world in the 21st century, you think? No. Try an 18th-century painting from rural Rajasthan.

I first went to the village of Samode in 2014. We set off from Delhi at the crack of dawn, to escape the heavy traffic that builds up after daybreak around the industrial hub of Manesar. It was a hot day in August, and the sun was bright even at 6.30 in the morning. After a five-hour drive, we arrived at a grand hotel in Rajasthan, 40 kilometres north of the state capital Jaipur. Built as a fort in the 16th century and then converted into a palace in the early 19th century, Samode Palace is now a heritage hotel. It has a magnificent Sheesh Mahal, or Palace of Mirrors, and its Darbar Hall is decorated from floor to ceiling with exquisite paintings. The palace is built in the syncretic Muslim-Hindu style of architecture, and the paintings all use vivid pigments. The artwork draws from themes both religious and secular—sensuous images of Krishna and Radha vie for space with our two women, who in turn rub shoulders with soldiers and sadhus. Desire is of the world, and it extends across what we now term hetero- and homo-sexuality, both of which co-exist happily alongside polyamory (Krishna with many gopis) and celibacy (saints with matted hair).

I am fascinated by these multiple versions of desire because these are the desires with which I grew up. All around me in the Delhi of the 1970s and '80s were Hindi films that celebrated same-sex attachments (*Anand*), older women desiring younger men (*Doosra Aadmi*), and cross-couple desire (*Angoor*). Equally, there was Bharatanatyam dance in which dancers played the parts of both men and women, lover and beloved. Sufi qawwalis that sang of mutual longing between two men. And dotting the landscape were transgendered hijras whom we were taught to respect at all times.

In the West, these multiple desires are greeted as new-fangled ideas, and in India now they are increasingly treated as foreign conspiracies. It was only after returning from 18 years of studying and working in the US that I was able to realize the complexity of this landscape of desire.

The legendary actor and singer Bal Gandharva,
who performed female roles in several
popular Marathi plays in the early 1900s.
Source: YouTube

When I first decided to move back to Delhi, friends and colleagues asked me how I would continue my work on queer theory in a country that was becoming increasingly puritanical and sexually violent. The pub attacks in Bangalore on Valentine's Day had already happened, reports of rape were on the rise, and misogyny was getting nationalized. Homosexuality had always been outlawed under an outmoded British law and was soon to be recriminalized after a brief reprieve.

But: despite a scant academic presence of sexuality studies in the form of syllabi, centres and university departments, India has a *lived* relation to desire that makes it much easier to speak about various desires to a wider audience. Millions of people know the stories of cross-dressing gods. Men hold hands freely. Women frequently sleep in the same bed. This is a country that is deeply homophilic even as it is often superficially homophobic. The intellectual and cultural histories of desire are both broad and deep: here, desire is not just, or even primarily, an academic subject. I soon realized that my interest in desire—my desire for desire—was not a *consequence* of my graduate work in the US. Rather, my graduate work on desire was a consequence of the fact that I had grown up in India.

Because desire here is everywhere. I daresay that is true all over the world, but both the restrictions and the permissions seem to be more intense here. What is considered taboo in the US—heterosexual men sharing the same bed, for instance—passes here without comment. And what elicits no reaction in other places—the length of one's hair, for example—is intensely policed and debated here. In India, even a law against homosexuality does not prevent a simultaneous law supporting transsexuality. Consistency is not the favoured mode in India, especially in relation to desire. We have very strict rules about What Must be Done: (heterosexual) marriage and producing children are flourishing businesses. But equally, we have long histories that valorize celibacy, and goddesses who model childlessness. So which one is the 'real' India? The answer—fortunately for us—is 'all of the above'. The history of desire in India reveals not purity but *im*purity as a way of life. Not one answer, but many. Not a single history, but multiple tales cutting across laws and boundaries.

What I find fascinating is how much this impurity offers a counterpoint to regimes of desire in other parts of the world. For example, sexual repression in India has historically been foisted on hetero- rather than homo-sexuality. As a gay man from Bangalore told the mathematician Shakuntala Devi in a 1976 interview she recorded in *The World of Homosexuals*:

> Some heterosexuals are much more oppressed. I couldn't have lived with Seenu for nearly four years so openly had he been a woman. I daren't be seen with a girl so often in public as I do with Mohan. Somehow people are so little aware of homosexuality in this country, though such a lot exists. Two boys, or for that matter two girls, can do anything they want, no one says anything. Not even parents suspect. But a boy and a girl can't get away with it.

One way of explaining the acceptability of this public camaraderie is that people here do not always recognize same-sex intimacy as being sexual. Heterosexuality is closely monitored in India because that is where people assume sex takes place. Unmarried men and women cannot mingle freely without inviting disapproval. But men together and women together in close and even intimate proximity do not elicit a second glance. They tend to fly below the marriage radar, and so their sexual activity or inactivity is not presumed. Equally, however, one might think of this laissez faire attitude towards same-sex intimacy as a historical reminder of what was once commonplace and continues to thrive in popular activities such as the launda naach, in which men dress as women and perform satirical plays and provocative dances.

A related reason for this seeming nonchalance towards same-sex intimacy is that sexualities have not always been *named* in India. The wide range of publicly sanctioned intimacies here would elsewhere be labelled as sexual identities. But in the Indian subcontinent, desires are multiple and names for them scant. Is a woman who gets married to a man but whose closest bonds are with another woman, a lesbian or a heterosexual? Bisexual, perhaps? All or none of the above? What about a man who sleeps with another man but does not have sex with him? Homo, hetero, bi, none, all? Escaping legal and reproductive constraints— whether through multiple naming, celibacy, tantric yoga, cosmopolitan nonchalance, life in a religious order, forest life, or a royal court—has a respectable history in several Indian traditions. Far from being seen as escapes from desire, they are viewed as desires that have escaped constraints. This is the reason why Vatsyayana's 3rd-century CE *Kamasutra* insists that 'passion knows no order'. So much so that even when his text provides an exhaustive taxonomy of sexual desires and acts, it regularly points out exceptions to its rules—desires that defy its own classification.

In the America in which I did my graduate work, desires automatically translate into sexual identities. But in the

religious, literary and performative histories of India, desire
is described repeatedly as the thing that escapes control. This
is why, when I went on to write my dissertation, my interest
was in queer theory—in desires that overflow the constraints
of identity. Desires that are not celebrated as the norm; that
take many forms. After all, I had grown up in a culture in
which every legend and myth has multiple versions. And
where impurity embodies the condition of desire.

But 'embodies' is the wrong word.

Famously, Kama, the Hindu god of romantic and sexual
desire, is ananga—without limbs, and therefore without a
body. Which means that historically in India, desire is seen
as being everywhere. Anything can be considered an object
or subject of desire. Desire is not confined to a (human)
body. The legend goes that Kama (in one version, born of
the creator, Brahma) is deputed to induce desire in Shiva's
breast so that an offspring of Shiva and Parvati might be
created to defeat the demon Tarakasura. Shiva is so incensed
at being awoken from his yogic meditations that he opens
his third eye and burns Kama to cinders. Shiva relents when
Parvati begs him to undo the consequences of his wrath. He
allows Kama to live, but only without a body. Thus is born
the bodiless god of desire.

These mythological and even pre-historic traces of desire
in India seem startlingly modern. According to Shakuntala
Devi, 'archeologists [in India] have found pre-historic cave
drawings showing female figures engaged in cunnilingus,'
which suggests early and intimate knowledge of what women
might do sexually with other women. And, she adds, 'In the
Ramayana, Rama is described as *Purushamohana Rupaya*—
so handsome as to be pleasing even to men,' which suggests

more than a passing knowledge, several centuries ago, of what kind of man might appear attractive to other men. Tales of amorous, sometimes adulterous, play among Radha, Krishna and the gopis have provided the richest vein for artistic production across the centuries and across schools of dance, poetry, song and painting.

Desire runs rampant across Indian Hindu traditions and texts. Kalidasa's celebrated 5th-century epic, the *Kumarasambhavam* (the Birth of Kumara), devotes an entire canto of 91 verses to a detailed description of Uma's erotic pleasures with Shiva. There are sculptures of anal sex—and bestiality and threesomes and orgies—on the walls of the Hindu and Jain temples at Khajuraho dating from over a thousand years ago. The *Kamasutra's* elucidation of people in India who have anal sex even provides a geographical location for them—according to Vatsyayana, and perhaps appropriately enough, they live in the South.

In Indian Islamic traditions, Mahmud of Ghazni—the first Muslim ruler of parts of what are now North India—was openly celebrated for his love of his cupbearer, Ayaz: Scott Kugle notes that 'In Persianate lands [including India, Iran, Afghanistan and Central Asia], Mahmud and Ayaz were always mentioned as a pair, on par with heterosexual romantic partners like Laila and Majnun, or Heer and Ranjha.' (And as Saleem Kidwai reminds us, Mahmud and Ayaz's love story is the only one in the genre that has a happy ending for the lovers.) Some Mughal rulers commissioned paintings that were frankly sensual, like the paintings of women bathing in the harem that were produced during Jahangir's reign. The 18th-century Mughal emperor Muhammad Shah II commissioned miniature paintings of himself having sex with his mistress.

Such explicit desire extends from the court to the commons, from the secular to the sacred, and from the school to the street. In Saleem Kidwai's translation of a 13th-century Hindavi poem, Amir Khusro addresses his Sufi master, Nizamuddin Auliya, thus:

My blossoming youth is red with passion
How can I spend this time alone?
Will someone persuade Nizamuddin Auliya,
For the more I coax him, the more he acts coy…
I'll break my bangles and throw them on the bed,
I'll set fire to this bodice of mine.
The empty bed frightens me
The fire of separation scorches me.

The mystical Sufis both celebrate the sexual allure of the body and make desire larger than the individual body before them. There are multiple Sufi orders or silsilas, each of which emphasizes a close—what many would today consider *too* close—bond between pir and murid, or master and disciple. This is the relationship that Khusro writes about so passionately. And the flipside of this passion—nonchalance—also marks desire, as is evident in the 18th-century poem by the Urdu great Mir Taqi Mir: 'If not him, there is his brother—/ Mir, are there any restrictions in love?'

But what is the relation between these texts and works of art and mystical traditions, on the one hand, and the fabric of lived social reality, on the other? There is not much that we know by way of historical data. All we can conjecture is that sexually explicit temple carvings, poems drenched in desire and same-sex mysticism were not unusual or atypical in ancient and medieval India. I should also emphasize that this book involves an active reading of these texts and phenomena. This reading is not meant to give us the *truth* of the past but rather an insight into what there might be in the past that can interrupt and complicate our drive to purity in a present that seems eager to sanitize our histories.

In this messy set of histories to which we are heir, India has been formed by multiple cultures in which same-sex desire, polygamy, polyandry and polyamory in general have been rife. The porousness of sexual borders has been of a piece with the openness of the geographical, trade and cultural boundaries of 'India' over the years. Ironically, this is one of the reasons why the British found it so easy to colonize the subcontinent—they walked right in because the borders were open. (And it is important to note that many of them walked in *because* they could find in India the sexual licence that they had been denied in England.) But unlike the hundreds of thousands of people before them who too had walked in— the Aryans, the Greeks, the Ghaznis, the Mughals, the early Syrian Christians, the Parsis, the Armenians, the Chinese, the Arabs—and woven their desires with what they found here, the British colonizers did something different. In response to the porousness of the borders that had let them in, they sought to close them down. In matters of desire, India was made part of an Empire that officially overlaid moral mores onto capitalistic concerns. Even as the colonial masters started to bleed India economically, they shored up their presumed moral superiority by policing what the 'natives' did sexually. Suddenly, they introduced a legal code against sexual proclivities that did not conduce to the reproduction of the missionary position. This continues to be the basis for the Indian Penal Code in effect in postcolonial India.

But despite the seeming rupture in the fabric of India's desires, the historical lines between an era of permissiveness and an era of repression cannot be drawn quite so neatly. India, before it was the political entity of India that we know today—which is largely a British invention—contained several of the same puritanical streaks that the British were able to exploit to their advantage. After all, if, as I have claimed, notions of desire across Indian cultures are marked by impurity, then surely such impurity arose as a reaction to a well-entrenched notion of purity?

And so it was: the sexually explicit *Kamasutra* sat alongside the sexually punitive *Manusmriti*; Sufism whirled around prohibitions against homosexuality; fluidity tiptoed on the heels of rigidity. There were strictures against bodily 'pollution' among the Hindus that restricted oral and anal sexual activities; there were restrictions on female sexuality across religions; the caste hierarchy strictly prescribed who is an appropriate object of desire and who is not—so much so that even the shadow of a lower-caste person was considered a contaminant for the upper castes. Consider, for instance, this episode narrated in Devaki Nilayamgode's *Antharjanam: Memoirs of a Namboodiri Woman* (Namboodiri is the term used to describe Kerala Brahmins; antharjanams are the women Brahmins who have historically led a horrific life based on deprvivation and steeped in misogyny.) In Indira Menon's translation of the text, the narrator describes some of the lines of purity that strictly policed a Brahmin woman in Kerala, well into the 20th century:

These helpers always went with antharjanams, walking ahead of them even on a trip to the nearest temple. One of their duties was to order the lower castes to make way for the antharjanam. Yet another duty was to carry the children; if an antharjanam had two or three, she would be allowed as many helpers. If a person of a lower caste strayed into their path, the woman would draw a line on the ground which the person was asked not to cross. Then she would measure the distance between them and the line to determine whether the antharjanam had been polluted by the untouchable. If the approaching person was a carpenter, then it was important to check whether he was carrying the measuring rule, because if he was, his presence did not sully the antharjanam.

The notion of ritual and sexual purity long predated the arrival of the British. What the British managed to do in their deadly political ploy was to tilt the balance away from permissiveness and towards purity. When politicians today speak about 'Indian values' in relation to sexuality, they mean a concoction of patriarchal British prudery and minority Indian practices that are now threatening to overwhelm the alternative histories sketched out in this book.

So where is this India we are talking about, and what is its desire?

Geographically and politically, India has not been 'India' for much of the history of this land. At its most expansive, 'India' has included what is now Pakistan, areas of Afghanistan, Burma, Nepal and Bangladesh. The current political entity of India is the result of a bloody Partition in 1947, and consolidations through persuasion and coercion after 1947. But parts of these borders continue to be disputed by India's neighbours. When we speak of desire in 'India', then, we do not stand on very firm ground. Desire in India has always been a desire that is not confined to one geographical entity alone. Instead, it has grown out of conversations *across* what are now physical borders. It has metamorphosed over centuries during which ideas did not require a visa to travel.

There is a 12th-century Javanese poem, for instance, that narrates Kama being rendered bodiless by the wrath of Shiva, suggesting that 'Indian' influences spread early on to countries that are not geographically or politically contiguous to the current borders of India. The story of Kama being reduced to ashes by Shiva first appears in India in the *Matsya Purana*, thought to have been composed between 250 and 500 CE. If you jump ahead 15 centuries, then the age-old 'Indian' understanding of desire as not being limited to or by the body sounds uncannily like the modern psychoanalytical understanding of desire. Sigmund Freud reminds us in his *Three Essays on the Theory of Sexuality* (1905) that desire is not always or only about sex. Sexual intercourse does not exhaust desire because our desire always exceeds the physical acts of sex. Even if we are married to the same person, and remain faithful to her or him for the rest of our lives, that will still not stop our desires from straying. We will continue to lust after Shah Rukh Khan or Sophia Loren even as we might stay happily married. This is the way desire operates— through fantasy rather than fact. Where would the world's glamour industries be without it?

Psychologist and author Sudhir Kakar notes that 'sexuality is a system of conscious and unconscious human fantasies, arising from various sources, seeking satisfaction in diverse ways, and involving a range of excitations and activities that aim to achieve pleasure that goes *beyond* the satisfaction of any basic somatic need'. Sexual intercourse or even sexual acts cannot dissipate the range of feelings, thoughts and images that make up desire. Instead, desire can attach to fantasy, object, story, person, institution, idea, or all of the above. Vatsyayana would agree with Kakar's description of sexuality as that which goes beyond somatic satisfaction. But to Kakar's suggestion that sexuality is a 'system', Vatsyayana would add that desire escapes systemization. Unlike the categories within which sexual orientations can be slotted, desire spreads out, widely and unevenly.

One of the many definitions of 'desire' provided by the Oxford English Dictionary is: '...that feeling or emotion which is directed to the attainment or possession of some object from which pleasure or satisfaction is expected.' Desire is not (only) love, and neither is it (only) sex. Love tends to capture desire within the sentimental framework of emotions, often through marriage. And sex focuses on acts of genital intercourse that may not always be the end goal or even the basis of desire. I cannot provide a definition of desire because it is precisely the thing that eludes definition. But what this book does claim is that desire in India has been, and has had a tendency to be, messy. It exists *across* what we now classify as sexual identities, subjects and objects, human and non-human, historical periods, geographical sites, street foods, and religious texts. Desire is surprising: it can strike us at moments when we least expect it to. Desire travels: it cannot be contained within strict boundaries. Desire is multiple: it resists being pigeonholed into this or that *thing*. But across its multiple definitions, desire is related to a shiver of pleasure, a shock of pain, an intensity of recognition.

In my case, the intensity of my desire for India is related also to my impurity as an onlooker, my mixed status as both insider and outsider. Between 1995 and 2013, I travelled every year between India and the US. These trips were intellectual and emotional journeys as much as they were physical and geopgraphical ones. I was always sad to leave Delhi, and always happy to return here. But I was also thrilled to be studying and writing and publishing in the US. For most of those years, my study of desire was focussed on Shakespeare rather than India. But *what* I said about desire in Shakespeare was always informed by the multiple histories with which I had grown up, histories in which Shakespeare's praise of sexually 'wanton words' (this phrase was also the title of my first book) resonates with Uma's cries of pleasure in Kalidasa's *Kumarasambhava*, and echoes Mir's come-hither poetry. These worlds of Indian desire are the opposite of swacch Bharat. We live in an intellectual stew that does not incline us towards the single and the clean. Rather, a tendency towards disorder is a way of life here—from the way we drive to what drives our desires.

Very little in these pages thus has anything to do with *pure* objects, ideas or histories. This book also does not focus on acts leading to sexual intercourse, or descriptions of sexual intercourse itself. Instead, each chapter visits a different site— whether object, relation, act or place—that plays a significant role in our *daily* lives. So many of us speak grammatically-inflected languages, go to college, do yoga (not me!), have grandparents, eat paan, and obsess about our hair. But what do these everyday sites have to do with desire? Well, one of the things they do is show us how widespread the ambit of our desires is. What is striking about desire in India is just how capacious it is. So each chapter follows a different idea and traces a history of its relation to desire. But equally, I can imagine a different set of chapters that might make up the roster of this book. Chapters on beedis and hookahs, for instance, or halwa. On medicine and call centres and bazaars. On water and widows and sarees.

Lady under a tree with a hookah.
Miniature from Bikaner, c. 1760

Such imaginative expansiveness is what allows for the simultaneous existence in this book of places, languages and ideas. I have finally been able to bring together my training in queer theory with Mir's haunting passions, the *Kamasutra*'s range of sexualities, Greek pedagogy, Persian poetry and the British desire to codify desire. English and non-English words coexist here without either being italicized or relegated to a glossary. What this means is that our reading will be interrupted, disrupted within the sentence itself by words that might not immediately be familiar. After all, one of the aims of this book is to highlight the idea that, like the kerosene in India, desire too is adulterated, and these adulterations run deep.

Let me end, therefore, with another example of adulterated desire, in a tale of two women. On 23 April 2017, *The Tribune* ran a story about a wedding in Jalandhar, Punjab. Manjit Kaur, a sub-inspector of police (some reports say she is an assistant sub-inspector), married her unnamed long-term girlfriend. Manjit (this can interchangeably be both a man's and a woman's name, which is common in the Sikh community) was dressed in a red turban, and wore a particularly impressive garland of money when she went in a baraat, or bridegroom's party, to wed her bride. (I don't think there is anywhere in the world other than North India and Pakistan where bridegrooms wear garlands made of currency notes.) So impressive was Manjit's garland of money that it is hard to see in the photos what she is wearing underneath it. Her bride is more recognizably dressed in a red and gold salwar kameez, with lots of gold jewellery, and all the markers of a North Indian Hindu bride. The newly-weds travelled home in a chariot after the wedding ceremony—'solemnized as per Hindu rituals', according to *The Tribune*—which took place in a temple and was attended and blessed by both families.

I would like to point out three things. First, this wedding involved a member of the *police* force in a country where the legal taboo around sex 'against the order of nature' hovers like a brooding British bird. Second, no punitive action has been taken against the married couple, even months after the event. And third, the participants in the ceremony have not classified themselves as anything other than lovers in the grip of desire.

In India, laws governing desire are usually not followed. Desires are erratic, not uniform. And passion is not easily codified. The chapters that follow are wanderings through Indian bylanes into which impure, erratic and not easily codified desires stray.

1

Dargahs

Kyaa haqeeqat kahun ki kyaa hai ishq
Haq-shanaason ke haan khudaa hai ishq
(What shall I say is reality and what desire?
For those acquainted with the truth, desire is god.)

—Mir Taqi Mir

It is the middle of the monsoon season. For several days I have put off my trip to the Mehrauli Archaeological Park, but finally decide to brave the puddles and take the plunge. Luckily, it is a breezy morning, and my guide awaits me at a side entrance to the park. Marvelling at the fact that despite being Delhi-born and bred, I have never visited this site before, I start taking in the wonders that await us a short distance inside the boundary wall. Old walls, and entire structures in various states of dilapidation. There is a new mosque on the left, at which I will stop, but not now.

This is the site of Lal Kot, one of the oldest versions of what was later to become Delhi. Founded by Anangpal Tomar in the 8th century, Lal Kot grew into a bustling fort-city under the Rajput king Prithviraj Chauhan in the 12th century. Under the Delhi Sultanate, which replaced Chauhan Rajput rule, it became a cosmopolitan space that flourished even after the Khiljis shifted the seat of power to Siri, a new fort-city some distance away. Many of the ruins around us in Lal Kot date from the 14th and 15th centuries, but there are hints of even older habitation. There is a sign for Balban's Tomb, built in the 13th century, which is widely regarded as the first structure in India to have made use of the arch. But before we get to Balban's Tomb, there is a small gate to the left. We round a corner and turn in through the gate to come upon a wonderful courtyard, with a flourishing tree in the middle of it, and a shallow well-like structure to the right—the wazu khana, where the faithful cleanse themselves before offering namaz. One can still see the underground aqueducts that drained water into the tank centuries before. This is where dusty, weary travellers from afar, and energetic, spiffy pilgrims from closer by, would have come together to clean themselves before entering the old mosque that rises majestically in front us.

A solitary watchman is on guard over this mosque. He sits in the shade provided by one of the arches, enjoying the breeze generated by the tree in the courtyard. He wanders over to chat, confirming that he does indeed get lonely in the absence of visitors. The mosque is a brilliant structure: designed by a Sufi saint named Shaikh Fazlu'llah and built around 1528, it boasts of unique architectural features, including the first recorded use in a mosque of the Rajasthani jharokha or latticed window. It is decorated also with the Star of David (or Daud), which was commonplace under the Mughals. The structure exudes a sense of serenity and beauty, but it is not at present an active mosque where the faithful can pray. Later, when I pause by the new mosque on my way out, the maulvi tells me that the old mosque is populated at night by jinns, creatures from a different dimension that have the power to pass into our world. I have heard this urban legend before, but decide to press the maulvi further. Why, I ask, would jinns come there at night, and how does the maulvi know that they do? The second question he considers unworthy of his attention, but in response to the first one, he provides a very interesting analysis. According to him, Allah does not like his places of worship to be empty, and since the old mosque is now a protected site, he sends jinns to add some life, as it were, to the place. Like people in this world, he adds, jinns too come in all shapes and sizes—some are drunkards, others gamblers, but then there are also the good-hearted ones, and they all together make up the ranks of worshippers in the mosque. Given how atmospheric the mosque is—tranquil, beautiful, caressed by the branches of an ancient tree—it is easy to believe the stories of hauntings by jinns without difficulty.

There is another gate, leading away from the mosque to the right. After ascertaining that we would like to go through this second gate, the security guard unlocks it, leading us into a different courtyard, with wide open spaces, and a flat-roofed structure towards the back left-hand corner. The site is both bucolic—washed clothes flutter lazily in the breeze on lines just outside the courtyard—and majestic—the sculpted archways through which I look out at the lazy linen are stunning.

But even the guard with the keys is powerless to let us into the structure around which the courtyard is built. Apparently the key to this particular building resides in the offices of the Archaeological Survey of India; it would take time, a trip to the ASI offices, and a special petition, before the doors can be opened to us.

This building—the dargah of Jamali-Kamali—has been described as a jewel box. And naturally, like any jewel box containing precious gems, it must lie under lock and key. One can peep into the small tomb through the latticed

'Jamali Kamali tomb' by Varun Shiv Kapur. *Source:* Wikimedia Commons

windows that adorn three walls of the structure. Squinting through the star-shaped holes, hoping to find the light at an illuminating angle, hopping from one positon to the next, I finally see. And what a sight it is. A domed roof painted in sumptuous blue and gold, with intricate patterns traced on its arches, and inscriptions—which I later learn are from the Quran and Jamali's poems—running around the base of the roof. What is interesting about this roof is that it is a dome only on the inside—the dargah is unusual in as much as it has a flat roof rather than a dome on the outside. What the reason for this might be, we do not know, but it seems to be a mark of humility. Rather than a tower or a dome reaching towards Allah, the Jamali-Kamali tomb has a flat roof on which to receive the word of god.

'Jamali' is the pen name of Shaikh Hamid bin Fazlu'llah, a Persian Sufi poet and traveller who died in 1536. At some point in his travels he made Delhi his home and was also known as Shaikh Jalaluddin Dehlwi, or Jalal—a name meaning 'wrath'—which he then changed to Jamali—meaning 'splendour' or beauty. He was also known as Shaikh Jamali Kamboh. Historically he straddled multiple reigns, beginning with the pre-Mughal Lodis at the end of the 15th century through the Mughal Emperors Babur and Humayun; he lived through several chronological periods, historical reigns, architectural styles and noms de plume. But the biggest mystery surrounding Jamali—some might say the reason why his dargah is kept under lock and key—is his relationship with the mellifluously named Kamali, alongside whom he is buried.

There are many theories about the identity of Kamali and his relationship with Jamali. Some say Kamali was Jamali's brother, victim of a parental desire to have rhyming names for their children. But this reason does not work since 'Jamali' was a name the Shaikh took on later in life. Others say, variously, that Kamali was Jamali's best friend, a staunch disciple, a fellow poet, a local villager, and even his wife. There is no documentary evidence to provide positive identification for Kamali, but what is incontestable is that he was a man. This can be seen from the fact that both graves in the dargah have pen boxes constructed on them. Traditionally, graves housing male saints have these pen boxes on top of the stone, denoting the instrument with which the commemorated saint wrote words of wisdom during his lifetime. Graves housing women—and there are several of these in the courtyard surrounding and adjoining Jamali-Kamali's tomb—are given flat tops to denote the paper upon which the pen writes. Interestingly, the roof of the building housing Jamali-Kamali's graves, as we have already seen, is flat. There is thus something androgynous about the building—woman on top and man below, female flat roof on the outside and male phallic pen on the inside—that adds to the central mystery of Kamali's identity. We do not know who Kamali is, except that he was close enough to Jamali in his life to warrant being buried next to the saint after his death. Urban legend and local chatter favour the homosexual theory that Jamali and Kamali were lovers in life and death. But once we accept that we cannot know for certain, what remains important for us to consider is the nature of a love between two men that was intense enough to warrant burial side by side. What does their love mean? And how was it coded?

Jamali-Kamali graves. *Image courtesy:* Vikramjit R. Rai

Often described as the gay Taj Mahal, Jamali-Kamali's tomb is understood to commemorate a same-sex attachment as intense as the one that inspired Shah Jahan to build the mausoleum for his wife; these tombs are part of the landscape of monuments that mark desire in India. Jamali-Kamali's dargah is not open for public viewing for fear of being defaced, and it is hard to see inside the dargah, just as it is almost impossible to see anything in the actual mausoleum room of Mumtaz Mahal. But while the Taj displays all its splendours on the outside, Jamali-Kamali keeps its beauty hidden, treasures only for a privileged few to see. This secrecy is also the reason why this tomb is not always referred to as a dargah. A dargah—literally 'door to the place' ('dar' from darwaza, 'gah' from jagah), a place of access—refers to the shrine of a Sufi saint that is visited by pilgrims and which hosts qawwali music to produce a mystical gathering, or sama, of followers. The Jamali-Kamali tomb is also the shrine of a Sufi saint, but it is not currently a site of pilgrimage or qawwali because of its protected status—a classic case of killing history in the name of preserving it. But it clearly once used to be a gathering place for qawwals and pilgrims. Belying its current bucolic surroundings, Jamali-Kamali's tomb was set in the middle of the still bustling fort-city of Lal Kot. And judging from the handsome courtyard that surrounds the tomb, the complex used to attract a great number of pilgrims. Equally, the courtyard has a clearly demarcated space right in front of the door to the tomb—an orange and beige chequered pattern with blue tiles still visible on a portion of it. Given that qawwali singers and musicians typically sit at the door of a dargah, one might speculate that Jamali-Kamali's tomb was a space that created frequent and thriving samaas. No matter, then, if one views this tomb currently as being a dargah or a qabr—grave—or a mazaar—shrine—the fact remains that a highly venerated Sufi saint, with a large number of followers who commemorated his poetry in ecstatic song, is buried here. Along with his boyfriend.

Or not?

In Sufi poetry, merging with god is described as merging with one's beloved. And that beloved is always coded as male. One reason for this coding is that much Sufi poetry in India was written in Persian (scholars suggest more Persian poetry was written in India than in Persia), and since Persian is a non-gendered language, the addressee is universally assumed, in a sexist manner, to be male. But far beyond this conventional privilege accorded to masculinity in which both god and devotee are grammatically deemed to be male, Sufi poetry often names its addressee by name as a man. Which is to say that Sufi poetry often *names* itself as homoerotic. The only matter of debate is whether the beloved thus named is considered to be a vessel of godliness or a vector of carnal desire. Or both.

Consider, for instance, that the 13th-century poet Amir Khusro, still considered by many to be the finest poet India has produced, describes himself repeatedly as the bride of his spiritual guide Nizamuddin Auliya. In one of his most famous qawwalis—'Chhaap tilak sab chheeni re mose nainaa milaaike'—he says that Nizamuddin seduced him with a single look. In his book *Muslim Shrines in India*, Christian Troll quotes another popular Sufi poem that describes this seductive aspect of the courtship between the pir and murid, teacher and pupil: 'I asked what is heaven, he said a glimpse of me / I asked what is contentment, he said a favour from me / I asked what is anguish, he said a yearning for me.'

Thus it was not only the grammatical vagaries of the Persian language that produced Indian Sufism's passionate homoeroticism. But just as one does not know for certain who Kamali is, so too is there no way to tell whether this passionate poetry was heavenly or worldly. At the very least, one presumes it must have been both. When it was written in Punjabi too, for instance by Bulleh Shah in the 18th century, the beloved was presented not only as male, but also as an erotic partner. 'Now Inayat will come to me on the bed in the morning,' says Bulleh Shah of his pir, Shah Inayat Qadiri; 'The bangles on my arms, the plait on my head and the bracelet on my wrist all look good. I am dyed with the delight of union with my beloved, and my whole being is filled with joy.' Legend has it that once, when Bulleh Shah fell out of favour with Shah Inayat, he taught himself how to dance and danced his way back into favour: 'Bullah, let us go and sit at the gate of Shah Inayat, who / made me dress in green and red. When I started / dancing, I found my way to him.' This repeated insistence on being the bride of the pir, of dressing in red and green, with bangles on the wrist and flowers in the hair, all suggest an erotic union. Some people will argue that these verses are an expression of 'real' homoerotic desire, while others will insist that they are metaphorical renditions of one's desire for god. But whether or not Khusro and Nizamuddin chose to consummate their relationship or Jamali and Kamali really were lovers matters far less than the fact that the couples were buried together in death after declaring their love for one another in life. How this love allows us to think about desire is the real legacy of the dargahs.

Given its Sufi provenance, this male-male love resulting in a shared burial site is attached to other tales that populate the faith. One Sufi tale claims that the mark of a real pir is that he can read the namaz prayers at his own funeral. This is what it means to possess the secret of the annihilation of the self—the raaz-i-fana: to still be present when the self is no longer there. Or absent while the self is still ostensibly present. This annihilation of the self is central to the tenets of Sufism in India. Qazi Hamiduddin, beloved of both the Chishti and Suhrawardi sects of Sufism (Jamali was a Suhrawardi), insisted that although the Lover and the Beloved seem different, they are in fact identical. The annihilation of the self is commonly understood in Sufism as a merging of the self with god, an immolation in the fires of devotional passion. The language with which Sufi poetry describes this process of annihilation—fana—is utterly erotic. But even more important is the power of this eroticism to destroy the self. In other words, what is erotic about Sufi desire is its power to eradicate that which is experiencing desire. The desire embedded in the dargah is fatal because fatality is what makes it erotic. But this fatality is not, or not only, literal.

Let us turn to Bulleh Shah, again speaking about his beloved Shah Inayat: 'He was Heer and then became Ranjha. Very rare are the / people who realize this. Once they do, all disputes / are resolved.' Bulleh Shah casts his poetry in the mode of popular romance—the story of Heer and Ranjha was for centuries the best-selling subcontinental version of Romeo and Juliet. The passionate love between members of different social classes is prevented by difficult parents and ends with the death of the two lovers. But Bulleh Shah also describes this passionate love as bringing to an end the reign of opposites. Heer and Ranjha are no longer two different entities but versions of the same phenomenon of desire, both of which are embodied by Shah Inayat. Realizing that the lover is both everything—Heer and Ranjha—and nothing—neither Heer nor Ranjha—adheres to a Sufi understanding in which erotic love is indistinguishable from religious love, in which disputes, or oppositions, are destroyed. At other times Bulleh Shah narrates himself as Sohni—the heroine of another popular love legend that bears an uncanny resemblance to the story of Hero and Leander, except that in the Punjabi story, as opposed to the Greek myth, it is Sohni, the woman, who swims every night across the river Chenab to meet her beloved Mahiwal. Sohni dies when her sister-in-law replaces the earthern pot she would carry to stay afloat in the water with one made of unbaked clay that quickly dissolves in the river. For Bulleh Shah, the insistence on death in love is simultaneously an instance of the dissolution of the self.

In their passion, the lovers move fluidly between states, between being Heer and Ranjha, Sohni and Mahiwal. He who was once Heer (the female protagonist) could then become Ranjha (the male protagonist), and vice versa. Even more, this ability to move between being Heer and being Ranjha allows us to resolve all disputes. 'Get rid of duality,' Bulleh Shah says later, 'there is no confusion. He is both Turk / and Hindu, there is no one else.' While the surface of the debate rests on whether the 'He' here is the mortal male pir or the immortal male god, the rigour lies in the idea that male homoeroticism for the Sufis seems to depend on an absence of boundaries. Or a recasting of boundaries so that they are no longer bounded.

Not only is Bulleh Shah here blurring the difference between Sufi pir and god, between male-female and male-male romance, he is also pushing against the difference of faith between the two major religions of India. 'I am not a Hindu, nor a Muslim. I have forsaken pride / and become unsullied. / I am not a Sunni, nor a Shia. I have adopted the path of / peace toward all. / I am not hungry, nor am I full. I am not / naked, nor am I covered... / Bulleh Shah, the mind that is fixed on God leaves behind / the duality of Hindu and Turk.' One of the ways to describe what Bulleh Shah is doing here is to say that he is asking us not to get attached to differences of religion, gender and species. We might be different from one another but those differences are not primary. For him, we are not Hindus or Muslims, men or women, but ecstatic devotees all. Some might think of this position as disingenuous. After all, Bulleh Shah's beloved is Shah Inayat—whom he variously addresses as spouse, husband, lord, friend and beloved—rather than, say, a woman. But the Sufi response to such an objection would be to say that what is being undermined is not gender, religion or species, but rather the fixity that we attach to them. Shah Inayat can be both Heer and Ranjha, female and male—and it is this lack of a fixed self that attracts Bulleh Shah to his pir.

Such a vertiginous lack of fixity has become visually the most recognizable form of Sufism—the whirling dervishes whose bodies dissolve in a swirling dance. The meditative dancing practice of the dervishes is said by some to have been invented by the famous Turkish Sufi saint Jalaluddin Rumi in concert with his male companion, Shams Tabrizi. Both Sufis of Persian descent, Rumi and Shams, or so the story goes, retreated into a cave for forty days during which

Shams taught Rumi the meaning of true knowledge. Rumi's students are rumoured to have murdered Shams out of jealousy over the fact that Rumi spent all his time in isolated retreat with him. The passion between Rumi and Shams, and the intertwining to which this desire gave rise, are all contained in the self-annihilating whirling of the dervishes.

Such a dancing desire uproots not only Sufis, but also their tombs. Bulleh Shah's dargah, for instance, moves as though in search of his pir (Shah Inayat is buried in Lahore). I was surprised to discover a sign pointing to 'Bulleh Shah ji ki dargah' on the way from Mussoorie, in Uttarakhand, to Chandigarh. When I asked my taxi driver about this sign, expressing surprise that it existed at all given that Bulleh Shah's dargah is in Kasur in Pakistan, the driver, taking pity on what he obviously saw as my ignorance, said that Bulleh Shah's dargah can be materialized anywhere because he is so widely beloved. He went on to add that there are many 'Bulleh Shah dargahs' all over North India. I have not been able to locate any of these other dargahs, but the one near Mussoorie exists, and even hosts an annual urs or anniversary of the saint; the dargah is referred to as a 'symbolic tomb' of Bulleh Shah. This idea of a travelling tomb is entirely in keeping with the Sufi love of mobile desire. In the case of Bulleh Shah's tomb, such movement flouts even the British-drawn boundaries between India and Pakistan.

As much of this history makes clear, for the Sufis in their dargahs, there is no boundary to desire since desire transgresses geography, gender, religion, culture, language, and the earthly realm itself. But arguably the two most distinctive barriers that the Sufi poets crossed were those of gender and religion—the 17th-century Jewish-born Sufi

fakir Sarmad Shahid and his student Abhai Chand are an
example of such incessant crossings. Another male couple
from Lahore—Shah Hussain and his disciple Madho Lal—
were so deeply in love that Shah Hussain changed his name
to Madho Lal Hussain. In addition to being a same-sex
couple, Shah Hussain and Madho Lal were also a cross-caste
and cross-religious and cross-generational couple: Shah
Husain was a lower-caste convert to Islam while Madho
Lal, some four decades younger, was a Hindu Brahmin.
They are buried side by side in their dargah despite these
differences, a feat that would not always be possible today.
As though paying tribute to this rich history of desire and
transgression, thousands still gather at the dargah every year
for Madho Lal's urs.

Like Bulleh Shah, Madho Lal Hussain too played
extensively with the romance legend of Heer and Ranjha—
'Ranjha is a Yogi and I his Yogini, what has he done unto
me?' he sang. The story of Heer and Ranjha—made five times
into films before Partition in 1947, and then several times
after that in both Pakistan and India—is a source of endless
fascination in the subcontinent. The masala of its tale not
only tracks the difficulty of love, but also emphasizes that
the lovers die for each other, and are then buried together.
Being buried together thus has a popular history of signifying
love's intensity. Since they are not Sufi saints, Heer and
Ranjha's historical burial place has not become a dargah,
but their grave in Jhang in Pakistan Punjab is nonetheless
visited frequently (like Juliet's alleged 'balcony' in Verona)
by hopeful lovers.

Playing Heer and Ranjha involves both a gendered and
religious transformation for Shah Hussain and Madho Lal,

and in traducing these boundaries, Madho Lal Hussain's poetry develops the best practices of both Hindu and Muslim art. Historically, all-women theatrical performances, called stree preksha, regularly presented women playing both men and women. The 4th-century *Harivamsha Purana* contains a detailed description of women playing scenes from Krishna's life. Legends of Krishna and Radha include tales of Krishna dressing up in women's clothes, while several grammatical and theatrical texts, including the *Natyashastra* (2nd-century BCE—2nd-century CE) describe men dressing as women, and women playing men. In the 19th century, Ramakrishna Paramahansa was only one among many saints who dressed as women in their devotions to various gods—Ramakrishna dressed as a gopi when he worshipped Krishna, and describes Sita merging into his body when he worships Rama; he also goes through a period of being a mother to the child Rama. So when Shah Hussain writes, 'If I play thus with the Beloved, I am ever a happy woman,' he speaks a language that has and continues to have a recognizable vocabulary and syntax in India. This language of desire is syncretic, crosses borders and speaks even from beyond the grave.

'Dargah desire' thus testifies to the lack of boundaries in desire rather than instating new borders around it—this is why locking up a dargah makes no sense at all. Heer and Ranjha are synonymous with Bulleh Shah and Shah Inayat, Shah Hussain and Madho Lal, Shams Tabrizi and Rumi. In one of Bulleh Shah's kafis, even the god Krishna and the human Ranjha are described in identical terms: as cowherds who pursue their passion. Both Bulleh Shah and Madho Lal Hussain perfect a poetic oeuvre that allows all to be equal, and equally, in the grip of desire. What is fascinating about this history of desire is that it actively demands not to be identified with just one thing or person. Indeed, the only thing about which we can be sure with dargah desire is that we do not know whose desire it is, and for whom. Two men are buried together, and their songs speak of intense same-sex love. But equally they speak of an intense longing for god. Rather than adjudicating between these possibilities, the dargahs present us with both options. There is no pressure to pick one over the other. Far from being seen as antithetical, religion and sexuality sing the same song of desire.

In early Europe, intense religious experiences called forth the same language of eroticism. From Margery Kempe's writings in medieval England to Bernini's 17th-century statue of St. Teresa ('Ecstasy of St. Teresa') in Baroque Italy, the nexus between erotic desire and religion was expressed in painting, poetry and sculpture. But unlike in India, where there is no recorded history of persecution against people for their desires, Europe rapidly developed a discourse around sodomy and non-normative desire that resulted in several violent deaths. Witches were burned at the stake and kings were skewered on red-hot spits. Laws were passed to prosecute 'unnatural desires' and religion and desire were quickly treated as distinct realms, the one sacred and the other profane. The difference between medieval Europe and non-European civilizations is that in the former the move from syncretism to demonization happened at a frightening pace and then continued apace. Same-sex desire, for instance, was hunted down and persecuted relentlessly. In stark contrast, and certainly up to the middle of the 19th century, if not beyond, India was dotted with the kinds of indeterminate desires to which the dargahs stand testimony.

In a second stark but related difference from Europe, the lack of persecution in India also ensured that neither homosexuality nor heterosexuality emerged as separate categories. While Europe came up with a taxonomy of desires into which fixed identities were slotted, desire in India was somewhat less determined. Vatsyayana's *Kamasutra* is certain only that it speaks of the man about town as its protagonist. To whom this man addresses his desires, and who else in this man's world feel and act on their desires, are matters left marvellously fluid. The text, which for long has been considered the final word on matters of desire and sexuality, speaks of people of 'the third nature' to describe (what we now understand as) homosexuals, except that the *Kamasutra* uses this term to refer only to men who take on the passive position in oral sex. Such third-nature men share a conceptual term with men who produce only daughters. Men wanting to have oral sex with other men do not always belong to the third nature. And anal sex is described as a heterosexual pleasure. Our current insistence on attaching uncertain acts to certain identities would have been completely alien to Vatsyayana and the dargah dwellers alike. They suggested instead a movement in which assigning a single name to desire was an impossibility. The advantage of not having an assigned name, of course, is that there are no fixed parameters within which desire can be constrained, or benchmarks it can be accused of dishonouring. Today the public assertion of identity by sexual minorities is considered a victory, but it also signals the defeat of a history of desire that was resistant to, and flourished by not, being named. Not because it did not dare be named for fear of god or the law, but because it participated in too many pleasures to be able to count them all.

Indeed, one of the meditative practices of the Sufis is to tell the 99 names of Allah in the full knowledge that such a list is not, and cannot be, exhaustive. What is astonishing about the imaginative horizons enabled by the architectural space of Sufi dargahs is that desire is divorced from sexual identity. Almost all the pirs were married and had children (with the notable exception of Nizamuddin Auliya, who thought that if he had children, they would mislead his disciples). But they almost all are buried with their male murids, or disciples. Many of them loved across religions and castes and languages. And not one of them thought of their desire as being contained in a category of its own.

The history of desire as it emerged in the dargahs is not a history that can be written down or told with any certainty. It is not a history of identity that can define the characteristics of a class of people. It is, instead, a history of *identification*; one that allows desires to cross borders and get attached to the most unlikely persons and objects. The desire of the dargah travels through space, time and people and never claims for itself a status of its own by which it can be known.

In his 1892 account of the dargah of Madho Lal Hussain, Muhammad Latif describes the association between the two men as follows: 'He became enamoured of a Brahman boy, named Madho, of the village of Shahdara, across the [river] Ravi, and his name to this day forms the prefix to that of the saint, as a mark of the strong attachment he had for him.' Latif, a district and sessions judge in a 19th-century India ruled by the British, found nothing troubling about this same-sex attachment and so does not refer to it by a special name. The legacy of Sufi annihilation—of getting rid of duality—was alive well into the 19th century. An 1858 account by Noor

Ahmad Chishtī of the basant (spring) festivities at Madho Lal Hussain's dargah emphasizes its key role in bringing people—Hindus and Muslims; he would not have had any vocabulary for hetero- and homo-sexuals—together. It is perhaps a testimony to the times in which we live that by popular account, the annual urs at Madho Lal Hussain's shrine in Lahore has now turned into a gay fest of sorts. The need to assert a vulnerable minoritarian identity flies in the face of what Madho Lal Hussain stood for; but it ironically finds a home in his dargah.

In a way, this inability to control where desire leads is a vital part of the desire celebrated by the dargahs. The Madho Lal Hussain dargah houses two tombs on an elevated platform with perfectly symmetrical space on all sides for devotees to walk around paying homage to the lovers. But most dargahs are not so symmetrical, since they are usually built to bury the pir, with the tomb of the murid following at a later date. Such flawed perfection also marks the Taj Mahal. It is said that Emperor Shah Jahan yearned for symmetry while building the Taj in honour of Mumtaz Mahal. And indeed, the Taj is perfectly symmetrical, with the exception of the cenotaph of Shah Jahan himself, which arrived at a later date and threw off the symmetry of the room in which Mumtaz is buried. In Jamali-Kamali's tomb, it is clear that Jamali was buried first, in the middle of the room (as Mumtaz Mahal was), and then Kamali was buried later on, towards the right-hand side. This later burial seems to testify even more to people's acceptance of Jamali-Kamali's relationship since presumably it was Jamali's disciples who buried Kamali in the same room, either in keeping with their pir's express wishes, or of their own accord as a mark of respect for the love between Jamali and Kamali.

But who was Kamali and what was his relationship with Jamali? This is the mystery with which I started on my exploration of the dargah in Delhi's Lal Kot on that monsoon morning, and it remains a mystery to this day. The maulvi I spoke to favoured the murid theory—Kamali was Jamali's favourite and favoured disciple—but then again, what prevents a murid from being a lover? If Jamali's Sufism revolved around the indistinguishability of the erotic and the divine, then this snatch of his poetry would find a place equally in anthologies of religion and homosexuality: 'My restlessness, for love of you, has passed all bounds; yet still I hope / you will have pity on my lack of calm!'

Dargah desire, then, is not 'the love that dare not speak its name'—which was the favoured descriptor of homosexuality in the West until very recently. Dargahs speak about the desires of their inhabitants eloquently and frequently, but what they say is simply not recognizable by a single name. Instead of a consolidation of desire, we get the annihilation that desire compels; instead of an identity, we get profusion; instead of stasis, we get ecstasy. A far cry from the dominant history of sexuality that would assign one identity to one person, dargahs provide us with a window onto a world of desirous possibilities, none of which are spelled out fully.

1.5

FRACTIONS

Just nipples meeting is not satisfying
Some dildo action now would be good.
> —Qais (trans. Ruth Vanita, in *Sex and the City*)

How do we see desire? Startlingly, the most common answer might be that we see desire mathematically. When we see *one* person canoodling with *another* person, then we recognize that as desire. We think of marriage as the legal consummation of *two* people. And when we seek romance, we often think of ourselves as looking for *a* partner. The marriage industry is fuelled by this idea of coupledom, and a well-oiled machine sustains the fantasy that two is better than one. Parents in India start imagining their child's wedding from the minute the child is born. And gay rights activists in the United States put all their energy into winning the right for two gay people to get married. There has never been a demand for the public rights of, say, threesomes, or celibates, because two is recognized as the locus of desire. If there is no couple, then it would seem like there is no desire.

This complex mathematical accounting of desire can be traced back to Aristophanes in Plato's 4th-century BCE text, the *Symposium*. For Aristophanes, desire works mathematically: one body is initially two conjoined bodies, which unit then gets divided into two separate bodies; each of these separated bodies searches for the other so that one plus one can make two again, and these two joined bodies are then divided conceptually to make one whole couple. Confused? According to his fable, all people were originally double, with two sets of arms and legs and two sets of genitals, until the gods cut them in half in order to stem the growing power of humans. Since that traumatic slicing, every human being has been in search of her or his 'other half'; this could be a man searching for a man or a woman, or a woman searching for a woman or a man. People continue to refer to their partners as 'their better halves' because in this romantic worldview, one and one is supposed to add up to one.

One and two are therefore the most common numbers of desire: 1+1 = 2, and then that 2 is made = 1 unit.

So what happens to *fractions* in this configuration of desire? How do we see desires that are both whole and partial? Desires that can perhaps be a little more than one but a little less than two? Desires that can both be seen and not seen?

Interestingly, the Hindi film industry presents us with a few answers to this question of fractional desire—desires that seem familiar but are also not easily recognizable *as* desire. Think of the dostana or male friendship films of the 1970s (for instance, Amitabh Bachchan and Rajesh Khanna in *Anand* and Amitabh Bachchan and Dharmendra in *Sholay*) which inundate us with heavy doses of male-male desire, only to replace that in the end with the heterosexual couple whose desire suddenly takes centre-stage. Is the hero thus engaged in one relationship or two? Which relation is the more desirous one? Does the one end when the other takes off? Hindi film songs too, many of them derived from Urdu ghazals and still written by Urdu poets like Javed Akhtar and Gulzar, speak of desire in a veiled manner, as that which cannot fully be named or seen. Consider, for example,

Gulzar's 2006 lyrics in *Omkara* for a song during the course
of which the heroine and hero fall in love 'Nainon ki mat
maaniyo re / Nainon ki mat suniyo. / Naina thag lenge'
(Never mind your eyes / don't listen to your eyes. / Your
eyes will betray you). Or these lyrics from the otherwise
unremarkable 2009 film *Ajab Prem ki Ghazab Kahani* (An
Incredible Tale of a Strange Love): 'Kaise batayein kyun
tujhko chahein / Yaara bata na paayein. / Baatein dilon ki
dekho jo baaqi / Aankhen tujhe samjhayen. / Tu Jaane Na, Tu
Jaane Na' (How do I tell you why I desire you / I can't seem
to tell. / All the remaining matters of my heart / Must be
understood through my eyes. / You do not know, you do not
know). The mode of communicating desire in Hindi cinema,
thanks also to the Censor Board that was set up in a prudish,
newly independent India, has historically taken recourse to
indirection rather than direction, to partiality rather than
wholeness, to not showing desire despite plastering it all over
the screen. Till recently, a gently shaking flower symbolized
a romantic kiss. A locked door suggests sexual intimacy,
dishevelled hair or an untucked shirt or a smudged bindi
stands in for just-concluded sexual intercourse.

Viewers of Indian cinemas have thus been trained to read
desire in the absence of explicit scenes of coupling. Or rather,
they have perfected the art of reading desires that lurk in the
cracks of filmic narratives. As though depending on this well-
honed skill of the Indian viewer, Abhishek Chaubey released
a film in 2014 titled *Dedh Ishqiya*, or One and a Half Desires.
The title does not make much sense in a world in which we
want desire (and sense) to be straightforward. *Dedh Ishqiya*
is a sequel to the director's 2010 film, *Ishqiya*, but that does
not explain why the sequel would be called one and *a half*

rather than, say, two, or the second.[1] Instead of privileging 1 or 2, the recognizable numbers of desire, the title of the film announces its attraction to fractions, to the one and a half.

It partly inherits this attraction from literature and literary traditions. Not only did the Hindi film industry grow out of the Bombay Parsi theatre, it has also made several films based on novels and short stories, especially those written by Urdu and Hindi's most famous writers. Some of these writers worked for the Hindi film industry—like Rajinder Singh Bedi, who wrote and directed *Dastak* (1970) and *Phagun* (1973), Saadat Hasan Manto, who wrote for Bombay cinema before moving to Lahore in 1948, and Ismat Chughtai, who wrote the stories for both *Ziddi* (1948) and *Garam Hawa* (1973). But it is perhaps another one of Chughtai's short stories, 'Lihaaf' ('The Quilt', 1942), that has the most to tell us about desire that can both be known and not known as desire.

'Lihaaf' is told from the perspective of a young girl, the narrator, who has been sent to her aunt's house while her mother is away. The aunt, Begum Jaan, is very close to one of her maids, Rabbu, and they even share the same bed. At night, the girl narrator, sleeping in the same room, notices heated activity going on underneath the quilt; she says it rises to form the shape of an elephant. Such activity

---

1. The film might also borrow its title from the commonplace saying in Hindi about 'dhai akshar prem ka' or the 'two and a half letters of love' from Kabir's famous 15th-century couplet, 'Pothi padh padh jug mua pandit bhaya na koi, dhai aakhar prem ka padhe so pandit hoi' (No one became wise by reading the best books in the world. But the person who has read the two and a half letters of love is a scholar indeed). Metaphorically, this suggests that even though 'love' seems to be such a small word, it is actually a big deal.

continues for a few nights, with increased passion. At the end of the tale, the narrator 'sees' what is going on beneath the quilt. She cries out loud as the quilt slips by a foot to reveal its secrets, but that is where the story ends, leaving us wondering what exactly has caused the narrator to exclaim. Chughtai never tells us what the girl sees, and never spells out what exactly the elephant-like activity is that goes on under the quilt.

This lack of transparency (the quilt is made of heavy stuff) stood Chughtai in good stead when an obscenity trial was brought against 'Lihaaf' in the Lahore High Court in 1944. Exceeding the skill even of Gustave Flaubert's lawyer in the obscenity trial against *Madame Bovary* in 1857, Chughtai's lawyer was able to win the case because he asked every witness if he could point to a single obscene word in the story. When none of them could, the judge was forced to throw out the case. The story of two women having sex in pre-Partition India tells the tale of their desire without using a single word that can publicly be identified as sexual. The two women are never described as a couple, even though their physical intimacy is laid out for us in great detail.

Based in part on 'Lihaaf', *Dedh Ishqiya* does not have a girl narrator who can plead ignorance of sex. But what it does have is a commitment to suggestive fractions, and suggestions. Posters for the film highlight the half—both women are shown with half faces; and the word 'Ishqiya' in roman script is preceded by 'Dedh' (one and a half) in Devnagari script and followed by the numerical 1½.

Begum Jaan and her maid Rabbu from 'Lihaaf' are in the film transposed onto Begum Para and Muniya. This latter couple plot and plan their way to escape from the

Poster of *Dedh Ishqiya*. *Source:* Shemaroo Entertainment

patriarchal constraints within which Begum Para is bound.
Their plan involves staging an elaborate marriage contest for
the hand of the Begum, who poses as a wealthy member of
the nobility. The Begum will marry the richest man among
her suitors, have herself kidnapped, demand ransom from
the new husband, and then escape with Rabbu and the
money to start a new life together with her. The plot goes
according to plan, and Muniya even manages to enlist the

help of two con-men who had initially set out to rob the seemingly wealthy Begum Para.

But the con-men who help the Begum and Muniya carry out their kidnapping plan also fancy themselves to be in love with the two women. This fancy comes to a crashing halt when the men 'see' the women playing love games with one another in the shadows. From being the subjects of male heterosexual fantasy, Begum Para and Muniya suddenly get converted into lesbians. Such a sight forces the two men in the film and us in the audience to revisit the entire story as it has unfolded up to that point. Were all those moments of intimacy between the women really *that* kind of intimacy? When they are finally faced with the fact that the women love each other rather than them, the men are completely crushed. But—and this is yet another interesting thing about the film—they bounce back soon enough and continue to think that the women are in love with them.

At these moments, the film is operating on three basic principles of desire that affect us all. First, it shows how easy it is to see heterosexual couples everywhere. Like Khalujan and Babban, the con-men in the film, we simply assume that two single women and two single men will merge together to form two sets of twos. And second, it shows us that non-coupled, non-normative desires are everywhere around us, even if we don't know how to *see* them. Like us in the audience, Khalujan and Babban both see and do not see the women's desire for one another. And this is because of the third principle with which the film works: there is always *more* and *less* to desire than meets the eye.

In *Dedh Ishqiya*, for instance, desire is continually see-sawing among various options. Begum Para pretends to be interested in marrying a man while simultaneously planning to run away with Muniya. This is also a lived reality, especially for women in India, who often have to hide behind the screen of heterosexual marriage in order to live their own lives. Ismat Chughtai herself pretended to be amenable to marrying her cousin (the pretence was with his consent) so she would be allowed by her parents to study on her own in Aligarh and Lucknow. Women across India, and across Bollywood, have to fight for their freedom to live their own lives. Not many of them are successful, but Begum Para and Muniya take advantage of another Indian custom by which to escape the restrictions placed upon them: *they do not hide their intimacy.*

This open expression of intimacy is a peculiar fact of the history of desire in India. Men can hold hands with other men without eliciting comment. Similarly, women can openly sleep with other women in the same bed without inviting censure. There is more than one way of reading these situations. On the one hand we can say that India today is so advanced sexually that we don't mind two men holding hands and two women sleeping together. On the other hand, we can say with equal validity that we are so fearful today that we cannot even imagine two men and two women having sex with one another. The women in *Dedh Ishqiya* fall between the cracks of these two positions. Or rather, the film suggests that cracks are the place in which their desire is to be found.

These cracks can be fleshed out a little when we look at British legal statutes that continue to govern same-sex desire in India today. An earlier version of Section 377 in the then newly-codified British Penal Code of 1797 states that buggery is 'a detestable and abominable sin among Christians not to be named, committed by carnal knowledge against the ordinance of the creator and order of nature by mankind with mankind, or with brute beast, or by womankind with beast'. This version of the law specifies that men having sex with other men is an 'abominable sin'. But women are not even imagined as being capable of having sex with other women. Women might have sex with beasts but not with other women. The 'one and a half' of our film's title, then, refers at one level to the legal and popular understanding of female homosexuals as not adding up to a 'real' couple. We do not see their desires because we cannot even imagine their existence.

Giti Thadani has pointed out that 'most Hindi-to-Hindi dictionaries do not have any explicit word to connote lesbian sexuality. The words *shanda/shandali* are translated as:

a woman desiring like a man
a woman having the properties of a man
a biologically deficient woman
a woman having no breasts
a woman not menstruating[.]'

In keeping with the blindness of the British statutes about what constitutes desire, these 'definitions' presume there is something about the body of a woman desiring another woman that is not—cannot be—womanly enough. One of the women must be a man, or at least, must be man-like, in order for their desire to count and be *visible* as desire. Otherwise, two women together cannot be *recognized* as desiring subjects.

Vijaydan Detha's blazingly brilliant story 'Dohri Joon'—

'Two Lives' or 'Double Life'—illustrates the ways in which this particular idea plays out in the social sphere. One girl who has been brought up as a boy prepares to marry another girl. This is a traditional motif in Indian literatures in which two rich men agree to get their offspring, often yet unborn, married to one another. In the folk versions of this tale, if both children turn out to be girls, then one of them jumps into a river and emerges from it as a man, thereby returning the relationship to heterosexuality. In Detha's satire, however, no one jumps into a river. Instead, the two married women are banished from their village, and their cause is taken up by the chief of a group of spirits, who gives them shelter in a magnificent palace. One of the women asks to be turned into an actual man since she has been brought up as one. But s/he is so horrified by the change in behaviour that masculinity occasions that s/he begs to be turned back into a woman. Startlingly, not only do the two women return to being a female couple, but they also ask for the foetus—which has been conceived during their brief tryst with heterosexuality—to be destroyed. There will be no child by which to identify their desire.

But before all these twists and turns of the plot take place, the girl who has been brought up as a boy prepares for the wedding. A neighour starts laughing at the prospect of such a marriage and teases the girl-boy by saying: 'Silly, if two millstones start grinding together, it doesn't matter how long they're at it, they can't make flour. There are some jobs only a pestle can do.' The idea of two women having sex does not seem to make anatomical sense to the nosy neighbour. In her worldview, the very definition of sex involves the coupling of a penis and a vagina in order to produce a child; nothing else counts. Homosexuality does not add up to public coupledom because it cannot prove its consummation with offspring.

Dedh Ishqiya injects a note of suspense in this atmosphere of simultaneous blindness and ubiquity in which women are assumed not to desire one another even as they sleep in the same bed. This suspense lies not only in the question of whether or not the ransom plan will succeed, but also in the question of desire: who will end up with whom? On the one hand, Begum Para and Muniya do not add up to two twosomes with the men. But on the other hand, the possible twosome of the women themselves cannot be comprehended by either the men in the film or the audience outside it. Both women, then, must count separately as one and one. But the film speaks of the *one and a half* of desire: neither one nor two. *Dedh Ishqiya's* one and a half is both an excess—more than one—and a paucity—less than two—that does not fit in with the socially-sanctioned form of the couple. Instead, its desire falls somewhere in-between the one and the two. The film presents us with the possibility that desire can confound us completely when it does not conform to the categories we already understand. In *Dedh Ishqiya*, we 'see' Begum Para and Muniya desiring one another, but we also do not see it. And what the film insists is that both these activites go together: we are *always* both seeing and not seeing desire around us, especially when that desire steers clear of the form of a heterosexual couple.

What we do see is a film set in a crumbling grand palace against a backdrop of gorgeous film heroines and luscious Urdu ghazals. *Dedh Ishqiya* is drenched in voluptuous desire. But instead of leading to a denouement in which desire adds up to one couple, we get the crack of the one and a half, in the crevices of which a twosome frolics. This fertile crack is where desire hides, lying in wait for the unsuspecting viewer to stumble upon it.

And because the law of the land does not confer upon Begum Para and Muniya the status of coupledom, the women in the film plot their own travels. They wander generically into a heist film, which is typically the bastion of men, and they wander romantically into one another's arms, when each would 'normally' be paired with a man. The women are both more than one and less than two. They defy the complex mathematics by which two ones become one two and then one one. They are not conferred the status of coupledom, which also means they do not have a label by which their desire can be captured. Instead, they remain one and a half, both more than we expect and less than we understand. The men still hope that the women will marry them some day. The women cohabit without being recognized as sexual partners. And everyone lives happily ever after.

Begum Para and Muniya thus outline a history of desire that is an alternative to the demand that all desires should be *recognized* by the State and its people. While we may long to express our desires freely and openly, it is also true that our desires are not always free and open. No matter who, what, or how we desire, we always have a mezzanine floor that cannot be accessed fully. Heterosexual couples have extra-marital affairs with other men and women; homosexual couples do the same. Rather than denying or dismissing these desires, *Dedh Ishqiya* asks how we can respect what is complicated about desire without needing to simplify it. Or rather, it insists that its desire is *both* heterosexual and homosexual, legal and illegal, visible and invisible at the same time. The women and men act in recognizably sexual ways—deep gazes into one another's eyes, conversations by moonlight, exchanges of gifts and bodily fluids. But equally, the woman and woman too act in exactly the same sexual way—deep gazes into one another's eyes, conversations by moonlight, exchanges of gifts and bodily fluids. We cannot watch the film as one *or* the other: there is always one story, and then there is something more. If anything, the film presents the singleness of desire as a stifling position. By contrast, the illegal twosome is ubiquitous in the film as it is in India. And its ubiquity allows it the freedom *not* to convert fractions into whole numbers. *Dedh Ishqiya* stubbornly refuses to be either a one that singularly tells us about a particular desire, or a two that is the resting place of coupled desire. In the process, it resists the craze for publicly acknowledged desires by insisting that desires can never fully be known or expressed.

Thus the demand for the visibility of desire in the world gets a twist in *Dedh Ishqiya* because the desiring women here both are and are not visible. They can be seen but not seen fully. If this fractionalism were to be acknowledged as the condition of desire, then we would not rush quite so quickly to pin down desire to whole numbers. *Dedh Ishqiya* is not a call to make desire visible. Instead, it recreates one of the voluptuous temple sculptures in Khajuraho that crosses the boundaries between the sexual and the sacred, the visible and the invisible, the one and the more-than-one. Begum Para and Muniya could well be sculptures on temples, engaged in various sex acts that are difficult to pin down. This new temple showcases desires that are centuries old. The delicate nuances of Urdu nestle in the delicate folds of brocade to reflect the desire between Begum Para and Muniya. *Dedh*

Ishqiya does not ask us to recognize, identify, condemn, or support what it shows, but it allows us to enjoy what we see. Begum Para and Muniya straddle the line between visibility and invisibility that troubles every experience of desire. Now you see it, and now you don't.

2

THE ZERO

My beloved has taught me a single dot.
The letters 'ain and ghain have the same shape. A single
Dot has created the havoc.

—Bulleh Shah (Trans. Christopher Shackle)

If we continue with the question of what mathematics and desire have in common with one another, then in India, one of the answers to that question is: Shakuntala Devi.

Variously described as a mathematician, child prodigy, and the 'human computer', Shakuntala Devi was born in 1929 into an orthodox Brahmin family in Karnataka. Her father rebelled against familial expectations and instead of becoming a priest, joined the local circus to become a trapeze-artist and lion-tamer. The daughter's own version of lion-taming came to light early on when she started learning card tricks at the age of three and quickly mastered them all. Sensing the extent of her prodigious talent, Shakuntala's father took the new show on the road and travelled around the world showcasing his daughter's mathematical abilities. They travelled around the UK, Europe, the US and Canada. Several academic institutions, as well as professors of mathematics and psychology, tested Shakuntala Devi's talents. She passed all such tests with flying colours, often proving even the early computers wrong. In 1980, she entered the *Guinness Book of World Records* for multiplying in 28 seconds two 13-digit numbers picked at random. And she accomplished all this without either formal education or recourse to mechanical devices like calculators and computers.

In 1977, the same year in which she mentally calculated the 23rd root of a 201-digit number faster than a computer did, Shakuntala Devi also wrote a book called *The World of Homosexuals*. In a documentary film made several years later, Shakuntala Devi said that she wrote the book after finding herself married to a gay man who, like countless gay people around the world, went along with a heterosexual marriage in order to keep up appearances. Responding to her husband's predicament with empathetic analysis rather than angry denunciation, Shakuntala Devi inquires into why society prosecutes homosexuality and homosexuals. Impressively, she advocates 'nothing less than full and complete acceptance...not tolerance and not sympathy', and says the blame for sexual violence lies squarely at the door of society: 'Heterosexual society dictates to the world how people should live and what they should do. Heterosexual society is based mostly on authoritarianism. The authoritarians are judges, priests and professors and their weapons of control are guilt, justice, punishment and fear.' Not many people know this side of Shakuntala Devi's brain that addresses social ills in addition to outstripping computers. But other than the personal connection of being married to a gay man (from whom she was subsequently divorced), might there be something else that links the mathematical mind to desire? Widely thought of as a subject that is objective and removed from the social sphere, does Shakuntala Devi's intervention allow us to reassess maths itself?

The World of Homosexuals begins with a historical overview of the ways in which different civilizations—and especially those of the Indian subcontinent—have been friendly to same-sex desire. Stating that 'homosexuality is as old as the human race', Devi notes India's long and pleasurable history of recognizing male-male and female-female desire. Although she sticks to a socio-historico-legal survey in her book, the organizing principle of *The World of Homosexuals* borrows from a mathematical concept that has for long been associated with sexuality.

I speak of the zero.

In *Figuring the Joy of Numbers,* one of her many popular books on maths that was written nine years after her lesser-known but arguably more path-breaking book on homosexuality, Shakuntala Devi announces: 'I have a particular affection for zero because it was some of my countrymen who first gave it the status of a number. Though the symbol for a void or nothingness is thought to have been invented by the Babylonians, it was Hindu mathematicians who first conceived of 0 as a number, the next in the progression 4-3-2-1.'

In fact, the origin of the zero is a subject of international mystery. Some people say that Indians, Mayans and Babylonians (the Babylonians got their numbers from the Sumerians, who were the first to develop a counting system) developed the concept of zero contemporaneously and independently. The Indian evidence for the invention dates, variously, from the 3rd, 5th, 7th and 9th centuries: the most recent reading of the Bakshali manuscript (found near Peshawar in Pakistan) suggests the earliest date of the 3rd century, 500 years earlier than mathemtaicians had previously imagined. Until now, the earliest text to use a decimal system, including a zero, was considered to be the

Jain text *Lokavibhaga*, which can be dated to the 5th century CE. Also in the 5th century CE lived Aryabhatta, the first of the major Indian mathematicians of the classical age, who is commonly credited with 'inventing' the zero, even though he does not use the symbol in his work. In the next century, Brahmagupta, another famous mathematician and astronomer following in the footsteps of Aryabhatta, seems to have used and theorized the concept of the zero as that which remains when a number is subtracted from itself. In *Finding Zero*, Amir Aczel suggests that we might be able to trace the zero to a circle found in a temple in Gwalior from the 9th century CE, after trade with Arabia had become common. Whether the zero on this wall came to India with the Arabs or was taken back to Babylon by them remains unclear (the Arab mathematician al-Khwarizmi, who became famous for the invention of the 'Arabic numerals', including the zero, referred to them a 'Hindu numerals'). Aczel also suggests that East Asia—present-day Vietnam—has a zero that dates from the 7th century CE. Europe only got the zero in the 13th century when the Italian mathematician Fibonacci introduced numerals to Europe; he presumably learnt them from Arab traders or from the Moors of Spain. The first known use of the word 'zero' in English dates as recently as the 16th century. The word itself comes from the Italian 'zero', which derives from Medieval Latin 'zephirum', which in turn is a bastardization of the Arabic 'sifr' or cipher, which is equivalent to the Sanskrit word 'shunya'.

Given this long trans-cultural, trans-geographic, trans-linguistic history, it is little surprise that the zero has many synonyms and related terms—nil, null and void, empty, vacant, nought, nothing, etc. In Buddhist thought, shunyata, or sunnata, signifies a void, emptiness—that which remains when something is subtracted from itself. In the Madhyamika Buddhist traditions from which shunyata derives, this would be the 'not-self'. Shunya denotes the presence of an absence, the nothing that can be apprehended and, according to Buddhist philosophy, rendered as a self that has no essence. As all these terms suggest, 'zero' straddles a faultline of being and nothingness: it is both something and nothing. This faultline puzzled the ancient Greeks mightily: how can nothing be something, and vice versa? After Fibonacci introduced the zero into Renaissance Italy, the powers that be were scandalized that anyone could introduce a void as a positive term when God is meant to have filled all holes and gaps in nature with his creative energies. Indeed, for the Catholic church, only the devil inhabits a void, and only hell is a place of infinite negation or nothingness. Thus Florence in 1299 banned the use of the zero in computation. But merchants loved it so much that they continued using the symbol in secret, making over the Arabic siphr into the modern-day cipher—that which is used in and as a secret code.

Historically in the West, then, the zero has been considered secret, hellish, opposed to God's creation, violative of God's will, precariously useful, conceptually difficult, theologically suspect, financially viable and philosophically rigorous. But in India, its reception has had positive reverberations in both mathematics and philosophy. It is the meaningful void—that which means nothing in itself but which allows meaning to be generated. Above all, it is positionally important. As Shakuntala Devi notes: '...the zero is a central part of our mathematics, the key to our decimal system of counting. And it signifies something very different from simply "nothing"—just think of the enormous difference between .001, .01, .1, 1, 10, and 100 to remind yourself of the importance of the presence and position of a 0 in a number.' But what exactly does it mean to be positionally important? In Buddhist ideas of shunyata, this means that everything has to be defined in relation to other things rather than as having an essential self to call its own. In mathematics, it means the position of the number is not random, but actually makes a difference to the meaning that we gather from the number. A zero placed before a '1' and a zero placed after a '1' make for entirely different meanings. Equally, the zero itself has no value; only its position in relation to other numbers does. Its position and its numerousness. The more zeroes there are after a number, the greater is its positive value.

The question that gets asked repeatedly about the zero is this: how can it be a number when it does not have any value of its own, any value that it can own? Isn't it rather unnatural in the scheme of numbers? How can nothing be something? As these questions suggest, the fear about the zero is that it is destructive of meaning. In *Figuring the Joy of Numbers*, Shakuntala Devi suggests that 'the power of 0 is its ability to destroy another number—zero times anything is zero.' Zero thus taints all with which it comes into contact: if it is loved by some for its ability to endow meaningfulness, then it is also feared by many for its ability to destroy meaning.

This fear that the zero might be the devil's handiwork, that it might have no value in and of itself, and that it might institute a void where there should be fecundity, all echo accusations that have in the West historically been brought to bear against homosexuality as well. Working with the zero as a concept can be helpful for thinking also about homosexuality, which allows us to understand a little better the eclectic itinerary of Shakuntala Devi's writings.

Like the zero, homosexuality too depends on where it is placed. If one encounters same-sex desire early on in life, then it is excusable. But if it appears later on in life, then it becomes inexcusable. Many people are expected to go through a homosexual 'phase', but if that phase lingers on, then it is malingering. This problem of positioning in a temporal sense—when is one allowed to have same-sex desire?—also becomes a problem of spatial positioning. Rather than a man being positioned on top of a woman, homo-sex allows for different spatial and political possibilities that can be dangerous to the status quo. As the 'human computer' notes in *The World of Homosexuals*, 'homosexual relationships break out of the norms prescribed by the needs of the monogamous nuclear family and...undermine the ideological foundation of the family'.

In Shakuntala Devi's searing analysis, then, homosexuality has been feared in the West because it questions our belief in the inevitability of the heterosexual family. Like the zero, homosexuality too suggests an alternative to what we consider to be the locus of meaning. There is, ultimately, nothing 'natural' about the 1 and the 2 as numbers that does not equally attach to the 0. And conversely, there is nothing 'unnatural' about the 0 as a number that does not also attach to the 1 and the 2. Homosexuality gestures towards the possibility that there might be more than one way of being in the world sexually, just as the zero insists that we take its 'nothingness' seriously. It is this embrace of the void—the alternative to received wisdom about meaning—that led to the zero being banned in Catholic states. Sexually, this void has been mapped onto the inability to reproduce, which puts homosexuality in the same category as the zero in allegedly having no intrinsic meaning.

What is fascinating, though, about this fear of meaninglessness and value is that, unlike in the West, it does not have a deep or rooted history in India. Both the zero and homosexuality have historically been met with disapprobation in the West, but not always so in either India or the Arab world. Indeed, eschewing the meaningfulness of reproduction is seen as a viable and even admirable strain of desire in India: witness the deep investment in the notion of celibacy, or even the worship of several hundred non-reproductive gods who, despite being paired up with spouses and having minutely chronicled erotic lives, do not reproduce. If reproduction has increasingly been seen as the goal of sexual intercourse in the West—and therefore also in the rest of the world as a consequence of Western colonialism—then that is only a part of our relatively recent history. The notion that reproduction is the justification for sex was not the dominant idea in the Indian subcontinent prior to the advent of colonialism. Instead, texts like the *Kamasutra* wallow in the notion of desire as a pleasure to be nurtured rather than as the means of reproduction. Even the seven verses in the Vedic marriage rituals do not mention reproduction as the desired goal of sex. But today we seem unable to separate marriage from reproduction. Far from disapproving of non-reproductive sex, then, ancient Indian texts devoted themselves to extolling its pleasures.

Sex without reproduction was certainly not shunya in the sense of being devoid of meaning, but rather shunya in the sense of not having any fixed outcome. Indeed, despite its general identification of desire as the thing that needs to be overcome, to be reduced to nullity, nullity is also the state to which Buddhists aspire. Unlike a Western tradition that sees homosexuality as the void, Buddhist traditions in India consider *all* desire to be problematic. While Western anxieties about nullity denounce only non-reproductive desires, Buddhism does not make such distinctions. It does not single out this or that *particular* sexual desire to condemn. The mathematician's attraction to 'the world of homosexuals' thus flowers in a soil that does not map desires onto numbers. Buddhist notions of desire do not equate heterosexuality with 2 and homosexuality with 0. Shakuntala Devi's passionate embrace of the zero and her active defence of homosexuality come together as part of a history of desire in an India where ancient Buddhist texts routinely asserted that no object or person has any inherent characteristics—svabhava—and that shunyata is the only reality. This concept of shunyata, which has given us the word that we continue to use for zero—shunya—is a desirable state, not one to be shunned.

In the land of the shunya, zero is not *no thing*: it is simply not *one thing*, and there is a big difference between these two designations. It is this long and complex history of the zero in India that allows Shakuntala Devi's book on sexuality to go where no 'polite conversation' has gone before. The mathematical genius has said that her interest in *The World of Homosexuals* stems from her own marriage to a homosexual man. But the book is also autobiographical in the sense that it stems from a mathematical mind keenly attuned to the many complexities of the zero. While homosexuality in the West has traditionally been equated with the nullity of the devil, Shakuntala Devi's book on homosexuality allows us to appreciate the complex history of desire in a land where the zero has for long been the hero.

3

AYYAPPAN

The seven verses (saptapadi) central to the Vedic marriage
ritual nowhere mention procreation.

—Ruth Vanita, 'Sexuality'

When I was six years old, my sister and I were taken by
our father and maternal grandfather on a pilgrimage to
Sabarimala in Kerala, the seat of worship for a god named
Ayyappan. My grandfather was an avid follower of Ayyappan,
and went on the pilgrimage about forty times in his lifetime.
My sister and I knew nothing about what was going on;
we were probably excited about going on an adventure.
In the hills! With my father and grandfather! Today there
are Ayyappan temples all over India—there is even one in
London and one in Paris—but now, as then, Sabarimala (the
hill of Sabari) was the major destination associated with
Ayyappan. Pilgrims are meant to fast for 41 days before
undertaking the pilgrimage (which we certainly did not
do), and abstain from shaving, and expressing anger. Even
more importantly, pilgrims have to abstain from having sex.
And most important of all, only men can undertake this
pilgrimage because women between the ages of 12 and 50
are not allowed to approach the Ayyappan shrine through
the main entrance. Only pre-pubescent and post-menopausal
women can ascend to the shrine since they are not considered
unclean. The eagerness to take my sister and me along for
the pilgrimage, then, was because we were still under the age

of 12. Did I know the real reason why my mother was not coming along with us? Probably not: even if I had been told why, I would not have understood the explanation. My only encounter with blood on that pilgrimage was when a leech attached itself to my foot as we walked back down through the dense jungles of the Western Ghats.

Ayyapan is a celibate god—this is the reason cited for not allowing women in the vicinity of his temple. This version of events ties in with predictable and drearily misogynistic narratives about (a) menstruating women being unclean, and (b) women more generally being seductresses. Clearly this is a symbolic ban—the keepers of the shrine cannot seriously fear that a god, materially made from sculpted stone, wood and metal, will be defiled by having menstruating women at his shrine. But Ayyappan's celibacy is such an oft-repeated theme that it is more than symbolic—not being around women seems to be integral to who Ayyappan is. So much so that all his male devotees too, as we've noted, need to abstain from having sex (with women) for over a month before undertaking the pilgrimage. This allows them to become 'Ayyappans' themselves because celibacy is the single biggest identifying marker of the god.

Ayyappan is one of the few gods in the Hindu pantheon who actively refuses to have sex with women by turning down offers of marriage. The most famous of Ayyappan's suitors is Malikappuram who emerges from the body of the female demon Mahishi, after Ayyappan has slain the demon. It is rather telling that the woman in love with Ayyappan is symbolically housed in the body of a demon whom he slays. His first love sprung from his first hate. Legend has it that Malikappuram begged Ayyappan to marry her, but he took refuge in his celibacy. She persisted, and was eventually told that he would marry her only when no new devotees come to visit his shrine. This entreaty for marriage followed by a rejection of the proposal is ritually repeated every year during the main pilgrimage to Sabarimala. Every year, Malikappuram's idol is removed from the shrine in which it resides, just a few metres away from the main shrine, and taken to see the number of wooden arrows—sharakol—deposited by first-time pilgrims to mark their attendance at Sabarimala. These arrows convince her that she will not be conjoined with Ayyappan and she returns disappointed to her role as the eternal consort-in-waiting.[2] In 1977, I was a part of that horde of new devotees who thwarted Malikappuram's desire yet again.

But even as Malikappuram's is set up as the shrine of disappointment, there are two more hopeful shrines en route to Ayyappan's. The first belongs to Kadutha, who helped to build the Ayyappan temple during Ayyappan's lifetime, and became so attached to the god that he refused to leave his side, choosing instead to spend the rest of his life with his lord.

The second, in many ways even more remarkable, shrine that a pilgrim worships at before approaching Ayyappan is dedicated to Vavar, a Muslim saint whose mosque in Erumely is en route to Sabarimala. Such a custom of inter-religious faith is startling enough in these times of communal strife. But there is more. Some legends say that Vavar was a pirate from Arabia, whom Ayyappan defeated in battle. Others say

2. Another famous celibate is Tirupati Venkatachalapathy, who refuses to marry Padmavati. In her case too, there is a temple dedicated to her, close to the shrine of the object of her affection. Every year she dresses up and waits for the lord but he never comes.

Vavar was a warrior who defeated Ayyappan in battle. Still others insist that these two men were so equally matched in bravery and valour that they acknowledged their mutuality before becoming boon companions. Many versions note that Vavar helped Ayyappan defeat the demoness Mahishi (from whose body Malikappuram emerged), which continues to be counted as Ayyappan's greatest feat of valour. No matter how many origin stories there are, though, they all seem agreed on the fact that Ayyappan and Vavar were inseparable in life, and closely connected after death. Legend has it that the demoness was finally killed at Erumely, which is now the starting point of the pilgrimage to Sabarimala, and the place at which Ayyappan asked his foster father, King Pandalam, to build a mosque for Vavar. This mosque is in addition to the shrine to Vavar in Sabarimala. Pilgrims believe they cannot approach Ayyappan without first praying to Vavar and making offerings of black pepper in honour of his pirate past. Like the two men buried together in many dargahs, Ayyappan and Vavar preside together in Sabarimala. Legend further has it that while explaining his attachment to Vavar, Ayyappan tells his father, 'Consider Vavar as myself.'

What might it mean to consider an other as one's self; Vavar as Ayyappan? Certainly, such a statement points to the existence of a close friendship. But usually, this language of interchangeable mutuality is reserved for married couples, the two of whom are said to make up a 'whole' uniting 'two halves'. Ayyappan and Vavar are not married—remember that Ayyappan's existence is legendarily opposed to marriage. He is very clear that he can never fulfil Malikappuram's sexual desire for him. Equally, Ayyappan was emphatic in his lifetime—or so the legends go—that his male companion be accorded the same status as himself. Given Ayyappan's nearly all-male following, and his refusal of heterosexual union, his relationship with Vavar points to a reorientation of desire that is fascinating from a historical perspective. Without suggesting that Ayyappan and Vavar should necessarily be considered a romantic couple, it is important to remember that the possibility of male-male union is not alien to Ayyappan since he is himself the product of such a coupling between Shiva and Vishnu.

The tale of Ayyappan's two fathers is widely known to devotees, not only of Ayyappan, but also of Shiva and Vishnu. In the case of Shiva, the tale of his coupling with Vishnu is only one of three tales of unusual desire that are regularly associated with him. (Indeed, in the light of these tales, it is tempting to think of Shiva the Destroyer as the god who destroys categories of gender, and opens up varieties of sexualities. He is, not coincidentally, one of the patron gods of the hijra communities in India.) The first tale of gender inversion involving Shiva produces the combination of male and female in the form of Ardhanarishvara—'ardha' is half, 'nari' is woman and 'ishvara' is a male god. This avatar of Shiva has a widespread iconographic presence in India, with everything from song and dance to films and poems and images being produced in its name. Almost universally, temples devoted to Shiva both in India and South-East Asia contain images of Ardhanarishvara in them. Tales about this form refer also to the equality between the male and female principles. According to one legend, Shiva and Parvati had an argument about who was superior between men and women, and settled on an equal partnership embodied in a form that contained halves of both. Significantly, the number of temples and rituals devoted to Ardhanarishvara is much higher in South India, especially in Tamil Nadu. The Ayyappan legend too has its roots in the same geographical zone—the border between what is now known as Tamil Nadu and Kerala, and what has been for much longer the forests of the Western Ghats.

Ardhanarishvara. *Source:* Wikimedia Commons

The second legend around Shiva's gendered and sexual ambiguity involves Vishnu—both Preserver and Destroyer come together in this tale to form the deity of Harihara, whose conjoined body is fully male, but made up half of Shiva and half of Vishnu. There are no real explanations for why Vishnu and Shiva should come together in one body (no argument about who is superior, like in the exchange between Shiva and Parvati). But they are joined together nonetheless, and worshipped together as Harihara. Sometimes this conjoined male statue is flanked by statues of Parvati and Lakshmi, Shiva and Vishnu's consorts. Harihara brings together the two most numerous sects in Hinduism—the Shaivites and the Vaishnavites—and is regarded as a form of the supreme being, both of whose halves are male.

This idea of a conjoined body made up of two men is not exclusive to Indian mythology. In its Greek counterpart— the origin myth about gender outlined by Aristophanes in Plato's *Symposium*—such a doubly male body is one of three primordial states to which human beings belonged. People were either male-male, female-female, or male-female before the jealous gods decided to cut them in half in order to reduce the doubled power possessed by humans. In Aristophanes' explanation of desire, each half then searches for its other in order to feel sexually and emotionally fulfilled. It is from this tale that we get the term 'my other half' with which to refer to our romantic partners. This is what Ayyappan seems to be saying about Vavar when he describes the Muslim pirate as 'myself'. In the Greek schema, heterosexual couples formed only one-third of the world's population, while both male-male and female-female couples populated the remaining landscape of desire.

Harihara forms the bridge between Greek myth and its Indian counterpart. But Shiva and Vishnu come up with yet another version of physical coupling that involves two men, one of whom is in drag as a woman. Indeed, the legend of

Shiva and Vishnu in his avatar as Mohini is a staple of the Hindu pantheon. This tale takes Hindu gods close also to their Roman peers who, in Ovid's legendary telling in the 1st-century AD *Metamorphoses*, are continually changing shape in order better to pursue their desires. Male gods change into swans and winds and seas and eagles in order to get their prey who are both female and male; the female gods are content with making other characters change shape while themselves remaining female. The Hindu pantheon is full of such shape-shifting gods; their malleability includes changing shape in pursuit of one another and also of humans. In such a landscape, Shiva and Vishnu are the prime examples of intra-divine desire.

As with all legends, the story of Shiva and Vishnu-as-Mohini has several versions. One version says that the demon Bhasmasura ('the ashes demon') performed severe austerities in order to please Shiva, who in turn granted the demon a boon, telling him to ask for whatever he wished. In a reversal of the Midas touch, in which the king asks for everything he touches to be turned into gold (which is one of the tales narrated by Ovid), Bhasmasura asks for the ability to turn into ashes anything that he touches. Shiva grants him this strange wish, at which point Bhasmasura immediately starts chasing Shiva in order to reduce the god to a pile of ashes and take over his power. Shiva hides himself in a tree and begs Vishnu for help. For reasons unclear to mere mortals, Vishnu decides to take on the form of Mohini, the enchantress, and seduce Bhasmasura into submission. The demon is so taken with Mohini's beauty that he gets side-tracked from his mission to incinerate Shiva and starts courting the enchantress instead. As part of their courtship routine, Mohini asks Bhasmasura to put his hand on his head and swear fidelity. The moment that the love-struck Bhasmasura does so, he is reduced to ashes.

Vishnu goes to tell Shiva of his success against the demon, and Shiva asks if he too can see Vishnu in drag as Mohini. When Vishnu obliges, Shiva is so flooded with passion that he spills his semen. The consequence of this encounter is Ayyappan.

A less lurid version of the tale focuses more on necessity than desire. The female demon Mahishi is determined to take revenge for the murder of her brother, Mahishasura, at the hands of the goddess Durga (Mahishasura had been granted a boon saying he could not be killed by any man, so the gods sent a goddess to perform the deed). After undergoing a formidable set of penances, Mahishi is granted a boon by the creator Brahma. When she asks for invulnerability, Brahma has enough good sense to turn her down. But then she makes a second supplication, asking for invulnerability to everyone except the son of Shiva and Vishnu. Once she is granted this boon, she starts ravaging the world with impunity, secure in the knowledge that no one can vanquish her. The gods beseech Vishnu, the preserver, to attend to the situation. Vishnu decides to reprise an avatar he had taken on earlier. On that previous occasion, he had become Mohini in order to rescue the divine nectar (amrit) from the demons who were refusing to share it with the gods. In this avatar, Vishnu had seduced the demons into giving up their hold over the nectar so the gods could gain immortality by drinking it. In the second reprisal of this role, Shiva and Vishnu-as-Mohini come together to give birth to Dharmashasta, of whom Ayyappan is an avatar. And Ayyappan, as we already know, goes on to kill the demon Mahishi, with Vavar's help.

Ayyappan temple with Vavar mosque.
'Vavar Mosque, Kerala' by Jay. *Source:* Wikimedia Commons

This second telling of the tale focuses less on the burning desire between Shiva and Vishnu and more on the pragmatic need of begetting Ayyappan. Interestingly, south Indian versions of the Shiva-Vishnu/Mohini tale tend to highlight the intensity of the erotic desire between Shiva and Vishnu, while tales emanating from the rest of the country tend to be rather more timid, even dour. Nonetheless, no version is able to deny the facts of a physical coupling between Shiva and Vishnu, and the birth of Ayyappan from that union. Ayyappan is the son of two men, and himself the boon companion of one man.

Such a lineage is unparalleled in the history of Indian Hinduism. Ayyappan is the god of men. The legends and rituals surrounding him might come across as misogynistic because of their insistence on male-male bonding. But despite this insistence on the company of men, Ayyappan beckons us to a history of desire that actively resists heterosexuality. And this resistance is not only to heterosexual union but also to the rules within which heterosexuality seems to be trapped these days in the Indian subcontinent. I refer to the insistence by the enforcers of heterosexuality on the issue of issue: a man and a woman should get married in order to have children. But before we get to a discussion of reproduction and children, we first need to take a detour.

The geographical layout of the temple at Sabarimala puts Vavar's shrine en route to Ayyappan's, and Malikappuram's nearby so that she does not have far to travel in order to get proof of her thwarted desires. This layout has been dispensed with in Ayyappan temples in the rest of the country and, one presumes, the world. In the temple in Delhi that I visited recently, and to which my grandfather used to take me often when I was a child, there is only one main shrine to Ayyappan, and an adjacent shrine to Shiva, one of his two fathers. Malikappuram is dispensed with entirely, as is Vavar, with the result that the Ayyappan temples outside Sabarimala present a denuded picture of the rich desires in which the Ayyappan legend is steeped. As I contemplated this picture of denuded desire—no evidence of male-male parentage, no proof of a male companion, no suggestion of rejected female desire—I was approached by a devotee at the temple in Delhi. She looked at me suspiciously and asked me if I was there as a believer or because I was 'just curious'. I said I was certainly curious, to which she replied that there was no place for curiosity in the Ayyappan temple, only for belief. By this point I had mustered up enough courage to say that I was not a believer, and that just as I would not tell her what she should be, she too should not tell me what I should or should not be. She marched off to the temple authorities to check with them. To their credit, the authorities told her that Ayyappan temples, unlike many other Hindu temples, are open to everyone, regardless of caste, religion or belief (the Ayyappan temple in Delhi is also open to all genders). She came back to tell me that apparently now I could stay with a good conscience, but her disdain of curiosity got me thinking about another legend surrounding Ayyappan.

Apparently once his shrine was built on Sabarimala—some date this to the 11th century, some say it is later—Ayyappan entered the sanctum sanctorum and promptly disappeared. The common belief is that he ascended to heaven, where he went to take his rightful place alongside the other gods, leaving behind a token that could be worshipped in his stead. Soon he became such a powerful god that he replaced Brahma as the Creator of the world. With his two fathers occupying the other pre-eminent positions as the Preserver (Vishnu) and the Destroyer (Shiva), this arrangement must have appeared to some of the gods as a family dynasty ruling the heavens. So even as Ayyappan ascended to the heights of power, envy started brewing among the gods. The reason for this, we are told in a popular Kannada song about Ayyappan, was not so much the power amassed by the god as what he planned to *do* with it. In this song, Ayyappan proposes with his power to put an end to the power of the gods. Perhaps predictably, the gods decide to mount a rebellion against him.

The startling idea that Ayyappan wanted to put into practice was that henceforth, human beings would not die. This was a decree not only about death, but also about birth. After all, as Ruth Vanita has pointed out in *Same-Sex Love in India*, the reason why goddesses in the Hindu pantheon do not give birth to children is because reproduction sets the stage for the replacement of the self. Reproductive sex is closely related to the idea of the imminent death of the self; having children produces one's own replacements. If we reverse this train of thought, then it becomes apparent that if birth is meant to ward off death, then the promise of no death would in turn ward off birth. The order of the world as we know it would change were we to get rid of both death and birth.

But having children is also the basis of heterosexuality. Or rather, the biologically deterministic argument goes that heterosexuality is 'natural' because a man and a woman can produce children through their sexual union. Quite apart from the fact that such sex is described in terms of necessity rather than pleasure, one could also point out that reproduction actually finds no place in relation to sexual pleasure in either ancient Hindu or medieval Islamic texts. The injunction to reproduce, for instance, does not exist in the *Kamasutra*'s treatise on erotics, which specifically uncouples desire from reproduction. Several medieval Sufi mystics refused to have children because for them the prescribed path was an ecstatic union with god, not a biological reproduction of the self. The emphasis on sex for the sake of reproduction exists in the Bible, which enjoins us to 'be fruitful and multiply' but it does not occur in the Vedic marriage rituals, for example, which do not mention procreation even once. Ayyappan's plan, then, tapped into a deep vein of religious and spiritual mysticism in India, while being utterly distant from our current obsession with biological reproduction. Hitting heterosexuality where it hurts the most, the god proposed doing away with both death and birth. This is an idea that seems shocking now, especially in the Indian context in which the injunction to have children is almost a sacred mantra. We now have blessings that extol a woman to be the mother of a hundred sons, but that blessing certainly does not come from Ayyappan.

But why were the gods alarmed by this plan? After all, they had already been given the nectar of immortality by Vishnu/Mohini and were themselves immortal. Why then were they upset by Ayyappan's desire that human beings should not die? This is where the Hindu gods again begin to resemble their ancient Greek and Roman counterparts. Tales about these gods paint them in utterly human colours: they are as riven by jealousy, violence and love as we are. Clearly, they feared competition from the newly immortal humans. But also, the gods were alarmed by Ayyappan's idea that there should be no more death and no more birth because they feared a significant reduction in the number of offerings made to them. After all, the desire to stave off death—with all the attendant warding off of disease—and the desire to reproduce in order metaphorically to stave off death, account for a large portion of the sacrifices made to the gods. Eager to protect their jurisdiction and influence, the gods employed Narada, the heavenly trouble-maker, to find a way of stopping Ayyappan in his tracks, to prevent him from preventing death and birth.

According to the Kannada legend, this was how Ayyappan left heaven and came back down to earth. On the instigation of the other gods, Narada approached Ayyappan and, during the course of conversation, posed a seemingly innocuous question to him. How, Narada asked, was Ayyappan related to Shiva's wife, Parvati, and to Vishnu's wife, Lakshmi? After all, Shiva was Ayyappan's father and Vishnu was his mother, so what relation did he bear to his father's wife and his mother's wife? Ayyappan was so perplexed by this query that he left Brahma's throne and withdrew into the forest to ponder the question. He remains there to this day. Atop a hill named Sabarimala.

This is the reason why Sabarimala is considered to be actually rather than just metaphorically sacred. Ayyappan is there: he came there from heaven while pondering Narada's question, and continues to live there. And Narada's question, we presume, is unanswerable, which is why Ayyappan is still pondering it. How is the wife of his mother related to him? And, perhaps the easier one, how is he related to the wife of his father? One presumes that the response to the latter question is that Parvati, by virtue of being his father's wife but not his mother, is his step-mother. But what of Lakshmi, the wife of his mother? What relationship can he draw for himself to the wife of his mother who is also a man and a god?

For one thing, the Mohini and Lakshmi relationship populates the landscape of divine desire with a female-female couple that vies for attention with the male-male couple of Vishnu and Shiva. Ayyappan is the son of one of these women who is married to another, but he is not directly related to Lakshmi at all. The question posed by Narada, then, is unanswerable because it cannot be comprehended within the bounds of the categories of relationality that we commonly inhabit. Ayyappan's relation to Lakshmi is as the son of Lakshmi's female lover who is interchangeably male and female. How does one describe this relation? The curiosity that the 'believing' pilgrim in the Delhi temple derided is precisely the reason why Ayyappan leaves the heavens. He ponders a puzzle, not knowing that it has been invented with the express purpose of thwarting his plan to reorganize the world wholesale.

Indeed, curiosity is crucial to the legends about Ayyappan because he is the counter-intuitive god: rather than encouraging belief, he embodies scepticism as his birthright. After all, which other god has been born of the union of two men? And which other god has wanted to stop death and birth? Both these ideas bear thinking about a little further. To be born of the physical union of two males is to interrupt the line that links sex with gender and reproduction. This seems to be the foundation upon which Ayyappan's thought is based. Having dispensed with heterosexuality even at the moment of his birth, Ayyappan is not initiated into the belief that differences between men and women should be arranged around the central idea of reproduction. If reproduction can take place between two men, or between one man and another man in drag as a woman, then our system of sex and gender can be slanted differently from its current organization; we can be freed from the need to enforce the distinction between the sexes in order to ensure reproduction. We already live in an age when men and women do not need to have sex with one another in order to reproduce—we have artificial insemination, surrogate mothers, egg donors, and IVF. In his questioning of the link between heterosexuality and reproduction, then, Ayyappan seems to have been far ahead of his time. He opposed the idea that reproduction is the fulfilment and pinnacle of (hetero)sexual life.

Indeed, Ayyappan's plan of getting rid of death marks

a radical chapter in the history of desire. If children are symbols, not of our immortality but precisely of our mortality, then getting rid of death also frees us from the need to create conduits of immortality. Ayyappan refuses to get married to a woman by insisting on his celibacy. Not only does he not have any children of his own, but he also actively spurns hetero-sex and insists upon celibacy for his devotees. His intense closeness with Vavar is celebrated even today. He leaves heaven because he cannot make sense of the categories of sexual relations within which we live. How are you related to your mother's wife, Narada asks Ayyappan? This is a question he cannot answer because his mother is also sometimes a father. In inhabiting this state of expanded sexual possibilities, Ayyappan can best be described as the god of non-reproductive and non-normative desire.

As the son of two men, and the boon companion of Vavar, Ayyappan is comfortable in an all-male world. He is one of the only Hindu gods in India whose temple is open to everyone regardless of caste, religion and belief. The only restriction is on women, and more accurately, on women who are reproductive; they are not allowed to ascend to the shrine through the golden 18 steps for as long as they are menstruating. This is, no doubt, a sexist practice. But given what else we now know about Ayyappan, we can appreciate that it is not *only* sexist. Women and men cannot mingle in his shrine, not because the fear is that Ayyappan will be tempted by women, but because the god does not preside over gendered reproduction. My initial verdict of sexism is more complicated now that I consider this restriction from the perspective of the history of desire. Ayyappan in his headquarters in Sabarimala presides over the possibility of an all-male community removed from the pressures of death and sexual reproduction. This community lives out, for a few days each year, the fantasy of what it might mean for separate sexes to live separately. Men mingle without fear of pregnancy. And, left to their own devices, women develop intimate bonds, like the one between Mohini and Lakshmi.

4

EDUCATION

Jisko mohobbat ka teacher kehete rahe
Who phateecher ek lesson mein fail ho gaya.
(The dude we used to praise as the teacher of love
Turned out to be a dud who failed in the very first lesson.)
—Kausar Muni, lyrics for *Ishaqzaade* (2012)

Devsingh's friend Kalyanchandra is in love. Devsingh's other friends surround him in the marketplace and urge him to reform Kalyanchandra's evil ways. The liaison that has upset them is between Kalyanchandra and a younger boy, to whom he writes love poetry. Transposing Kalyanchandra and his young beloved into the roles of an older teacher and a younger pupil, the conversation soon drifts to a general lament on the state of modern education in India:

Modern education draws people to such sins...Our ancient education system didn't make us so impure. These days, after fuelling the fire for twelve years in an English school in Delhi, educated young men set out to try all the shops of sin. As soon as they learn four words of English, they set up on a white horse, go to the white market, and shamelessly start sweeping the chocolate path with the broom of desire, under the veil of beauty, love and discovery. God has not yet given me a son, but if that day comes and I think it necessary to send my son to school or college, I will shoot him before I do that. Ha, ha, ha, ha—no, don't laugh; it's not a joke. I'm absolutely convinced that our present-day educational institutions are not fit for us to rely on. We cannot send our sons—the lamps of our lineage, the fame of our families—to them without feeling nervous. In twelve years, our schools do turn their brains into museums, but because the education system and the teacher training programmes are foreign, their hearts become hellish. Oh! The meaning of education is to make life happy, but how many of the educated in our country today can purify their environment with true happiness? Very few. Almost none. I say that if I have to send my son to today's educational institutions, I will shoot and kill him.

In this story, 'modern' refers to 1927, the year in which Pandey Bechan Sharma 'Ugra' published *Chocolate*, his collection of short stories featuring Devsingh and Kalyanchandra, among other characters. Ruth Vanita's terrific translation of these stories makes clear that 'chocolate' was a slang term for male homosexuality and it was extremely well-known in the India of the 1920s. 'Sweeping the chocolate path with the broom of desire' was shorthand for indulging in homosexual activities. In Ugra's story, Devsingh's friend insists that schools and universities teach boys how to be homosexuals. In an outburst of violent anger, he says he would rather kill his son than send him to these breeding grounds of unnatural desire. According to the friend's nationalistic analysis, the blame for homosexuality in educational institutions lies squarely at the door of 'foreign' pedagogical models.

There are several instances in early 20th-century India of similar outrage over an educational system that breeds sodomites. Shakuntala Devi reports that in 1934, the Minister of Education in the Punjab Legislative Council replied to a question about the condition of schools in the province by saying that 'the number of cases of seduction amongst the secondary department of the schools during the last five years was 31; 10 of the offenders were dismissed from the services, two were awarded rigorous imprisonment by the Court of Law, eight cases were under consideration of the authorities, while in 10 cases the charges could not be proved'. There also seemed to be a widespread understanding, made clear by Devsingh's friends, that homosexual activity was rampant in boarding schools and private schools that followed a 'foreign' model of pedagogy. Boys who lived together and studied together under a foreign influence, they seemed to fear, also had sex together.

Mostly these accounts of 'the foreign hand' blame the malign influence of the British. But sometimes it is also the Persians, as it was for Mufti Muhammad Zafiruddin, who warned that the sodomy spreading in educational institutions was a consequence of the unseemly appreciation of beautiful boys by Persian and Urdu poets. Part of this disapproval was fed by the large-scale revision of Urdu and Persian poetry in the late 19th century by the British, whose Victorian horror at the sexual explicitness of such poetry led to the downgrading of Persian as an educational language.

But while the 'foreigners' blamed for this educational model vary, the tide was most fully against the British. It is in this context that even Mahatma Gandhi joined the debate about sodomitical education. In response to a complaint from Bihar that the 'unnatural vice' was flourishing in boys' schools there, Gandhi noted: 'I have had literature too sent to me from other provinces inviting my attention to such vice and showing that it was on the increase practically all over India in public as well as private schools. Personal letters received from boys have confirmed the information…Boys who were clean before they went to public schools have been found to have become unclean, effeminate and imbecile at the end of their school course.'

Ugra's story about Devsingh and his 'dissolute' friend Kalyanchandra was first published in 1927 as the Indian independence movement was gaining in strength; Ugra himself was an ardent nationalist. Indeed, his anti-British rhetoric in this short story might be driven more fully by anti-colonialism than a conviction that the British encouraged sodomy in schools. As other stories in the same collection make clear, Ugra and his characters seem aware of the fact that the most famous sodomitical educational system in history was the one practised by the Greeks rather than the one imposed by the British in India. Plato's *Symposium*, for instance, written around 385 BCE, is a paean in praise of pedagogical sodomy: Socrates, the master, is drawn to the beauty of youth who are in turn drawn to the wisdom of the Philosopher-Teacher. Education for Plato can only happen in the presence of desire; without it, there is no learning. Indeed, the path to knowledge of the Forms—which for him signify the highest good, and the best knowledge—takes a necessary route through the love of boys. Devsingh's friend seems to assume that the British have inherited the Greek pedagogical tradition. If Indian education were to be conducted in keeping with Indian values, he thinks, then there would be no dilution of learning by the pollutant of desire.

Let us take Devsingh's friend seriously. Or rather, let us think carefully about the relation between education and desire, and wonder whether this relation is indeed a foreign import or whether there is something about education itself—anywhere—that depends on desire. After all, in the century before Ugra's didactic story denouncing all-male educational institutions, Vivekananda was an ardent disciple of Ramakrishna Paramahansa. Four hundred years before that, Chaitanya Mahaprabhu had an intimate association with his disciple Nityananda. And a hundred years before that, Amir Khusro was united in ecstatic verse with his master, Shaikh Nizamuddin. India, it seems, has a long history of pedagogy interwoven with desire.

'Amir Khusro'. Miniature from a manuscript of Majlis Al-Usshak by Husayn Bayqarah. *Source:* Wikimedia Commons

Vivekananda, in fact, went to Ramakrishna Paramahansa in order to be educated. While studying William Wordsworth's poem 'The Excursion', Vivekananda and his peers at the General Assembly's Institution in Calcutta were told by Professor William Hastle to visit Ramakrishna at his ashram

'Chaitanya Deva Listening to the Bhagabata', by
Dinesh Chandra Sen. *Source:* Wikimedia Commons

in Dakshineswar in order to understand the meaning of the
'trance' about which Wordsworth writes in his poem. This is
exactly what Narendra (as Vivekananda was known at that
point) did in 1881. And after that, there was no looking
back. In Swami Nikhilananda's biography of Vivekananda,
Ramakrishna is apparently astounded when he first sees his
future disciple entering the room, unmindful of body and
dress and the outside world in general. Ramakrishna is said
to have told Naren that he had been waiting for him: 'My

ears are almost seared listening to...worldly people. Oh, how I have been yearning to unburden my mind to one who will understand my thought.' Significantly, it is Ramakrishna's mind that is first caught up in Narendra's aura. It is this organ that convinces Paramahansa he is in the presence of a soulmate, that his dishevelled disciple has a divinity within him. What follow are five years of an intensely loving partnership, from 1881 until Ramakrishna's death in 1886.

Narendra becomes Vivekananda under Paramahansa's tutelage, remains celibate (like Socrates in the *Symposium*), and sets up the Ramakrishna Order after his teacher's death. So intense is the emotional-pedagogic charge between Vivekananda and his master that the Ramakrishna Order is tasked precisely with setting up educational institutions where male disciples can learn from male masters, recreating the relation between Vivekananda and his teacher. All disciples have to remain monastic; indeed, Vivekananda was as, if not more, critical of sex than Ramakrishna had been. 'In my first speech in Chicago,' he said, 'I addressed the audience as "Sisters and Brothers of America", and you know that they all rose to their feet. You may wonder what made them do this, you may wonder if I had some strange power. Let me tell you that I did have a power and this is—never once in my life did I allow myself to have even one sexual thought. I trained my mind, my thinking, and the powers that man usually uses along that line I put into a higher channel, and it developed a force so strong that nothing could resist it.' To this day, guest houses attached to the Ramakrishna Mission have only narrow single beds, even in their double rooms. These beds are attached to the wall so as to be immoveable. 'No physical sex, please,' the followers of Vivekananda and Paramahansa seem to be saying, 'we are lovers of education.'

For, contrary to what Devsingh's unnamed friend fears, the intense charge in education is not always, and not only, and not predominantly, genital. The vice against which he would guard is less a matter of two men having sex with one another and more a matter of the desire generated between two men by the fact of education itself. The primary task of Plato's *Symposium*, for instance, is to outline the seductions of *education* rather than the *seductions* of education. And the seductions of education allow us to think of desire as something far more capacious than genital contact alone. Rather than involving sexual intercourse (though it can), education engages with the organs—eyes, ears, brain—all of which Ramakrishna adduces as nodes of pleasure connected with his pedagogic relation to Vivekananda. For him, his disciple is a sight for sore eyes, a balm for tired ears, a vent for eager minds; Ramakrishna is reportedly swept away by the sound of Narendra's voice lifted in song. Vivekananda replaces his sexual thoughts with thinking belonging to, in his words, 'a higher channel'; his erotic investment is in thought rather than the genitalia. Indeed, the name 'Vivekananda' itself translates into 'one who desires, and derives pleasure from, learning'. Learning for these two men, in all its intensity, engages organs that are not genital but that are nonetheless desirous. Which is to say, Devsingh's friend is correct to assume that educational institutions are the sites of intense desire between men. But he is incorrect to think that this intense desire is genital alone.

In Plato's text, Socrates is famously described as an ugly person. But Alcibiades outlines Socrates's seductive powers as being quite outside the ambit of physical beauty. After comparing him to the satyr Marsyas—ugly to behold but bewitching with his flute—Alcibiades says of Socrates: 'You have the same effect on people. The only difference is that you do it with words alone, without the aid of any instrument. We can all listen to anyone else talking, and it has virtually no effect on us, no matter what he's talking about, or how good a speaker he is. But when we listen to you, or to someone else using your arguments, even if he's a hopeless speaker, we're overwhelmed and carried away.' The bewitching words of the master are intoxicating for both their sound and sense.

This intoxication has historically characterized education in India. After all, why does the *Bhagavad Gita* describe the world as standing still while Krishna instructs Arjuna? And why does the teaching conclude by advising Arjuna to surrender to Krishna, the master? The relation between teacher and student has a long history of being linked to complete immersion in one another, total surrender. But this dissolving into one another is not necessarily the kama we would identify with genital pleasure. Rather, surrender in the Indian pedagogic tradition is just as strongly to be understood as ravishment experienced by the ear, the eye and the mind such that two people become as one in their enjoyment of the senses.

In the *Sakinat al-Auliya*, the Mughal prince Dara Shikoh—heir apparent to Shah Jahan's throne—describes his orgasmic initiation into the Qadiriyya order: 'He [his teacher Miyan Mir] exposed my chest, and having pulled the clothing away from his own chest under the left nipple, rubbed it against my nipple on the same side, and declared, "Take that with which I have been entrusted." And such a multitude of dazzling lights from his blessed chest entered mine that I cried, "Enough!"' Dara's sister, Jahan Ara Begum, who too was a committed

Sufi, writes of her pir in her mystical memoirs, *Risalah-i Sahibiyya* (1641): 'Your passion takes me in embrace and caresses me…Every moment I am anointed by your rapture… Oh Shah! You have finished me with one glance.' Education is what Socrates's teacher Diotima describes as philosophical rather than biological reproduction—it is the outcome of a process as intense as sex. But the organ involved is the brain.

The Panchavargika—the Buddha's first five disciples—were ravished by sound. At first they refuse to accept the Buddha as their master, but the sound of the Buddha's voice and the sheer charisma of the Buddha's speech, to which multiple texts testify, convince them of his brilliance and they become his first disciples. As recorded by the biographies written soon after his death, the Buddha's charisma as a teacher apparently resided both in the content of his sermons and in the cadences of his voice. This double dynamism also resulted in the conversion of one of his most promising disciples, Udayin, who was swept away by the sound of the Buddha's words. Not only does Udayin go on to become an arhat or enlightened disciple of the Buddha, but he too is described as a charismatic teacher in the manner of the Buddha and converts several other disciples to his faith. Indeed, the very principle of conversion depends on this notion of charisma, what a dictionary describe as the 'compelling attractiveness or charm that can inspire devotion in others.' Charisma makes even wayward difficulty seem like the most pleasurable thing in the world. It makes the out-of-the-way seem like the path to enlightenment.

This possibility of wayward enlightenment is written into the very idea of education. Etymologically, the word 'education' derives from the Latin educare, which signifies the ability to lead forth, lead away and, significantly, lead out of (the tried and tested path). The most common term for education in Sanskrit is 'vinaya', which has the same etymological sense of leading away (from ignorance). Education is what leads you astray, and that is its job. To be educated means surrendering to the intense attractions of thinking and behaving differently. After all, teachers such as Nizamuddin, Ramakrishna, the Buddha, Mirabai, Gandhi compelled their disciples to leave their way of life in order to embrace a different order—of asceticism, enlightenment, religious ecstasy, non-violence.

Another famous master-disciple couple whose belief system revolved around waywardness is Chaitanya Mahaprabhu and Swami Nityananda from 15th-century Bengal. So intimately are their lives connected that they are even given rhyming nicknames—Chaitanya is Nimai and Nityananda is Nitai—much like Jamali and Kamali. Proponents of a Vaishnavite devotion, their chosen god was Krishna, and their preferred persona Radha. According to Sudhir Kakar—in his essay in *Freud Along the Ganges*—for Bhakti worshippers like Chaitanya, 'the adulterous world was symbolic of the sacred, the overwhelming moment that denies world and society, transcending the profanity of everyday convention, as it forges an unconditional (and unruly) relationship with god as the lover'. And Bhakti, he adds, 'is preeminently feminine'. For Chaitanya, worship involves a route that *violates* everyday conventions of desire. In the case of Bhakti worshippers, this violation is exemplified by the adulterous dalliance between the married Radha and unmarried Krishna, which becomes emblematic of rebellious devotion.

After all, if education requires us to move away from the path that we have been given, then another way of describing education is that it requires us to be adulterous. By allowing us to explore options that have not been sanctioned socially, adultery becomes the opposite of fidelity. Radha's adultery is the metaphor for a desire that moves beyond given notions of the world into an ecstatic realm in which she is united with Krishna. According to the Bhakti poets, we cannot learn how to love Krishna without such a moving away. An education in Krishna worship thus by definition involves adulterous and mobile desires; it is 'vinaya' indeed.

But rather than being the marker of any one particular pedagogical system or any one religion, this rebellious desire forms the basis of *all* education. Desire that challenges the norm is or should be a fundamental feature of education itself. This is the reason why education has always had the potential to be dangerous. This is also the reason why Socrates was condemned to death by the State on charges of leading his students astray. Across the ages—and certainly until the British in India insisted that education become an acquisition of instrumental knowledge alone—education in India has been respectful of the colourfulness of charismatic conversion that marks the province of the pedagogic. Whether it is in the ecstatic poetic mehfils of Hazrat Nizamuddin, or the philosophically celibate cells of the Ramakrishna Mission; in the seductive sounds of the lute, or the charisma of the Buddha's words, India has historically not separated education from desire.

But now we seem to be shutting our brains and eyes and ears to this connection. The historically close relation between desire and education has in present-day India been confined to a strange sub-field of study known as 'Sex Education'. And even (sex) education in schools does not mention the word 'sex'. For example, the Central Board for Secondary Education (CBSE) includes a chapter on 'Reproduction' in its Class X Biology textbook as the entirety of its offerings on sex. In schools today, desire is considered to be either functional—hence the emphasis on sexual reproduction—or genital—thus the shame attached to it— rather than a wide, all-encompassing ethos that blooms in educational encounters. There is no sense of leading away in such an education, no smell of intellectual novelty, no threat of new desires. These CBSE textbooks belong to the same civilizational soil as the *Kamasutra*. But the older text discusses desire at great length *as something that needs to be taught and learnt,* and does not mention reproduction at all. Desire today is not understood as an integral part of education—we are too busy insisting on vocational safety to make room for adulterousness. And were the topic of desire ever to come up, it takes the form of a denuded science that would scarcely be recognizable to someone like Amir Khusro. Where education once meant a comfort with transgression, it now means the safety of the expected. Where education was once inseparable from the vagaries of desire, it now insists on sanitized truths. Where education once pointed to the necessity of leading away, it now subscribes to staying put.

5

GRAMMAR

I am Indian, very brown, born in
Malabar, I speak three languages, write in
Two, dream in one. Don't write in English, they said,
English is not your mother-tongue. Why not leave
Me alone, critics, friends, visiting cousins,
Every one of you! Why not let me speak in
Any language I like! The language I speak
Becomes mine, its distortions, its queernesses
All mine, mine alone.

—Kamala Das, 'An Introduction'

In 1976, when I was five years old, I had a double hernia operation. I remember vividly the many moments of intense discomfort, the multiple trips to the hospital, and the slow and painful recovery after the operation. On one of my early visits to the hospital before the surgery was scheduled, the doctor took my mother aside to express his doubts over my diagnosis. He said it was quite unusual—almost unheard of—for such a young girl to be diagnosed with a double hernia. There was no question that I needed the operation since I had pieces of my inside spilling out on a regular basis and needing to be pushed back in again. But his theory was that rather than having a double or even a single hernia, I had undescended testicles that needed to be removed.

I did not hear about this counter diagnosis until 35 years later. My mother had been unnerved by the conversation with the doctor in 1976. And she was even more traumatized when a well-meaning nurse told her to make sure that word of my 'condition' did not get around for fear that I would be kidnapped by hijras before the operation had taken place, and made one of their own.

There are only two areas in which gender plays a defining role in our lives. The first is in determining the identity of living beings, both human and animal. And the second is in defining the rules of grammar. Indeed, Sanskrit grammar texts like Panini's *Ashthadhyayi* and Patanjali's *Mahabhasya* in the Brahminical tradition, and Buddhist and Jain texts written in Pali, all assume that animate and inanimate people, objects and concepts, have gender. These grammar books make clear that the way in which we think of gender in language affects the way in which we think of gender in persons. The same term—napunsaka—is used in these texts to describe the state of being neuter in person as well as the state of being neuter in grammar.

From at least the 3rd century BCE onwards, the mark connecting biological and grammatical gender in Sanskrit and Pali traditions has been that of the linga, Shiva's 'phallus'. Those of us who have suffered through classes in Sanskrit will know that the linga is the category into which different words are placed: stri-linga for feminine words, pu-linga for masculine words, and napunsaka-linga for neuter words. If you put the wrong word in the wrong gendered category, then your sentence construction is, simply, wrong. The linga separates Man and Woman and Neuter in person just as ruthlessly as it separates the masculine, feminine and neuter case in grammar. The dilemma with which my mother grappled in 1976 was both a grammatical and an existential one. She was faced with the possibility of my sliding from the feminine to the neuter case in both body and language. My seemingly female body, she was told, might not belong in the grammatical category of the feminine.

But even as gendered identity in grammar and life are considered essential to a 'proper' state of being, they are not so easy to ascertain. Even the handbooks of grammar find it hard to limit themselves to the three cases of masculine, feminine and neuter. For instance, these three gendered categories were augmented in Jain texts from the 5th century CE with a fourth case that offers two versions of the neuter or napunsaka gender. One is the masculine napunsaka (or purusha-napunsaka) for those men who occupy the penetrative position during intercourse. And the other is the feminine napunsaka to describe those men who are the receptive partners in sexual intercourse. This fourth gender expands the notion of the neuter by suffusing it with masculine and feminine. Suddenly, the three 'separate' genders become less distinguishable from one another. This expansion of the neuter accords also with the taxonomy laid down in the *Kamasutra*, in which people of 'the third nature' are described as being either masculine or feminine. What is interesting about this proliferation of terms attached to the neuter gender is that the neuter is often understood as an *absence* of characteristics rather than a profusion of them. A lack rather than an excess. But the historical debates about Sanskrit grammar and gender suggest a profusion of content despite seemingly rigid forms.

What is also interesting about Sanskrit is that it traces its roots not just to the gendered family of languages known as the proto Indo-European that has given rise to German, Italian, Spanish and French (in fact, all Indo-European languages including Sanskrit, Urdu and Hindi, are gendered; almost one-quarter of the world's languages use gender in their grammatical structure)—but it is also related to the non-gendered family of languages known as the proto Indo-Iranian, such as Farsi (Persian) and Pashto. The primary verb for 'being'—asth—is common both to Sanskrit and Farsi. Persian is a non-gendered language, while Urdu, Hindustani and Hindi—all derived from confluences between Persian and Sanskrit—are gendered with a vengeance.

As we remember, though, grammatical gender in Sanskrit and its related languages is rigid while also being expansive. This expansiveness might suggest a ghost memory of Sanskrit's non-gendered roots in Persian, and is possibly the reason why the seeming strictness of gender in Urdu and Sanskrit is more fluid in reality. For instance, despite being a gendered language, Urdu did not have a vocabulary term for the word 'unnatural' until the 20th century (according to Scott Kugle 'be fitri' became the 'ungracefully literal translation of "unnatural"'). And even though almost all current Indian languages owing their descent to Sanskrit—Hindi, Marathi, Assamese, Punjabi—use gender, many of these languages assign gender to nouns in hilarious ways. For instance, in Hindustani—the umbrella language for both Hindi and Urdu—the word for manliness—mardangi—is gendered feminine.

This means that all Hindi- and Urdu-speaking manly Indian men are grammatically transgendered.

Even more, the most prominent nouns signifying desire in Hindi and Urdu—ishq, pyaar and prem—are gendered male. This means that a woman expressing desire is automatically a transvestite. Since the noun signifying a woman's desire is masculine, a woman in love in Urdu and Hindi is a woman-man.

All Indian women who desire in Hindustani are grammatically transgendered.

Indeed, the lingering allegiance of Sanskrit and Sanskritic languages to non-gendered desire might be the reason why Jain texts and the *Kamasutra* allow for so much variety in gendered being. Gender is not as important to desire in the *Kamasutra* as it seems to be for us today. In that text, gender refers to and is a reflection of sexual position rather than sexual desire. As in the Jain texts, being penetrative or receptive determines the gender of your biological and grammatical case rather than the presence or absence of certain genital markers. Masculinity depends on whether you are sexually penetrative or penetrated. This is why the ancient texts, though written in gendered Sanskrit, had a strong sense of the masculine and feminine *neuter*.

These expansive definitions of gender have been present in the languages and peoples of the Indian subcontinent for over 3,000 years. The napunsakas are mentioned in ancient Sanskrit texts like Patanjali's 2nd-century BCE grammar that predate Hinduism and also in what are considered Hindu texts, like the *Ramayana*. Indeed, if all the tales of cross-dressing men and women and gender-shifting gods and goddesses are any indicator, then the 'neuter-masculine' and the 'neuter-feminine' have been abundantly and visibly present in India for centuries. And the neuter in person has inevitably been presented as steadfast, loyal, intelligent and reliable. Legend has it that Rama dismissed his subjects who were ready to accompany him into 14 years of exile by exhorting all 'the men, women and children' to go back home from the edge of the forest. The neuters, fitting into none of these categories, remained where they were for 14 years, awaiting the return of Rama. Touched by their devotion, Rama granted them the special powers of benediction for which they continue to be known today.

The Mughal courts regularly understood 'hijra' etymologically as a term describing the Prophet Muhammad's flight from Mecca to Medina in 622 AD. The Islamic calendar—the hijri—begins from this date in 622, and the subsequent years are denoted by the appendage of an H for hijra or AH for anno hegirae in Latin. This association with a flight from persecution has historically marked hijras as a noble people, seeking sanctuary and freedom from barbarism, and standing steadfast in the face of ruthless political pressure. Hijras are people who flee persecution— whether of royal whims, religious sects, or the draconian orders of gender.

Indeed, so high was the religious regard accorded to hijras/ napunsakas across languages that it is quite possible—had my counter diagnosis taken place in 1476 rather than 1976—that my mother would not have been as terrified by the possible 'demotion' of my gender from the feminine to the neuter. But the lower social status would still have been a problem for her, though, since hijras were in lived reality subject to many depredations, including at the hands of slave traders, and sometimes were boys who had been forced to undergo castration.

There is very little historically that has been written by hijras themselves (A. Revathi's *The Truth about Me* and Laxmi Narayan Tripathi's *Me Hijra, Me Laxmi* are recent exceptions to this rule), and so it is difficult to glean historical details about their lives in India apart from the religious myths that surround them. While they were appointed to high positions in court—in the Mughal courts, they were regularly keepers of the harem—they were also subjected to normative jokes. They were trusted as loyal soldiers, but also regarded as lesser beings because of their lack of lineage. They were invoked as auspicious people, but also shunned for being undefinable. Linguistically too, their path is strewn with irony. While the fiercely gendered Sanskrit and Urdu languages celebrate gender-bending napunsakas and hijras in their literatures, the English, with their *non*-gendered language, started the process of prosecuting the hijras in person.

Indeed, shocked by the gender 'confusion' displayed by the hijras, the British passed the Criminal Tribes Act in 1871, under which hijras were classified as belonging to a 'criminal caste', a category of caste invented by the British themselves. This category included individuals who 'are reasonably suspected of kidnapping or castrating children, or of committing offenses under section 377 of the Indian Penal Code, or of abetting the commission of any of the said offences'; or 'who appear, dressed or ornamented like a woman, in a public street or place, or in any other place, with the intention of being seen from a public street or place'; or 'dance or play music, or take part in any public exhibition, in a public street or place for hire in a private house'.

This Act is the source from which my mother's fear derived before my operation. This is why she was warned not to let news of my condition become common knowledge lest I be kidnapped. During the Raj, hijras were forced to be registered with the colonial authorities, and were arrested if they were caught doing any of the things that they had historically done. Under the British, 'hijra' became ungrammatical, a deviation at odds with the laws of the land, an example of the too-muchness of desire that inhabited this jewel in the British Crown. But despite the phobia generated by the Criminal Tribes Act, the Indian subcontinent continues to harbour the idea that there are more than two genders in the world. Indeed, at least the recognition of hijras is one of the few policies on desire that ties the partitioned subcontinent together. Nepal, Bangladesh, Pakistan and India all recognize hijras officially as 'the third gender', with varying access to civil and political rights.

What is interesting, however, about the British attitude to the 'confused' gender of the hijras is its complete variance from the grammar of the language they themselves speak. English is not a gendered language, and stands out among the world's prominent languages for its lack of commitment to gender. Even though Old English was an extremely gendered language, modern English only retains the gendered vestiges of 'he', 'she' and 'it'. Other than that, it has no gendered nouns or verbs. I am not gendered in current English, and neither are you. The clarity of separation that gender is supposed to provide for both people and grammar does not exist in English. Which makes it all the more surprising that the English colonizers could not tolerate in the realm of desire what they quite happily embraced with their tongues.

And so, unlike gendered Sanskrit and Urdu, ungendered English responded aggressively to the neuter in person. It would seem that the history of India has had an inverted relation between grammatical and biological gender. The reign of Sanskrit and Urdu saw the sprouting of various genders, while the rule of English saw the shutting down of gendered possibilities. Hijras flourished for about 3,000 years before the English arrived, but have been in steady decline ever since then.

This general genital-gendered confusion lies at the heart of present-day India's love-hate relationship with hijras. Men in Hindi are feminized, and women's desire in Urdu and Hindi is masculinized. Hijras are welcomed as harbingers of good luck at auspicious events because they embody both male and female principles, but they are also driven to begging and prostitution because they cannot make a living. But love them or hate them, hijras are marked by a *profusion* that defies the potentially denuding conventions of grammar. The grammatical neuter went by various names in ancient and medieval India, and hijras today too have various names in the subcontinent. They are known as khwaja saras in parts of Pakistan, aravanis (or thirunangai) in Tamil Nadu, hizra in Bangla, napunsakaa in Telugu. Then there are the zenanas—men who dress as women without undergoing surgical reassignment; kothi—men who take on the feminine role in sex without reassignment surgery, and do not live in communities; and khusras—transgendered individuals who do not necessarily live together. These are but a few of the many names by which hijras, transgendered, transsexual, non-gender normative people have been known in the Indian subcontinent for centuries. The Sanskrit and Pali terms used prior to the Persian hijra of the 16th century, and which continue to exist alongside hijra, include tritiyaprakriti, kliba and napunsaka.

Despite being brought increasingly under disciplinary surveillance, hijras have if anything increased the degree of contradiction they carry in their bodies and tongues.

Hijras across India, Pakistan, Bangladesh and Nepal all speak a language called Hijra Farsi that seems to embody the rootlessness and restlessness of the word hijra itself. A blend of non-gendered Persian and gendered Punjabi, Hindi and Urdu, Hijra Farsi is syntactically close to Hindustani. Also known as Koti in some parts of the North, Koudibhashai among hijra communities in the South and Gupti (hidden) Vasha or Ulti (opposite) Bhasa in Bengal, Hijra Farsi has local variations in different regions, but the basic vocabulary remains North Indian and gendered. The irony that Hijra Farsi is a gendered language can perhaps better be understood when we remember that it was developed as a tool of self-protection at the time of the British criminalization of hijras in India. As happens with so many marginalized people who take on the categories of oppression used by their oppressors, the hijras too took on the masculine/feminine distinction that the colonizers used against them. But they kept it secret. And they called it by the name of a language—Farsi—that allows them to flee the persecution of grammatical gender.

Hijra Farsi is accompanied also by distinctive bodily gestures that challenge the regime of gender. Indeed, it is the specific way hijras highlight their relation to genitalia that brings the idea of bodily grammar to the fore. The hijra practice of lifting sarees and exposing the genital area to those who have been rude to them is an extremely effective mechanism for shaming people. In an inversion of the typical situation in which the exposure of the genital area causes shame to the person so exposed, the hijra exposure shames the person doing the looking. And why? Because if the hijra has retained her masculine genitalia, then the disjunction between the saree and the penis engenders shock. Suddenly we are in the presence of the 'masculine-neuter' of the *Kamasutra*. And if the hijra has gone through the 'nirvana' ceremony of excising the penis and testicles, then what is exposed is the hole where once the penis used to be. The neuter in what was once masculine. Or even the feminine in what was once presumably masculine. The 'feminine-neuter' of the Jain texts. Hijra genitals defy gendered and grammatical determination, and therefore seem shocking to our colonized selves. But rather than being a simple rejection of masculinity for femininity or a rejection of both masculinity and femininity—as the prefix 'na' in napunsaka seems to suggest—hijra grammar provides us with a profusion of options.

This proliferation is unlike the terms used in the Rights of Transgender Persons (Protection of Rights) Bill, 2016, which is poised to become law in India. Even though the law marks a huge step forward in transgender rights, it cannot quite come to terms with the profusion that marks the grammar of hijras. Instead, it defines hijras as '...biological males who reject their masculine identity and identify either as women, or "not-men", or "in-between man and woman" or "neither man nor woman"'. These proliferating definitions nonetheless keep intact the separate categories of men and women. But what about the beings that the Pali and Sanskrit texts describe as masculine-neuter and feminine-neuter—what we might term neither/nor/both/and? Not a third gender but a term that points to a proliferation of genders and grammars? This would take us closer to the idea of hijras who combine both masculine and feminine principles while simultaneously being neither male nor female. This is why hijras are considered auspicious in the first place: because they play with grammatical and embodied gender not by negation but, rather, by voluptuousness.

And this voluptuousness shows through in everything having to do with hijra culture. From their clothes to their names, hijras are multiple. All hijras in India have at least two names, one male with which they are named at birth, and one female with which they are named during the hijra initiation rites. In Hyderabad, this duality gets doubled also with two religions. Here, hijras usually have one female Hindu name by which they are known in everyday life, and a male Muslim name by which they are officially entered into the hijra register. These are in addition to the male names they might have been given at birth. They practice sharia rituals prescribed for both men and women, but they also style themselves as devotees of a Hindu goddess who goes by the name of Bahuchara Mata, or closely aligned regional variations thereof. Hijras take on, then, not only the two major genders of the world, but also the two major religions of the subcontinent, and live to tell the tale. Far from being the embodiment of grammatical negation, they speak a language of linguistic excess.

This excess is what Tamil hijras channel when they style themselves aravanis after Arjuna's son, Aravana, in the *Mahabharata*. Aravana offers to sacrifice himself in order to ensure victory for the Pandavas. But as a reward for his sacrifice-to-be, Aravana wants to have sex before he dies. Since no woman is willing to marry him just for one night, Krishna comes to Aravana in his female form as Mohini, and has sex with him. Aravana is thus both sacrificial and acquisitive, a martyr and a married man, a celibate and a sensualist.

Far from opposition or negativity, then, Aravana, like the aravanis, occupies a force-field of multiplicity. This multiplicity of the neuter in India extends to both desire and grammar; the neuter is prolific rather than empty or negative. Not conflicted, confused, uncertain, violent and criminal, as hijras are commonly described these days, but rather, plenitudinous, cultured and, above all, reflective of a lived reality of mobile desires that marks our everyday lives. The neuter in India has given us persons who defy the categories of two fixed genders. And it has given us grammars that every day mark our language as transvestite: grammars that recreate the exquisite echoes of English and the prolific passions of Persian. If we are Hindi- or Urdu-speaking men and women, then we are neutered by the grammatical effeminization of mardangi and and the masculinization of ishq or prem. In Hindustani, English, as well as in many Eastern and Dravidian languages, we are all grammatically hijras, and have been so for a long time. Perhaps it is time again to acknowledge that like our grammars, our desires too might not fit only one category at a time.

6

CELIBACY

'My attitude is celibate. I don't give a f**k.'

—Anonymous

Why should a book on desire pay any attention to celibacy?
Let us ask Mirabai.

A 16th-century devotee of Krishna, Mira was convinced
early on in life that Krishna was her spouse. Nonetheless, she
was married off at the age of 18 to Bhoj Raj, the heir apparent
to the throne of Mewar. According to legend, Mirabai never
consummated her marriage and, increasingly in the throes of
passion for Krishna, would wander the streets in an ecstasy
of song and dance. Such behaviour was not only lineally
irresponsible since it did not produce a son and heir, but
it was also scandalous since Rajput women did not go out
openly and behave in such a brazen manner. Rumour has it
that Mira simply merged with her lover—disappeared into
Krishna's statue—when she was being forced to return home
to Mewar. In the meantime, she had become a significant
Bhakti poet and saint, with apparently hundreds of poems
to her credit. These poems are love poems to her lord, but
speak also of her right to live as she pleases, and defends
all those who are oppressed by the shackles of caste and
gender. Mirabai is an early example of a woman who uses
celibacy to redirect her energies into socially non-sanctioned
worship rather than marriage. She stands out because such a
move goes directly against a Rajput culture that frowns upon

women in the public sphere, and requires them to be sexually subservient to the institutions of marriage and reproduction.

Indeed, religiously ecstatic celibacy is one of the few routes available to women who want to opt out of getting married. Consider in this regard the Basran sect of female Sufi mystics who lived in Syria around the 9th century CE, and whose practices are supposed to have influenced later women Sufis from India to China. The most famous among them is Rabi'a bint Isma'il, who, like her fellow mystics, used celibacy as a way of escaping the circumscribed female roles of wife and mother and domestic labourer. In a tradition harking back to the Christian mystics, and forward to Mahatma Gandhi, Rabia organized a 'spiritual marriage' for herself with the Sufi Ahmad ibn al-Hawari after making it clear to him that she was drawn only to the Sufi way of life and had no interest whatsoever in a sexual relationship with him (or anyone else). She rebuffed all his amorous advances, and with her considerable financial wealth, even arranged for dowries to be paid for Ahmad to marry other women and satisfy his sexual cravings. Rabia's intense desire was to fast during the day and devote herself to worshipping god at night; nothing else mattered, and sex played no role in her desires.

Celibacy allows entry into a different kind of community that is not based on the imperatives of heterosexual marriage. This is the kind of renunciate celibate community that gathers each year before the pilgrimage to Ayyappan's shrine, for instance. Historically, in India, women have used celibacy as a means of moving away from a community that tells them to conform to the lusts of men.

Two of India's most famous women saint-poets predate Mirabai in exemplifying this tendency. Mahadeviyakka, a saint from 12th-century Karnataka, betrothed herself to Shiva at an early age. Nonetheless, like Mira, she was forced into an earthly marriage with the local chieftain, Kausika, whose paeans of love impressed Mahadevi's parents, if not her. Even though the marriage seems to have taken place, it is clear that it was never consummated. At one point, it seems that Kausika tries to force Mahadevi into having sex with him. This is the cue for her to leave him altogether. Mahadevi renounces not just husband, home, parents and village, but she also gradually sheds her clothes, and wanders about covered only by her long hair. Reminiscent of other Shaivite yogis, as well as of a later Sufi poet, Said Sarmad, who too shed his clothes in the ecstatic service of god and in rejection of heterosexuality, Mahadevi embraced celibacy as the path to freedom from a patriarchal world that serves only to harness her desires for reproductive purposes. Mahadevi is clearly in love, but her desire does not tend towards having sex with men. Or women. She wants to be one with Shiva, and celibacy is the only route by which she can achieve her ardent desire.

We know of at least one other woman poet-saint from South India who walked away from community, husband and family life in order to follow her desire. Like Lady Macbeth, from Shakespeare's famous tragedy, the 6th-century Tamil poet Karaikkal Ammaiyar 'unsexes' herself, but this time in order to escape the eyes of men. Contemporary accounts suggest that she converted herself from being a beauty to someone who struck terror in the hearts of men. In her own words, she had:

Sagging breasts and swollen veins
protruding eyes, bare white teeth and sunken belly

reddened hair and pointed teeth
skeletal legs and knobbly knees
has this female pey (ghost)

She devoted her life to the worship of Shiva, whom she insisted on addressing as appa (father), and who, she wrote, addressed her in turn as ammai (mother). The crux of her desexing is to remove herself as an object of attraction from the register of (human) sexual desire. Thus the emphasis on being physically unappealing is important in her case: by all accounts a beautiful woman before her celibate transformation, Karaikkal Ammaiyar got rid of her beauty in order to enjoy her desire, which had nothing to do with having beautiful flesh.

Instead, her celibacy celebrates Ammaiyar's devotion to the dancing Shiva. It also allows us to recognize—as in the case with education—that physical beauty and genital sexuality are not the only recognizable embodiments of desire. Celibacy revolves on the axis of desire, but that axis can be spiritual devotion just as intensely as it can be sex acts. It can be an escape from the constraints of physicality, especially for women who want to shun the lascivious advances of men. This is why female Sufi saints too have a history of celibacy despite Islam not regarding celibacy as either necessary or desirable. In all these cases, celibacy allows for the fulfilment of desires that are specifically not socially sanctioned. Interestingly, in this version of desire, sex is what is socially sanctioned while celibacy is the rebellious child who wants to live dangerously.

Celibacy is thus both elevated by religion for being a sign of devotion, and feared for being an anti-reproductive force. This tension is perhaps best exemplified by a famous male celibate in Indian mythology: Bhishma in the *Mahabharata*. In fact, the story of Bishma brings to the fore the tension between religion and celibacy precisely over the question of desire.

In order to smooth the process for his father Shantanu to marry Satyavati, the daughter of a fisherman, Bhishma promised that he would never marry and have children of his own, thus assuring the throne for Satyavati's children after Shantanu's time. Bhishma—whose name means 'he of the terrible oath'—was much venerated for his oath of celibacy and was even granted the boon of choosing the moment of his death.

Famously, Bhishma died at the hands of Shikhandi, the reincarnated male version of the Princess Amba, who had been humiliated by Bhishma in a previous life. Bhishma had kidnapped the three sisters Amba, Ambika and Ambalika on the day that Amba was due to pick Salwa, the man she loved, as her husband. Bhishma wanted all three sisters to marry his younger brother Vichitravirya, but 'returned' Amba when she made her love for Salwa known. Salwa, however, refused to accept what he thought of as soiled goods. And Vichitravirya too refused to take her back. Amba then turned to Bhishma and asked him to marry her, but Bhishma turned her down on account of his vow of celibacy. In a fury, Amba asked Shiva for the boon of being the one to kill Bhishma, whom she understandably held accountable for ruining her life. She was granted the wish but had to be reborn as Shikhandi in order to do this. The story from this point on gets rather convoluted. But suffice it to say that Amba was reborn as a woman who then turned into a man and caused Bhishma to bow before her. Since Bhishma could choose the moment of his death, Shikhandi succeeded only in having him pinned down with arrows. Bhishma chose to die soon after the Pandavas won the war, but the conditions for the death of the celebrated celibate had already been created by the trans-gendered warrior Shikhandi.

In the Jain *Mahabharata*, Bhishma castrates himself in order to prove the seriousness of his vow of celibacy and ensure that he will never have children. What is interesting in the case of both Bhishma the Castrated Celibate and Shikhandi the Woman/Man is that they are considered complete human beings. Like Tiresias in Greek mythology, Shikhandi too has seen life from the perspective of both a woman and a man, which gives him a power rarely accorded to mere mortals. This is the same power associated with hijras, which is why historically in India their blessings are sought on auspicious occasions. The Ardhanarishvara (half man-half woman) aspect of Shikhandi grants him/her the power to cause the death of even the most powerful warrior of the time, a feat that no one else is able to achieve. And by giving Bhishma the boon of choosing his own moment of death, the gods also recognize the supremacy of the celibate. Bhishma stands in a unique position in the *Mahabharata*—he is accorded perhaps the highest status in the tale as the embodiment of self-sacrifice. But equally, his sacrifice is lamented because not having children (especially sons) dooms him to a dark fate according to the scriptures of Vedic Brahminism. Bhishma is known as the complete human being, the complete warrior, and the complete teacher. But his completeness stands in a state of tension with his childlessness.

Bhishma's role in the *Mahabharata* points to an interesting faultline between the imperative to reproduce and the worship of celibacy. It also outlines an important chapter in the development of many modern Indian religions— Buddhism, Jainism and Hinduism—and the differences among them.

Scholars have suggested that around the middle of the 2nd millennium BCE, sects and religions arose to challenge the Brahminical emphasis on marriage and procreation. What later came to be known as Buddhism and Jainism started to make celibacy a central tenet of their practice, so much so that celibacy became the most recognizable component of the new religions. Even though Buddhism enjoined it only upon monks and nuns, celibacy quickly became central rather than peripheral to the theory and practice of the religion. Indeed, a belief in the high value of celibacy presented itself as a resistance to Vedic rituals, of which marriage was an important part. Marriage, desire and attachment to the world—samsara—were all bundled together as practices to be shunned in order to attain enlightenment and freedom from pain. The Vedic insistence on the married (male) householder as the norm around which the Brahminical worldview is articulated started being criticized by religions that saw both marriage and householding as adding to, rather than freeing us from, sorrow.

Thus was set up a contest between two ideals of sexuality and asceticism, with each trading barbs against the other. Patrick Olivelle records a poem from the 2nd millennium BCE, a staged conversation between Raja Harishchandra and the sage Narada, in which Narada outlines the importance of producing sons and the horrors of indulging in celibacy. In the poem, Harishchandra says:

Now, since they desire a son,
Both those who are intelligent and those who aren't:
What does one gain by a son?
Tell me that, O Narada.

And Narada replies:

A debt he pays through him,
And immortality he gains,
The father who sees the face
Of his son born and alive;

Greater than the delights
That earth, fire and water
Bring to living beings
Is a father's delight in his son.

By means of sons have fathers ever
Crossed over the mighty darkness;
For one is born from oneself,
A ferry laden with food.

What is the use of dirt and deer-skin?
What profit in beard and austerity?
Seek a son, O Brahmin,
He is the world free of blame.

The Vedic patriarchal insistence on producing sons in order to ensure the happiness of fathers in the afterlife is, in Narada's narrative, challenged by the imagined ascetic who renounces the world altogether. The Brahmin writing the poem clearly assumes there is no 'profit' to be had in the celibate life, and encourages the ascetic to renounce renunciation, and beget sons. In fact, this begetting of sons is considered a business of extreme urgency. For example, poor Bhishma, the 'complete human being', is destined to be trapped in a hell-like realm because he has no sons who will perform his last rites and repay the debt to his ancestors. The 'profit' represented by sons is a profit to be reaped in the afterlife for the Brahmins, while for the Buddhists the afterlife is itself the thing to be shunned. Since both Buddhism and Jainism promulgate their teachings as a means of attaining freedom from the afterlife, the begetting of sons does not feature prominently in either religion.

Alarmed at the attractions that this rejection of ritual seemed to pose, the Brahmins came up with a compromise formula that was to mark the Vedic religions for the rest of their history: the concept of the four ashramas or stages of life. In this theory, Hindu men are encouraged to be celibate during three of the four phases of life—first during brahmacharya (as a student), and then during the two stages that follow the householder stage (grihasta): vanaprastha (forest-dweller) and sanyasa (renunciate). This compromise formula allowed people to indulge in the attractions of celibacy but only before and after they discharge their sexual duty and produce children.

What is particularly interesting about this compromise formula is that it recognizes that people find celibacy attractive. In a panic about the encroaching inroads being made by religions advocating celibacy, Vedic Brahminism starts developing a version of itself in which men are told that they can have *both* sexuality and celibacy. Buddhism encourages you to pick one over the other but, Vedic Brahminism seems to be saying, 'come to us, and you don't need to choose because you can enjoy the pleasures of each'. In fact, the scramble to accommodate celibacy within sexuality has led to fascinating formulations within the Vedic traditions that claim, for instance, that having sex only at night is the same thing as staying celibate. Or that engaging in intercourse only to produce children is tantamount to being celibate. Only non-reproductive sex, in this instance, seems to count as sex.

The infamous Manu, whose 2nd-century CE book of repressive laws, the *Manusmriti*, was adopted by the British as the basis of Hinduism, even suggests that having sex with one's wife only during permitted nights amounts to remaining celibate. He seems here to be confusing chastity with celibacy, or the insistence on being virtuous while sexually active with the renunciation of sex altogether. And how many nights of sex are permitted in the *Manusmriti*? In *Intimate Relations*, Sudhir Kakar takes us through the proscriptions: A husband should only approach a woman in her season, which is a period of sixteen days within a menstrual cycle. But among these the first four, the eleventh and thirteenth are forbidden. Since sons are conceived only on even nights, while daughters are conceived on uneven ones, the number of recommended nights straightaway shrinks by a half. Then there are the parvas, the moonless nights and those of the full moon, on which sexual relations lead either to the 'hell of faeces and urine' or to the birth of atheist sons. In addition, there are many festival days for gods and ancestors which are forbidden. This leaves at best about five 'permitted' nights a month for sexual intercourse.

Vedic Brahminism thus mingles a suspicion of sex with an insistence that people should reproduce, which makes for a rather confining, not to mention confusing, atmosphere. It is in this atmosphere that the attractions of celibacy become evident. Less a giving up of desire than a different organization of one's desire, celibacy suggests a way out of the ritualistic loathing of and longing for sex. Its alternative organization moves us away from a communal monitoring of desire to a more private enjoyment.

Getting rid of the rituals for marriage and reproduction laid down by an oppressive community amounts to a radical call for freedom. Celibacy becomes desirable as a way of escaping religious control over one's desires and asserting independence in the face of repression. Resisting the dominant call to marry and reproduce can be a liberating experience. By definition, then, celibacy is seen as the anti-social choice, the one that flies in the face of what the Brahmins have prescribed.

Such an appreciation of celibacy suggests that desire cannot be understood narrowly only as sexual desire; desire is often at its most intense in its renunciation of sex. This understanding runs counter to our current emphasis that marriage and reproduction are the most appropriate expressions of desire. Celibacy is considered desirable until a point, after which the need for sexual activity regulated by marriage takes over with a vengeance. Indeed, the insistence that reproduction should follow hot on the heels of marriage is made clear by the growing number of IVF centres all over the country.

Given the current population of India, the need for IVF centres is perhaps less evident except as the fulfilment of a social compulsion to reproduce. Indeed, what celibacy does in such a situation is point to an alternative and more radical regime of desire, which is why it is considered a threat to social stratifications of sexuality. Working backwards, celibacy makes it obvious that neither reproduction nor marriage is necessary in this overpopulated world. Celibacy can be seen as a desire not to allow desire to lead to reproduction. It becomes a way for women of all religions to resist the patriarchal imperatives of marriage. Celibacy allows for a personal freedom from the constraints of sex, but it also encourages the formation of communities based on the collective rejection of a narrow understanding of desire. The Brahma Kumaris, a spiritual order founded as the Om Mandali in Sindh in the 1930s, and comprising primarily women right from the start, is only the most modern example of such an established female community. The Brahma Kumaris insist on celibacy for all its members—male, female, married and unmarried. This is their core requirement for full membership. In 1938, when the Om Mandali insisted that its women members could choose whether or not to be celibate in their conjugal relations, the husbands of the women picketed the organization for destroying their marital pleasures. Giving married women the right not to have sex with men was a huge step forward in ensuring non-servitude for the women. Female Om Mandali members could now focus on their own desires instead of catering to those of their husbands.

Rather than being defined negatively as shunning sexual contact with other people, then, celibacy can also be celebrated, singly or communally, as the heightening of desire within one's self. Such an understanding of celibacy is woven into the very fabric of desire in India. In the 8th century, the philosopher Adi Shankaracharya founded a set of mathas, or monasteries, in which men were divided into two groups—those who studied scripture and those who studied weapons. What is now known as the akhada in India derives from this lineage of the matha in which celibate students learn from a dedicated guru. Indeed, the Hindi word 'akhada' is related to the Greek word 'academy' and indicates a group (of men) living and learning together. Today akhadas refer largely to schools of wrestling in North India, and some of them are open also to women. Akhada members desire to learn a sport, or wrestle, or in Shankaracharya's time, study scripture, and this has to take priority over the desire to have sex. All members of the akhada are meant to be celibate while they are a part of the akhada, and focus primarily on attaining their non-sexual desires, either of body or mind. For an akhada member—often from the lower class or lower castes—following a strict exercise and diet regimen, and being celibate, is a way out of straitened material circumstances. Joseph S. Alter quotes one of them as saying: 'If wrestlers are brahmacharis then they will do well.' He also reports a conversation with a guru at an akhada: 'When I asked him, "Guruji, why is it that you have never married?" he answered, "Who says that I'm not married? I have married wrestling and the children of this marriage are my disciples."' For over two thousand years in India, then, celibacy has provided an alternative to the straitjacket of social imperatives, allowing people instead simply to follow their desire.

7

YOGA

'Be a part of a new fitness craze combining the philosophies of yoga with the pleasure of beer drinking to reach your highest levels of consciousness.'

—Online invitation to join a
Beer Yoga event in Indore

'This is an attack on Indian culture.'

—Part of the campaign that ensured
cancellation of the Beer Yoga event

Despite appearances to the contrary, yoga is perhaps the best example of the mixture and impurity that marks the history of desire in India. Indeed, the first space of impurity is yoga's complicated relation to desire. There seems to be no link between the *Kamasutra*'s sexual positions (outlined about a century before Patanjali's 4th-century CE *Yoga Sutra*) and the later asanas of yoga. Even though Wendy Doniger describes the *Kamasutra*'s postures as 'the erotic counterpart to the ascetic asanas of yoga', the yoga asanas are meant to still desire rather than excite it. But kama does shed important light on the history of yoga in India. Or rather, thinking about kama and yoga together gives us a snapshot of the mixtures that mark Hindu philosophies of body and mind. One of the ways in which these philosophies have historically dealt with cultivating, renouncing, shaping, rejecting, enjoying, dismissing, energizing and depleting the desires of the body has been through studies of yogashastra, or knowledge/

science of yoga. And another way they have exerted control over the body has been through studies of kamashastra, or knowledge/science of desire. Kama and yoga are conjoined twins that have been separated in order for each to survive.

Scholars are at pains to note that these two strains of yoga and kama *coexisted* with one another rather than either one trying to stamp out the other. Nonetheless, what remains true is that Patanjali yoga in India seems to have developed as the opposite of kama rather than as an expression of it. Yoga focuses on freeing the mind and stilling it, while kama studies the means by which to excite the body and heighten its pleasures. Many centuries after Patanjali, Gandhi becomes the embodiment of these two conflicting strains. As Sudhir Kakar points out in *Intimate Relations*, Gandhi's 'excessive' interest in sex as a young householder gave way to an obsession with celibacy. Much of this obsessiveness, says Kakar, grew out of intense conversations between the young Gandhi and his jeweller friend Raichandra: '...it is evident that a central concern of their earnest exchanges was the relationship of sexuality to "salvation", the transformation of sexual potency into psychic and spiritual power.' In other words, how to use yoga to overcome kama.

While the *Rig Veda* accords pride of place to kama as the very first thing that came upon the creator, the later *Upanishads* (around 800 BCE) suggest that kama might not be the only or primary path available to its followers. In addition, they outline the path of the renunciate, the ascetic who gives up on bodily pleasure in order to tame the mind. This latter tradition was embraced by the Buddha as he tried to still the upheavals of an uncertain world by anchoring the mind away from the distractions of the body.

The downgrading of the body for him took several forms, all of which revolved around the renunciation of desire— starvation, celibacy and meditation. The Buddha lived sometime between the 6th and 4th centuries BCE, and the first mention of the word 'yogi' to mean 'ascetic' dates from between the 2nd and 4th centuries BCE. But the *Yoga Sutra*'s emphasis on meditation (rather than asanas) does not focus on the deprivation model that formed the core of Buddhist meditation. For Patanjali, yoga is not about self-mortification, but rather, about reflexive self-restraint. But even as the *Yoga Sutra* does not prescribe deprivation, it is far removed from the sensuous indulgence of the *Kamasutra*'s postures.

This debate between yoga and kama, stillness and excitation, is also a debate *within* the histories of yoga. If Patanjali yoga sought to create ascetics who control the body and mind, then the tantric traditions that arose around the 2nd century CE (and flourished towards the end of the millennium) problematize that understanding of yoga. For the tantrics, that which binds you—desire—is also what will set you free. Tantric scriptures did not outlaw alcohol or meat from their recommended yogic diets. Neither did they outlaw sex. In fact, for many tantrics, the inner energy that yoga sought to distil was to be found in bodily and sexual fluids that are otherwise considered taboo. According to David Gordon White, ritualized orgies were organized—often in graveyards—between tantric yogis and female 'messengers' of the goddess who were termed yoginis.

With its close alliance to both gastronomic and sexual pleasures of the flesh, tantra yoga defied most of the ascetic practices of Hinduism, Buddhism and Jainism. What tantra also shows is the faultline along which yoga has historically been constructed. Hatha yoga, the postural yoga that developed out of tantra between the 11th and 15th centuries, considered the body as a hydraulic system that needed to be worked upon in order to channel sexual fluids. Unlike Patanjali's yoga, which was incredibly cerebral, hatha yoga both arouses the body and allows for mastery of that arousal; it highlights the centrality of a desire that must be controlled. It draws the line between the sensualist who accumulates karma by allowing his seed to spill, and the ascetic who moves his seed upwards and therefore gets out of (obtains moksha from) the cycle of karmic accumulation.

Little wonder, then, that the majority of tantra yoga practitioners are Shaivite, or followers of Shiva, the God of Destruction. Being a tantra yogi is to harness the sensual power of Shiva and turn it into millennia of yogic meditation. This is why many tantrics continue to this day to wander

'Sadhu with Long Hair' (ref. CSWC33/
OS16/28). Courtesy of the Centre for
the Study of World Christianity
at the University of Edinburgh

around naked with ash smeared over their bodies, and hair grown out in matted locks in imitation of what Shiva is assumed to look like.

For tantrics like the 10th-century CE Kashmiri yogi Abhinavagupta, the point of yoga was to unite the male and female principles—Shiva and Shakti—within one's self. This union is pointedly non-sexual even as it is deeply physical. The figure of Shiva embodies this paradox—the erotic intensity of his unions with his first wife Sati and then with the reincarnated Parvati is the stuff of legend. But an equal part of the legend is his ascetic lifestyle and secluded abode on top of Mount Kailash. Shiva is both sexual being and renouncer of sexuality. He is a renunciate who understands the intensity of sex. And a sexual being who embraces the value of renunciation.

When Sati immolates herself to protest her father's refusal to accept the rough and rude Shiva, the god goes mad. Ramesh Menon's retelling of the *Siva Purana* describes Shiva's state of mind and body after Sati's death:

> Initially, my distraught mind would not be still and her face haunted my every thought as a peerless fury. I saw her in life and death. I saw not merely her face; I saw her body with its velvet folds, each a vale of Brahman to me. I saw her breasts, nightblack nipples taut; I heard her whispered and screamed ecstasies. Ah, why was I punished so cruelly? Then, I took firm hold of myself. I shut her out from my mind as irrevocably as she had shut herself from my life by dying. Slowly, peace came back to me, absorption... In time, my dhyana was immaculate again and I knew nothing save eternity then... I lost myself, as I never had before there was Sati. Fleetingly, I thought this was why she came into my life, to make my tapasya purer when she left.

In Patanjali's *Yoga Sutra*, the main goal of yoga is samadhi, or absolute absorption in the moment. Shiva's reaction to Sati's death reveals the conditions of turbulence in which yoga can intervene to restore the stillness of the mind. That this turbulence is inevitably sexual is another of hatha yoga's insights. In Ramesh Menon's fictionalized narrative, Shiva talks about the absorption that is required in order to still the self and acquire a bliss comparable to the bliss he enjoyed with Sati. For Shiva in the *Puranas*, the bliss of samadhi is as intense as erotic bliss—the latter gets channelled into the former once Sati leaves the scene.

The non-Shaivite branch of yoga—Vedanta—has sought to undertake a systematic 'purification' of yoga to leach it of any tantric influence. Its most eloquent spokesperson was Swami Vivekanada who, in the 19th century, led the movement both to purify yoga and make it more 'scientific'. He was strict about discarding all pleasures and excesses of the flesh: his version of yoga was aspirationally pure. For Vivekananda, tantra was the evil to be shunned because it would routinely run afoul of the dominant social mores—it moved with ease across caste, class, religion, and even gender; its flirtation with desire seemed to him to be the opposite of both purity and modern science. But despite his adherence to Patanjali—the 1896 *Raja Yoga* is Vivekananda's influential reinterpretation of Patanjali's *Yoga Sutra*—the Swami also incorporates asanas from the tantra tradition into his yoga. This is because his 'scientific' outlook made him interested in building the body, and seated meditation alone was not conducive to building a six-pack. But equally, Vivekananda was also interested in the question of desire, though he completely disavowed the sexual realm. It was Vivekananda who popularized the notion of the kundalini, or the coiled feminine energy at the base of the spine that is to be tapped by yogic practice and sent upwards into the brain. The kundalini was understood to be the seat of the body's sexual energy. Symbolized by a triangle with a serpent coiled up in it, the purpose of yoga for Vivekananda was to harness the power of this sexual energy.

Thus, even as the Vedanta school tried to leach yoga of all its tantric trappings, it nonetheless held on to the relation between yoga and desire. Patanjali's text, in comparison, makes no mention at all of the kundalini. For Patanjali, yoga is vai-raga or lack of desire, but for the tantrics, yoga is raga, or desire. Tantra yoga takes sexual desire seriously, but here too, the understanding of desire involves an absolute absorption in the moment—to be in the moment without shame or the accumulation of karma. For both the tantrics and the Vedanta-adherents, the non-accumulation of karma depends on the non-spillage of semen. The 'vital fluids' have to be maintained within the body and sent upwards into the brain rather than being 'wasted'. This rechannelling of desire seems to be the fundamental principle of yoga.

Consider what a present-day yoga guru and holy man, Sadhguru Jaggi Vasudev, has to say about the relation between tantra and sexual desire:

> The Guru-shishya relationship is to deliver the shishya to a higher dimension of consciousness, not trap one into the compulsive nature of sexuality. Above all, this sacred relationship is definitely orgasmic, but not sexual. I am talking about upgrading your technology. You don't have to huff and puff to get into an orgasmic state. If you sit with your eyes closed, you can drip with orgasms in every cell of your body. Those who have failed to achieve an

orgasmic state of existence will associate an ecstatic state with sexuality because that's probably the highest level of experience they have known.

One of the main goals of yoga is to overcome desire and tame it. But yoga does this, especially in the tantric tradition, by exciting desire, by engaging the body if only to go beyond it. What is interesting from a historical perspective is that this desire seems to get rid of the couple form—it is desire that feeds only (on) itself. The bliss created by yoga is orgasmic, but without a sexual orgasm. It is post-coital without the coitus.

Such an experience can perhaps best be described by reference to the Pali word sukha. The *Yoga Sutra* follows the Buddha's lead in relation to the concept of sukha (joy, bliss, happiness) and sthira (stillness, stability, peace), both of which are described as characteristics of the yoga asanas. In the Buddhist canon, sukha refers to a state of lasting rather than transient bliss, to be gained by meditation and centred in the stabilized self. This is the sukha that is divorced from worldly pleasures and absorbed in meditation. For Patanjali, sukha is to be achieved by yogic meditation and attention to breathing. But in the present-day, sukha (or sukoon) also refers explicitly to sexual pleasure. In North India, one of the blessings given to newly-married women is sada sukhi raho—be happy at all times—where 'sukh' is understood to mean the state of marital/sexual bliss. This is also the meaning of 'sukh' in the popular phrase 'shadi-shuda jeevan ke sukh bhogna' (reaping or consummating the pleasures of a married life). Equally, in slang terms, one speaks of 'nain sukh prapti', which means achieving pleasure with/for the eyes.

This is usually the ironic term used to describe voyeuristic pleasures that cannot be translated into genital ones. Sukha is today the term popularly associated with material sexual desire even as yoga has tried for centuries to remove it from the sphere of the sexual.

Indeed, it is this doubleness of the relation between yoga and bliss—is it sexual or is it not?—that has made yogis sexually rampant beings in the popular imagination. The famous American songwriter Johnny Mercer hilariously expresses this vexed relation between desire and yoga in his lyrics for a song in the 1941 film *You're the One*:

The Yogi Who Lost His Willpower

There was a yogi who lost his willpower
He met a dancing girl and fell in love.
He couldn't concentrate or lie on broken glass
He could only sit and wait for her to pass.
Unhappy yogi, he tried forgetting, but she was all that he
    was conscious of.
At night he stretched out on his bed of nails
He could only dream about her seven veils
His face grew flushed and florid every time he heard her
    name
And the ruby gleaming in her forehead set his oriental
    soul aflame.

We remember, of course, the split tendencies in Hindu philosophies out of which both yoga and kama are born. Is 'Hinduism' to be defined by the yogic practice of material detachment, or by the kamic practice of sensual attachment; by sukha or sukha? This question is rarely one of stark binaries in the history of India. For example, even Vatsyayana, who wrote the *Kamasutra*, was a practicing ascetic (and in all probability a yogic one) as he wrote about the 64 sexual positions. Sudhir Kakar even titles his fictional biography of Vatsyayana *The Ascetic of Desire*.

Yoga depends for its existence, then, on mixing with kama. Indeed, this kind of impurity seems to be the very ether in which yoga thrives. Even though it is marketed now to the world as an 'ancient Hindu' tradition, yoga, like almost everything in India, is the product of a syncretic history. The first mention of 'yoga' is in the 15th-century BCE *Rig Veda*, where the word denotes neither meditation nor austerities but rather a chariot in which the yoke holds together the wheels and the horses. 'Yoga' is etymologically linked to the English word 'yoke'. Several hundred years later, in the *Mahabharata* (circa 4th century BCE), this yoking of horse and chariot starts to be understood metaphorically as the coming together of the body, senses and the mind in a unified whole. Later sections of the *Mahabharata* (200-400 CE) develop this idea of yoking from materials available in the 3rd-century BCE *Katha-Upanishad*, which in turn picks up on the breathing meditations outlined in Buddhist and Jain sources to gain control over body and mind. Patanjali's *Yoga Sutra* codifies these meditations with the goal of achieving samadhi, or absolute stillness of body and mind, oblivious to all that is external to the self.

The Sufis then picked up on this yogic desire for meditative control over one's baser instincts, and embraced it eagerly. So much so that the Shattari tariqa (or Order), which was the Sufi tariqa in India most closely associated with yoga, adopted not only yogic mechanisms with which to control breath, but also took on board vegetarianism and abstinence from liquor. Dara Shikoh, the Sufi brother of Aurangzeb, belonged to the Shattaris; his absorption in the sufic-yogic world of meditative practice cost him the crown of Mughal India as the ambitious younger brother stole a march upon the ascetic older brother.

In fact, the Muslim interaction with yoga in India was so profound that it has shaped what we understand by 'yoga' today. The dissemination of the *Yoga Sutra* in India was helped greatly by al-Biruni's Arabic translation in the 11th century, which rekindled interest in Patanjali. But what is remarkable is that the yoga in Patanjali's *Yoga Sutra* (both the Sanskrit version and al-Biruni's Arabic translation) does not quite resemble the yoga that we now practice. One fundamental difference is the attention paid to asanas or postures. Patanjali mentions asanas in only 1 out of 196 sutras. For him, yoga is more about the practice of mindful meditation and less about bodily contortion. It is only texts like the *Hathapradipika* (Light on Hatha) from the 15th century that draw on Sanskrit texts on asanas from the 11th and 13th centuries to start outlining multiple bodily postures. One of these earlier texts proclaims that there are 84 lakh asanas (8,400,000), even though it describes only two.

The 17th-century *Hatharatnavali* (String of Jewels of Hatha) and the nearly contemporaneous *Yogachintamani* (Wish-Fulfilling Gem of Yoga) started to describe asanas in greater numbers—84 are named in the former book and 35 are described in the latter. But the embodied asanas that we now associate with the practice of yoga derive from a Persian text—the *Bahr-al-hayat* (Ocean of Life)—that dates from the 16th century. This Persian text is the translation of an Arabic source—the *Hawd-al-hayat*, or The Pool of Life. In turn, *The Pool of Life* claims to be a translation of a Sanskrit text by the name of *Amritakunda* or The Pool of Nectar. But to date research has not been able to locate any such text in the Sanskritic tradition. Scholars speculate that *Bahr-al-hayat*'s composer—the Sufi Shaykh Muhammad Ghawth Gwaliyari—might have consulted several living yogis because none of the asanas outlined in his text appears in any earlier written version. In his text, these asanas are described in great detail and matched by beautiful illustrations that were commissioned by Prince Salim, the future Emperor Jahangir. *The Pool of Life* describes and depicts 21 yogis performing complicated asanas.

The yoga that is traceable back to Patanjali, then, does not emphasize asanas. And the asanas we practice today derive from an illustrated Persian manuscript. Such is the complicated provenance of yoga in India.

But when the British were faced with a culture in which desires and religions were hopelessly mixed up with one another, they decided that the practice and practitioners of such mixed-up desire needed to be demonized. First, they discredited yogis as criminal troublemakers, whom they finally managed to squash in the so-called Sannyasi and Fakir Rebellion in late-18th-century Bengal. (Hordes of yogis had, throughout the course of the 18th century, managed to convert pilgrimage routes into trade routes, directly competing with the British for wealth and influence.) And then they decided that 'Hinduism' was irrevocably sensual, and therefore dangerous. In *Reading the Kamasutra: The Mare's Trap and Other Essays on Vatsyayana's Masterpiece*, Wendy Doniger cites an English 'Supreme Court ruling from 1862 that states that "Krishna...the love hero, the husband of 16,000 princesses…tinges the whole system (of Hinduism) with the strain of carnal sensualism, of strange, transcendental lewdness." India is both transcendental (or yogic) and lewd (or carnal). For the British, the sukha of yoga was inseparable from the sukha of sexual desire. It was all just 'strange'.

As though responding to this British view of tantra yoga, Sadhguru Jaggi Vasudev takes care to separate the lewdness from the transcendentalism:

> People always try to take recourse in the Krishna-Gopi relationship. As the legend goes, Krishna gave an orgasmic experience to 16,000 women simultaneously. This cannot happen with sexual union. A shishya can establish a very intimate relationship with a Guru. Intimacy is generally understood only as two bodies touching. The body is not intimate enough for one who is on the spiritual path. The physical body is an accumulation from outside, so in the tantric and yogic systems, the body is never considered an intimate part of you. Only when energies meet and mingle and a Guru's energies overwhelm and override the shishya's energies, it leads to an orgasmic experience—a union, but not of the sexual kind.

Yoga's relation to desire, then, is a multi-layered one. It seems clear that yoga re-channels sexual desire into lasting bliss of a non-sexual kind. But it seems equally clear that this non-sexual bliss can only be apprehended in, and has to be routed through, the mode of sexual bliss—what Sadhguru calls 'orgasmic' desire. In fact, both sukha and yoga are closely related etymologically—they derive from words that describe the beneficial joining of the hole and the axle. Sukha and yoga are both blissful, and replete with fulfilled desire. They acknowledge desire, but also want to clean it. They invoke ancient texts but also cater to timeless desires. They fit the axle of the head into the hole of the body.

The desire for India—for its ancientness, its 'wisdom', its beauty—is now inextricably bound up with a desire for yoga. As an indicator of this inextricability, global celebrity involvement in India has tended for many decades to be routed through a desire for yoga. From the Beatles' sojourn with the Maharishi to Marilyn Monroe being photographed in yoga poses, from Beyonce's figure to Madonna's spirituality, from George Clooney's body to Jack Kerouac's prose, yoga has been the gateway drug for an interest in an 'authentic' India. The syncretic history of yoga—Hindu and Muslim—has been made only more cosmopolitan over the years. It is now also English, American, Russian, vegetarian, non-vegetarian, sexual, non-sexual, hot and served at room temperature. Everyone, it seems, desires yoga.

8

SUICIDES

But,
I must pose.
I must pretend,
I must act the role
Of happy woman,
Happy wife.
I must keep the right distance
Between me and the low.
And I must keep the right distance
Between me and the high.
O sea, I am fed up
I want to be simple
I want to be loved
And
If love is not to be had,
I want to be dead, just dead.

—Kamala Das, 'The Suicide'

The history of 'love suicides' runs deep in India, and is represented by tales of intense desire. In some versions of a story told about Shiva, his first wife Sati kills herself so she can be reborn to a different father who will approve of her husband. Sati's father, Daksha, is a rich king who looks down upon Shiva's ascetic life and does not consider it good enough for his daughter. He insults Shiva, and does not invite him to a sacrificial yagna that he organizes and to which he invites all the other gods. Sati insists on attending anyway, without Shiva, and commits suicide at the yagna itself. And indeed, after her love suicide, Sati is reborn as Parvati and becomes Shiva's 'second' wife.

In 16th-century Rajasthan, Mirabai 'merges' with the idol of Krishna in a temple in Dwaraka. Persecuted for wandering about in public and writing love songs to Krishna, Mirabai finally settles in Dwaraka, thought to be the birthplace of Krishna. Legend has it that the new ruler of Mewar, Udai Singh, sent a contingent of Brahmins in 1547 to bring her back to her home state. When they reach Dwaraka, Mirabai asks them to give her one night before complying with their wishes and returning with them to Mewar. During the night, she merges with the idol of Krishna, and is not to be seen again. This is a classic example in the Bhakti-Sufi tradition of becoming one with a god who is also the object of desire. Nothing can now separate Mira from her beloved Krishna.

Love suicides in India are thus paradoxical events. Lovers are ostracized for mating outside their caste or religion or within their gender. They are threatened with violence. Suicides are occasioned by social, sexual, religious, regional and even linguistic divisions. They are seen by the lovers as the end of the line—that beyond which nothing exists. But in India, the strong belief in rebirth (for Hindus), and the deep desirability of merging with the Beloved (for Muslims and Hindus), makes love suicide resonate in more than one key. Suicide might be the end, but it is also the desired beginning—the point after which love can bloom without inhibition. Love suicides are viewed with horror but also accorded respect. They take a stand—it is the lovers against the world, and the lovers win in the long-term. Pain and helplessness mingle here with desire and agency. Death in a love suicide parts the lovers from the world but never from one another. In the reports, myths and tales reproduced below from multiple traditions developed over many centuries, we see this overlap between the pain and desirability of suicide. The lovers hover between shame and triumph, giving in and holding out, losing their lives and winning their loves.

* * *

Valmiki, the 'Sundara Kandam' from the *Ramayana* (2nd centuries BCE-CE):

'Separated from you, reduced to bones, with no blood in the body, and having no further chance of meeting you, I, that chaste wife, am in a desperate situation, and the vow of chastity that I have observed, and the rule of having only one wife which you have been observing, have both become meaningless and vain. I pray from the bottom of my heart that you at least may return safe to your country and rest in happiness... O Rama! I am one whose mental functions have always rested on you exclusively. But still, unfortunate that I am, my austerity and vow have proved to be fruitless. So I have resolved to commit suicide. I should have ended my life quickly with poison or a sharp instrument, but in this city of Rakshasas there is no one to procure me poison or a sharp sword.' Bemoaning her fate thus in many ways and with her body trembling and mouth dried, and also remembering Rama constantly in her mind, Sita Devi approached that great flowering Simsupa tree. Then expressing her sorrow in many ways and deeply immersed in grief, she held her braid of lock and said, 'I am going to the abode of Yama this very moment, strangling myself with the binding cords of my braid of locks.' Saying so, she who was noted for the beauty of all her limbs stood there for a moment holding a branch of that tree.

* * *

Waris Shah, 'Hir-Ranjha' (1766), translated by Charles Frederick Usborne:

[Hir, more commonly spelt as Heer, is a beautiful woman born into a wealthy Jat family of the Sial tribe in Jhang (now in Pakistan Punjab). Ranjha is also a Jat of the Ranjha tribe, who leaves home after a quarrel with his brothers. Ranjha reaches Heer's village and falls in love with her. Heer's father offers Ranjha a job herding his cattle. Heer becomes mesmerized by the way Ranjha plays his flute and eventually falls in love with him. They meet each other secretly for many years until they are caught by Heer's jealous uncle, Kaidu. Heer is forced by her family to marry another man named Saida Khera. Ranjha is heartbroken. He wanders the countryside alone as an ascetic and eventually arrives at the village where Heer now lives. The two lovers return to Heer's village, where Heer's parents agree to their marriage. However, on the wedding day...]

* * *

And the brethren said to Kaidu, 'Brother, you are right. Our honour and your honour are one. All over the world we are taunted with the story of Hir. We shall lose fame and gain great disgrace if we send the girl off with the shepherd. Let us poison Hir, even if we become sinful in the sight of god. Does not Hir always remain sickly and poor in health?'

So Kaidu in his evil cunning came and sat down beside Hir and said, 'My daughter, you must be brave and patient.'

Hir replied, 'Uncle, what need have I of patience?' And Kaidu replied, 'Ranjha has been killed. Death with a glittering sword has overtaken him.'

And hearing Kaidu's words Hir sighed deeply and fainted away. And the Sials gave her sherbet and mixed poison with it and thus brought ruin and disgrace on their name. The parents of Hir killed her. This was the doing of god. When the fever of death was upon her, she cried out for Ranjha saying, 'Bring Ranjha here that I may see him once again.' And Kaidu said, 'Ranjha has been killed; keep quiet or it will go ill with you.'

They buried her and sent a message to Ranjha saying, 'The hour of destiny has arrived. We had hoped otherwise but no one can escape the destiny of death. Even as it is written in the Holy Quran, "Everything is mortal save only God."'

They sent a messenger with the letter and he left Jhang and arrived at Hazara, and he entered the house of Ranjha and wept as he handed the letter. Ranjha asked him, 'Why this dejected air? Why are you sobbing? Is my beloved ill? Is my property safe?' The messenger sighed and said, 'That dacoit death from whom no one can escape has looted your property. Hir has been dead for the last eight watches. They bathed her body and buried her yesterday and as soon as they began the last funeral rites, they sent me to give you the news.'

On hearing these words Ranjha heaved a sigh and the breath of life forsook him.

Thus both lovers passed away from this mortal world and entered into the halls of eternity. Both remained firm in love and passed away steadfast in true love. Death comes to all.

* * *

Heer-Ranjha's tomb in Jhang, now in Pakistan.
Photo by Khalid Mahmood. *Source:* Wikimedia Commons

Shakuntala Devi, *The World of Homosexuals* (1977), p. 117:

Homosexuals have been oppressed in all societies. They
have been considered the negation of heterosexuality and
of the nuclear family structure, and as such they have been
driven from their jobs, families, education, and sometimes
from life itself.

* * *

Ruth Vanita, *Love's Rite: Same-Sex Marriage in India and the West* (2005), p. 141:

In India, the idea that no one can separate those destined to be together is very powerful and is interwoven with the idea of love-death. In the 1988 film *Qayamat Se Qayamat Tak* (From One Apocalypse to Another), two feuding families react with great hostility when the daughter of one and the son of the other fall in love. The girl's family tries to forcibly marry her off to another man. The lovers then elope and marry each other without witnesses, by garlanding one another in a ruined temple. This is a modern representation of a gandharva marriage. The woman's family sends hired killers to kill her lover but by mistake they kill her, whereupon he commits suicide. Her dying words to him, 'Now nobody can separate me from you,' invoke the normative Hindu idea that death does not sever attachments. Almost identical words are found in every same-sex couple's suicide note.

* * *

Meerut, *TheTimes of India*, 11 January 2006; 'Girl Attempts Suicide over Lesbian Marriage':

Chafed by her family's opposition to her same-sex marriage, an 18-year-old girl on Wednesday attempted suicide by consuming insecticide and was admitted to a nursing home in Kankerkhera.

The two, who have grown up in the same locality and known each other for several years, 'solemnized' the marriage at a Shiva temple in Kankerkhera after which the girl brought her 20-year-old 'bride' with 'sindoor' (vermillion) on her head to live in her Jawaharpuri house on Tuesday evening.

The family, however, disapproved of the union and sent the bride back to her house in Badam Mandi. The 'groom' was then locked inside a room and allegedly consumed some insecticide kept there. She was rushed to a private nursing home where her stomach was flushed out. Doctors attending on her said she was out of danger but kept under observation. The girl said at the nursing home that the two had made a choice and would continue to live together. She said they had been 'living as husband and wife' for the last five years.

A probe had been ordered into the incident, District Magistrate Rama Krishan said. No police report had yet been filed in this connection, Senior Superintendent of Police Rajiv Ranjan Verma said, 'Prima facie, no case has been filed but we are seeking the legal opinion on the matter.' Affronted by the lesbian marriage, VHP and Shiv Sena activists staged a demonstration in front of the Deputy Commissioner's office.

* * *

Chennai, *The Times of India*, 22 May 2008; 'Tragic End for Lesbian Couple Tormented by Family Pressure':

A lesbian couple who committed suicide by setting themselves on fire have been put to rest in a joint cremation this week. Christy Jayanthi Malar (38) and Rukmani (40) set themselves ablaze after their families took objection to their 'unnatural' relationship.

It has been reported that the two women had suffered years of torment from their families who objected to the closeness of the couple. Although being in a relationship since their school days the women both had husbands.

This is common in India where there are huge social and legal pressures to live a heterosexual lifestyle. The alarm was raised when smoke was seen coming from Mrs Malar's home. When neighbours went in they found the bodies of the two women held in an embrace.

It is thought that the women committed suicide after an argument that Rukmani had with her relatives. Police told reporters that the two doused themselves in kerosene before setting themselves alight. In an ironic twist, the families who tried to separate them agreed for the bodies to be laid to rest in a joint cremation.

A senior police [official] told *The Times of India*: 'We can't say the relatives pushed the women into suicide. They might have verbally abused them, but that was to bring them back to normal life.'

* * *

Kochi, *Mathrubhumi*, 27 June 2008; 'Youth and Student Immolate Themselves':

A youth running a barber shop, and his friend, a student, have been discovered dead due to burns in a rented house. Sivanarayanan (32), from Perumbilavu in Trichur, presently residing near Ajantha Theatre in Pandikkudi, Mattancherry (Kochi) and Deepak (17), son of Srikesh, R.G. Pai Road, are the deceased and their badly charred bodies were spotted in a room of the rented house Sivanarayanan had been occupying. The incident seems to have taken place at around 3 a.m. on Thursday (26th). Both the bodies have been completely burnt. Police recovered a petrol can from the precincts. Police assumes that the two, who were intimate friends, had committed suicide together.

Deepak's family had been objecting to his relationship with Sivanarayanan. As a result, Deepak had even attempted to run away from his house a few days back. On Wednesday, Deepak had been watching TV till 12 at night and must have sneaked out after that to go to Sivanarayanan's house. Police added that he had even created a human shape on his bed with a pillow and covered it with a blanket to avert the suspicion of his family.

The police have come to the conclusion that the trauma caused by his family's discovery of his unnatural relationship with Sivanarayanan must be the reason for his suicide. Sivanarayanan, who came from Perumbilavu to Kochi a few years back, had been running three barber shops in the city.

* * *

Vijaydan Detha, 'Chouboli' (Oral tale, written down in 2010):

Once there was a village where a Rajput and a Jat lived. They were the best of friends. They spent every moment of the day and every moment of the night as close to each other as shadows... The two had their houses built next to each other on adjoining plots. The love they had for each other was deeper than that of brothers.

When the Rajput went with the Jat for his mukhlavau to retrieve his bride from her parents' home, his friend's in-laws treated him better than their own son-in-law... After a few days it was time to set out for the Rajput's mukhlavau... The whole journey the Rajput couldn't stop wondering how his in-laws would treat his friend. It would be horrible if they were to slight him in any way. When they drew close to a temple, he stopped the carriage. The Rajput was a devotee of Guileless Mahadev. The Rajput stood before the image of Shankar Bhagwan with folded hands and prayed that his in-laws would attend to his friend with the same care and concern as they would to him. He pledged an eleven-rupee offering that everything might turn out just as he hoped. But he vowed that if there was any discrimination, he would come back to take his life at that very spot.

The Rajput's in-laws received the Jat as coolly as they would a menial. They treated him just like a servant. They discriminated against him in the way they served the food, in the way they served the drinks, in the way they talked to him. The Rajput's heart went out like a snuffed candle.

On the way back he stopped the carriage in front of the Shiva temple. He stood in front of the image of Guileless Shankar and pulled his sword out of its scabbard with a swoosh. And without stopping to ponder his resolution, he drew his sword across his neck. Blood pooled on the floor in puddles.

The Jat waited a while and then went into the temple himself. And the sight he saw no one should ever have to witness! When he saw the red blood flowing from his friend's body, his face went white as a ghost's. There was no need to think any further. He grabbed the same sword to slice his own neck and fell next to his friend. While alive, both friends' hearts beat as one. Now even their blood began to mingle. They began to dissolve into one another.

* * *

Lucknow, *Express* News Service, 19 May 2016; 'Man Kills Self, "Wife" Consumes Poison at Grave':

A 22-year-old woman on Wednesday attempted suicide at the grave of a Muslim man in Muzaffarnagar, a day after he died allegedly after consuming poison. Danish Qureshi, 25, had reportedly committed suicide Monday when his parents refused to let him marry the woman who is a Hindu. The woman, who had reached Muzaffarnagar from Uttarakhand, was rushed to hospital by people present at the graveyard. Her condition is stated to be stable.

On Monday, Danish came to Muzaffarnagar to discuss with his parents his plans to marry the woman. A heated exchange followed and Danish left home. When he returned home in the evening, his condition had started deteriorating. He had allegedly consumed some poisonous substance and died before the family could take him to a hospital. The family buried the body without informing the police.

Upon learning of his suicide, the woman boarded a bus and reached Muzaffarnagar Tuesday. She visited Danish's house in Kasaban locality the following day and collected information about the place where he had been buried. She went there and consumed the poison, police added. The police found a suicide note, in which she identifies herself as Danish's 'wife' and terms his death as the reason behind her 'taking her own life'.

'We are yet to record her statement in detail about when she got married and whether Danish's parents knew about it. She has yet to produce any evidence to corroborate her marriage,' the SHO said. Danish's father has refuted the woman's claims that his son was married.

* * *

Delhi, Catch News, 21 July 2015: 'In the name of love: what drove 4,168 Indians to death last year':

It's not hard to see why being in love in India is no easy thing. Consider the restrictions on courtship in public places, the moral policing of young couples, the stigma around relationships before marriage and outside one's caste or community. Consider the stories of parents crying rape and kidnapping against the 'unsuitable' boys their daughters elope with. Consider the number of inter-community relationships that end in honour killings.

The social realities that govern relationships in India often feed into a sense of failure, disappointment, disruption, estrangement—and push vulnerable people to suicide.

In 2014 alone, the NCRB [National Crime records Bureau] attributed 4,168 suicides to 'Love Affairs', or 3.2% of all suicides in India. Fewer people, 3,647, died due to 'Drug Abuse/Addiction'. The NCRB report does not explain precisely why love affairs are driving people to suicide.

City dwellers are taking their lives for love at higher rates than the country as a whole. Such suicides, as a percentage of all city suicides, is higher than the national average of 3.2%. Among cities, Delhi witnessed most love-attributed suicides (63) in 2014, followed by Bangalore and Chennai (54 each), Bhopal (48) and Mumbai (46). Men seem more lovesick than women, having a significantly higher rate of suicides, except in West Bengal and Odisha where the trend was reversed last year.

In Meerut, a whopping 46.8% of all suicides in 2013 and 32.4% the year before were attributed to love, the highest of any city. The best places for lovers: Srinagar and Nagaland. Neither has seen a love-related suicide in three years.

* * *

New Delhi, *The Indian Express*, 26 July 2015; 'Delhi has Highest Number of Suicides over "Love Affairs"':

Last year, the national capital witnessed the highest number of suicides over 'love affairs' among 55 cities, according to a report of the National Crime Records Bureau (NCRB), which analysed data on reported cases of suicides in these cities. As many as 63 people, including 38 men and 25 women, committed suicide over 'love affairs', said the report. The capital's neighbouring cities recorded fewer cases of suicides over 'love affairs', according to the report. Chandigarh recorded 21 such suicides, while Jaipur and Ghaziabad recorded seven and 10 cases respectively, it stated.

* * *

Mysore, *New Indian Express*, 14 April 2016; 'Suicide or Honour Killing? Mystery over Girl's Death':

Distressed by her parents' attempts to thwart her love for a lower-caste boy, a 20-year-old girl allegedly committed

WHAT THE NCRB REPORT SAID

City/UT	Population in lakhs	Suicides related to 'love affairs'
Delhi (City)	163.2	63
Delhi (UT)	202.8	65
Bhopal	18.8	48
Ghaziabad	23.6	10
Chandigarh	10.3	21
Jaipur	30.7	7

suicide on Tuesday. Police are not ruling out the possibility of an honour killing. The incident, reported from Chandrawadi near Nanjangud, came in the wake of her family's repeated attempts to make her 'uphold the respect of the family'.

Madhu Kumari, hailing from an upper caste, was in love with Jayarama. Her parents, who did not approve of her choice, had fixed her wedding with a relative. They had even started distributing cards for the wedding, slated for March 29. Madhu had resisted the alliance and wanted to marry Jayarama against the wishes of her family, a source said. This led to a furore. A distressed Madhu allegedly committed suicide on Tuesday. The family performed her funeral in a hurry, without informing the police.

* * *

The Urdu and Hindustani term for suicide is khudkushi, which derives from the Persian words khud—self—and kushtan—to kill. This is the way in which all Hindi/Urdu-English dictionaries render the term for suicide. But the colloquial rendition of this word is khudkhushi—with a second 'h'—which translates quite literally as self-pleasuring. 'Khud-kushi' turned up 87 results on Google, and 20,800 without the hyphen. 'Khud-khushi' turned up 4,51,000 results, along with graphic images of suicide, and 3,33,000 without the hyphen.

Sexual pleasure, it would seem, is widely associated in India with the idea of death. To kill onself is also to pleasure oneself. The fact that one of these words is etymologically incorrect does not diminish its power in the popular imagination. Colloquially, speakers of Hindi and Urdu in India speak a language of death that is also the language of desire.

9

LAW

VS: When we first started, we didn't know the name for it...
We only knew that we made each other happy and that's
what counted most.

SD: Did you feel guilty?

VS: No. Not till we found out that what we were doing had
an actual name for it and that if we were caught we'd be
punished by law.

SD: Did it deter you from continuing that kind of relationship?

VS: Not at all. To be frank with you, in a way it made the
whole thing more interesting for us...you know, the feeling
that we were doing something that was a criminal offence...

—Interview in Shakuntala Devi's
The World of Homosexuals

Two curious things happened in the Indian Supreme Court
in two consecutive years.

In December 2013, the Supreme Court overruled the
Delhi High Court's 2009 decision to 'read down' Section
377 of the British-promulgated 1860 Penal Code. Section
377 states that 'Whoever voluntarily has carnal intercourse
against the order of nature with any man, woman or
animal, shall be punished with imprisonment for life, or
with imprisonment of either description for a term which
may extend to ten years, and shall also be liable to fine.' The
marginal explanation clarifies that 'penetration is sufficient
to constitute the carnal intercourse necessary to the offence
described in this section'. Even though 'carnal intercourse

against the order of nature' might refer to any sex act that does not lead to reproduction, the law was widely considered to be discriminatory against homosexuals. And even though there have been no convictions of homosexuals on the basis of this law in the higher courts of the land, Section 377 has been used rather liberally, often by the police, to harass and intimidate gay people around the country.

The Delhi High Court's landmark ruling did not get rid of Section 377 altogether. But it did rule that the law was discriminatory against the Constitutional guarantees of freedoms of life, liberty and equality for those people targeted by this law. This included, first and foremost, private consensual sexual relationships between adults of the same sex. Section 377, the court said, could only apply to cases of non-consensual non-vaginal intercourse, or intercourse with minors. That is, Section 377 should penalize only homosexual rape (heterosexual rape is covered under Section 375 of the Indian Penal Code), and the rape of minors regardless of sexuality. The Court held that this justifiable punishment of forced sex could not in any way be interpreted to refer also to consensual sexual relationships between adults of the same sex. The Delhi High Court verdict was greeted with much jubilation.

Three and a half years later, the Indian Supreme Court in December 2013 overturned the Delhi High Court judgment, and upheld Section 377. The judgement was a strange mix of aggressive ignorance and legal special pleading. It says that homosexuals constitute only 'a minuscule fraction of the country's population'. One of the judges said in court that he did not personally know a single homosexual. And the judgment stated that since only Parliament can change the law, the Delhi High Court acted beyond its jurisdiction in reading down Section 377. The partial overturning of the law was thus fully overturned.

And then a few months later...

In April 2014, the same Supreme Court of India (albeit a bench consisting of different justices) affirmed the fundamental legal and constitutional rights of transgender people. According to the NALSA judgment (so called because the case was argued between the National Legal Services Authority and the Union of India and Others), discrimination against transgenders violates their rights to equality and freedom of expression and dignity. These were the same rights whose violation was dismissed in the case of homosexuals by the Supreme Court four months earlier. Even more, the Court now asserted that gender identity is a matter of one's intellectual and emotional choice rather than medical intervention. In other words, one does not need to be anatomically male in order to identify as a man and anatomically female in order to be recognized as a woman. This is a huge leap forward in thinking about gender since it also takes into account one's desire: how do I see myself and how do I want to be seen by others? Under the new dispensation, desire is no longer based on anatomy, but rather on what one *wants*.

Perhaps even more importantly, the Supreme Court judgement understands and supports the idea that the word 'sex' as used in Articles 15 and 16 of the Constitution of India to mean a characteristic on the basis of which discrimination is prohibited by law, should be understood to refer not only to biological sex but also to psychological sex, gender identity and sexual orientation. (This last stipulation puts the transgender judgement directly in conflict with the 377 judgement.) The Supreme Court judgment is very much in keeping with the spirit of a postcolonial India that sought to distance itself from several pernicious aspects of British law. The Criminal Tribes Act of 1871, for instance, which included 'eunuchs' among other tribes, castes and social groups whom the British considered to be criminal from birth because they did not conform with gender stereotypes, was one such law. Independent India's first prime minister, Jawaharlal Nehru, repealed the 1871 law in 1952 after referring to it as 'a blot on the law book of free India'.

Indeed, the Bill on transgender rights passed in the Rajya Sabha, the Upper House of the Indian Parliament, in 2015 is an attempt to reinforce and re-implement Nehru's vision with even greater force. This Private Member's Bill is based on the spirit and letter of the Supreme Court judgement. It defines a transgender person as 'a person whose gender does not match with the gender assigned to that person at birth and includes trans-men and trans-women (whether or not they have undergone sex reassignment surgery or hormone therapy or laser therapy etc.), gender-queers and a number of socio-cultural identities such as—kinnars, hijras, aravanis, jogtas etc.'

The Rights of Transgender Persons Bill states: 'The provisions of this Act or the rules made there under shall be in addition and not in derogation of any other legislation, rules, orders or instructions which provides any entitlement or benefit to transgender persons.' Such a stipulation seems to open the door to undoing the criminal status accorded by 377 to people of the same sex having consensual intercourse. After all, since the transgender judgment and Bill have lifted the requirement for anatomical alignment between body and gender identity, presumably one of the men having sex with another man could claim, should he so desire, to be transgendered. This is one of the loopholes being examined in the version of the Bill currently circulating in the Lok Sabha. Completely disregarding the Supreme Court's judgement that the space of the third gender can be occupied by whoever psychologically feels distanced from the gender binary of male and female, the government has sought 'clarification' on who exactly and empirically should be included in the category of the third gender. And then, even more perniciously, the Transgender Persons (Protection of Rights) Bill, 2016—which is the current version in circulation in the Lower House of Parliament, the Lok Sabha—officially removed the right to psychological self-determination provided for by the Supreme Court judgement.

But even if Parliament changes the Supreme Court's definition of a transgender person as someone whose identity is not dependent on anatomical rigidity, even if it refuses to allow sexual orientation as one of the ways in which the use of 'sex' in the Constitution can be understood, even if it refuses to overturn 377, *even then* the curious legal situation generated in 2013 and 2014 will remain. How can the same court strike down the rights of sexual minorities in its judgement on 377, and then uphold the rights of sexual minorities in its judgment on transgenders? This two-faced legal tangle has generated much perplexity in its wake. Does the Supreme Court, the country's highest judicial authority, believe that sexual minorities should or should not be protected under law?

One reason for this curious situation is that the Supreme

Court, unlike its counterpart in the US, does not sit as one unified body to hear its cases. Instead, different benches of judges are constituted for different cases, which makes the arbitrariness of the law and its interpretation startlingly obvious.

However, even as the law's seeming two-facedness in relation to sexual minorities seems deeply perplexing, there is an underlying uniformity that marks both judgments. Despite the progressive nature of the NALSA judgment and the regressive slant of the 377 verdict, both judgements are sex-phobic. 'Carnal intercourse against the order of nature' in Section 377 is met with revulsion because it specifies sexual activity as its ambit, and the Supreme Court judges recoiled from such a blatant reference to sex. Equally, the transgender judgment focuses firmly on the gender identity of a person rather than on their sexual acts. Of the 286 mentions of the word 'sex' in the NALSA judgment, only a handful refer to sex acts, and those are inevitably in relation to Section 377, on which the Court explicitly says it will not pronounce. The phrase 'carnal acts' is never used. It is almost as if the judgment assumes that transgender people do not have sex.

In its avoidance of sex, the Supreme Court judgement is joined by the hijra community's historical association in India with celibacy. Post-op hijras who have undergone 'nirvana' are meant to abjure sex absolutely, and are often punished if they violate this rule. While several hijras go into prostitution by compulsion or desire, and have sex by choice, they are not supposed to do so. Celibacy is a requirement of the true hijra—going beyond gender also means going beyond sexual desire. This is why for so long, and continuing to this day, hijras are considered to be holy—because they fit

the bill of a celibacy that all Indian religious traditions hold
to be sacred. It is not difficult, then, to see a deeper affinity
between the 377 and transgender judgements since they are
joined together in an avoidance of sex.

Even though the NALSA judgment delivered some
revolutionary ideas in terms of gender, it did so at the
expense of dealing with sex. It expanded the understanding
of gender from biological to psychological gender, but it did
not pronounce on the sexual attractions that might be tied
to such a psychological gender. The judgement made illegal
the need for sex reassignment surgery in order to qualify as
a transgender person of the third sex, which is a huge step
forward from thinking of gender as being entirely embodied.
But it did not specify that such members of the third sex
can *also* be men and women who have sex with other men
and women. The judgment boldly said that no one should
be discriminated against on the basis of sexual orientation,
but it equally noted that it would not comment on the one
law that explicitly peddles such discrimination. Indeed, in
many ways, the judges were operating in a sex-free zone,
which perhaps made it easier for the Court to deliver the
progressive judgement that it did. The judgement was bold
because it brushes sex under the carpet. This absence of
explicit sex is now allowing the government to try and get
away with excluding sexuality from being protected under
the ambit of NALSA.

The legal sphere in India is sex-phobic, then, whether
actively or by omission. This does not only mean that courts
cater to phobias about sex, although they do that too. But
even more, they refuse to think about sex even and especially
when they pronounce judgements that mark a step forward

in matters of gender identity. While it is a sound move to uncouple gender from sexuality—after all, one's gender should not automatically determine one's sexual desire or even suggest that one should have sexual desire of any kind—it seems egregious to refuse to pronounce on sex acts at all in a judgement that has far-reaching consequences for who has sex with whom.

Indeed, two things seem evident about laws governing desire in India today: they are averse to talking about sex acts, and when they do talk about them, they talk only about heterosexuality. The underlying impulse of Section 377—to distinguish between 'natural' and 'unnatural' sex and then penalize the 'unnatural' so designated—has a deeper reverberation in the law, quite independent of Section 377. The Criminal Law (Amendment) Act of 2013, for instance, which has made the rape laws in India more stringent, cannot even conceive of sexual activity as being anything other than heterosexual. Male victims of male rapists are not protected by the amended law and female perpetrators of sexual violence against women or men are not even allowed to exist.

In *Talking of Justice: People's Rights in Modern India*, her account of serving on the Justice Verma Committee charged with providing recommendations for laws on sexual assault and harassment at the workplace, Justice Leila Seth describes her views on the law's sexual blind spots:

> When I had helped draft a bill regarding sexual offences for the 172nd Report of the Law Commission, of which I was a member, we had made rape gender-neutral, which meant that the perpetrator could be 'any person' and the victim could also be 'any person'... (This was also the accepted position in Bill No. 130 of 2012, pending in the Lok Sabha.)

But there was considerable weight of opinion pressing for this offence to be made gender-specific... After a great deal of brainstorming...we arrived at a consensus: though the perpetrator was identified as a man, the victim was to be categorized as gender-neutral, thus covering males, females and transgender persons... // The government ordinance issued immediately after our report was submitted kept the gender neutral with regard to both perpetrator and victim, but when the Criminal Law (Amendment) Act, 2013...was passed by Parliament, it made the offence of rape gender-specific with regard to both perpetrator and victim.

The Justice Verma Committee report sought to make the law gender-neutral in terms of allowing both men and women to be perpetrators and victims, and also allowing transgender people to feature in the law as sexual beings. But the law rejected such neutrality (some might say capaciousness) because it cannot imagine that two men and two women might be in sexual relationships with one another.

Several curiosities are immediately on display in such a scenario. First, the law punishing rape ossifies the roles of men and women in society as powerful and powerless. Sexual crimes are always committed by men, and the victims are always women. Such a reinforcement of victimhood does very little to empower women with a sense of dignity and self-worth. Second, and this was pointed out clearly in the Committee report, allowing the sexual harassment law to deal in the familiar binaries of male and female ignores the reality—especially in India—that transgendered people have always existed among us. Third, even if the law wanted to specify men as perpetrators and women as victims in order to recognize the asymmetry between the social power

accorded to men and women—of which there is no doubt—
there is no reason why other sexual configurations cannot
also be allowed under the scope of a sexual harassment law.
Why not recognize that sex happens not only between a
man and a woman? The refusal of such recognition means,
fourth and finally, that the law does not consider sexuality
when thinking about the issue of sexual harassment. State-
sanctioned gender alone rules the roost. The laws of the land
thus veer from criminalizing same-sex sexual activity to not
mentioning it at all.

What is interesting is that India has historically *both*
mentioned varied sexual activities *and* not criminalized
any of them more than the other. If we look at some 11th-
century sculptures from temples in Khajuraho, then what is
immediately noticeable is that they contain sculptures only of
the kinds of sexual acts that our current laws seem unable to
name but are happy to penalize. There is not a single image
of what the law would today understand as procreative
heterosexuality. Instead, we have anal sex, oral sex, sex with
dildos and group sex. Not gender identity, not criminalized
sexualities, but only multiple forms of desire. On a temple
wall. 'Indian' law is now uncomfortable with what Indians
seem to have been comfortable with for a thousand years.

In all fairness, though, and despite the astonishing sexual
explicitness of temples in Konark, Khajuraho, Gwalior and
other places, hierarchizing sexual acts and punishing violators
is not only a British import into India. The *Manusmriti*, for
example, which dates from the 3rd century CE, takes very
seriously its self-endowed mandate as prescriber and enforcer
of the laws. Not only does it firmly outline the caste system
within which all Hindus are meant to be cast, but it also

'Depicting Plural Congress on the Walls of Khajuraho'
by Krishna Sastry. *Source:* Wikimedia Commons

clearly delineates a gendered hierarchy in which women
are inferior to men, and a sexual hierarchy in which sex is
for reproduction alone. Bringing together a Brahminical
insistence on caste purity with an aggressive insistence on
reproduction, Manu says that upper-caste men who have
anal sex will automatically lose caste. But the *Manusmriti*
is not too outraged by such men, advocating only that
Brahmin men who have sex 'with a man or a woman in a
cart pulled by a bullock, in water, or during the day' should
have a purifying bath while fully clothed, or else they will
risk losing caste. Despite its remedies, then, the *Manusmriti*
allows sexual 'deviations' to get off rather lightly even as it
points out what those deviations are. In another example, a
woman who is alleged to have deflowered a younger virgin
woman is not only to have her head shaved and two of her
fingers cut off, but is also to be paraded around town on an
ass. This is a much harsher punishment than that reserved

for the men having anal intercourse, but even here, the text at least acknowledges that women can and do have sex with other women.

The *Manusmriti*'s desire to prescribe and proscribe sexual deviance, though not as virulent as its caste stipulations, has nonetheless made its way into an Indian legal system already groaning under the weight of Victorian morality. As Suparna Bhaskaran points out in 'The Politics of Penetration': 'A charter of 1833 instituted a series of law commissions that met from 1833 onward to codify a uniform criminal and civil law for the whole of India. Although the British intended to "carefully" consult scriptures and/or scriptural experts like pundits/Brahmins, maulvis, and qazis while establishing the "personal laws" of Hindus and Muslims, British law was the basis of codification... Those who prepared the Indian Penal Code [IPC] drew on English law, Hindu law, Muslim law, Livingston's Louisiana Code and the Code Napoleon. Disregarding the numerous complex variations of customary law and practice prevailing among Hindus and Muslims in different parts of the country, Macaulay decided that all Muslims were governed by the Quran and all Hindus by the *Manusmriti*.'

In a fantasy of subjunctive history—imagining a history that is not but that could have been—we might consider how different our laws on desire would have been today if the British had chosen the *Kamasutra* as the text on which to base its laws for Hindus. After all, both the *Manusmriti* and the *Kamasutra* are roughly contemporaneous, and both enjoyed huge popularity. Unlike the *Manusmriti*, the *Kamasutra* does not pronounce any sanctions against sexual variety; indeed, it encourages it. But when it came time to pick, the British lawmakers went for the more conservative text, perhaps because it echoed their own sentiments. If the *Kamasutra* had become the basis for the British legal system in India, then we would be inhabiting a very different set of assumptions about sex, desire and sexuality. But we can now only fantasize about a world that once was such but seems destined never again to be.

10

PARKS

No flower
No leaf
No tree
No bird
Only kama's play
Musk scent
The sound of dry leaves underfoot
O my love, O the beauty of gardens!

—Namdeo Dhasal, 'Gandu Bagicha'

In December 2005, Sub-Inspector Mamta Gautam had not read the *Kamasutra* when she barged into Meerut's Gandhi Bagh. If she had, she might not have abused, kicked, slapped and chased couples who were canoodling in the bushes. After all, in the *Kamasutra*, desire is a walk in the park. Not that it is easy, but rather, that it is public, something to be indulged in outdoors. Desire involves several people, various go-betweens, varied outings. For men, the rules governing desire include going on picnics, owning a house with an orchard, and playing games in public. Women too are instructed on how to brush against the man of their choice when they encounter him in public. All desiring encounters are attended by many servants, and the cultivation and expression of desire takes place among other people in open areas.

Especially in parks or public gardens. Urdu poetry stands testimony to the many pleasures of gardens. As Scott Kugle notes in *When Sun Meets Moon*: 'In Islamic theology, the garden represents paradise. But Muslims went far beyond mere theology and constructed actual gardens, especially in the Persianate world that included South Asia. The garden is a place of leisure, where strolls and picnics provide the context for roving eyes and chance meetings, where lush verdure provides cover for secret meetings, where arbors harbour trysts that are impossible or dangerous in the routine spaces of social life.'

In one of the folios of his 16th-century autobiography, *Baburnama*, Emperor Babur supervises the construction of a garden identified as the Garden of Fidelity, just outside Kabul. The intricate details of the painting reveal contours that are recognizable even today: a charbagh or four-square Persian-style garden (called a chahar bagh in Farsi) with a central fountain and plenty of trees. The inscriptions state that 'there are pomegranate trees around the hawz, all three gardens are lush green', and refer to a spot that is 'the centre of the garden, when the oranges ripen'. The last line of the text gives the name of the artist, Bishandas, who is known for his figurative art.

Charbaghs had four streams, echoing both the Islamic rivers that flow from paradise and the Hindu rivers that flow north, south, east and west from the sacred mountain Meru. These gardens were organized around a central feature at which all four paths converged. Along the paths, and in the gardens enclosed by these paths, grew plenty of trees both big and small, as well as flowers. By building paths and hedges and walkways and fountains and clusters of bushes around which people from different classes, religions, and sexualities, could mingle, these vast parks certainly provided an alternative to the routine spaces of social life.

Babur himself talks about spending time in gardens, notably in the context of his passion for his beloved: 'In those days I discovered in myself a strange inclination—no, a mad infatuation—for a boy in the camp's bazaar, his name Baburi being apposite. Until then I had no inclination of love and desire for anyone, by hearsay or experience... In that

Folio from a *Baburnama* manuscript (c. 1590-98) depicting Mughal Emperor Babur supervising the laying out of the Garden of Fidelity; the artist is identified as Bishandas. *Source:* Wikimedia Commons

maelstrom of desire and passion…I used to wander…through orchards and vineyards. Sometimes, like mad men, I used to wander alone over hill and plain; sometimes I wandered in gardens and suburbs, lane after lane.' Feeling too shy even to look Baburi in the face, Babur instead resorted to writing poetry: couplets to describe his love. One of them announces: 'Desire overwhelmed me, made me reel, / What every lover of a comely face does feel.' And in passions that continue to be familiar to us today, this builder of both gardens and the Mughal dynasty in India says helplessly: 'Nor power to stay was mine, nor strength to part; / I became what you made of me, O thief of my heart.'

Whether or not Babur and Baburi—the Emperor and the 'thief'—had actual trysts in the garden, the chahar of the chahar-bagh and the chah of chahat (desire) share an emotional if not an etymological root. Mughal gardens— the great charbaghs of India—include trees and bushes that generated both shade and what we currently consider to be shady activities. In post-British India, with space running low and numbers running high, the gardens of Vatsyayana and Babur have become the preferred spot in which to indulge in the excitations of the senses. Which is exactly the role that gardens played for Vatsyayana and Babur as well, in extremely formal and elegant terms.

But all this public elegance and public sex existed about 1,800 years ago in India. Now is the age of 'Operation Majnu', the codename given to sting operations mounted by the Uttar Pradesh police in a bid to counter the molestation of women. But even the name of 'Operation Majnu' nudges us in the direction of a more spectacular history of desire. After all, the namesake of the crude police action in Meerut is also the name desired most by male lovers. The Arabic legend of Laila and Majnu was popularized by its Persian rendition by Nizami in the 12th century. The plot, like that of Shakespeare's *Romeo and Juliet*, revolves around a blazing love that encounters the barriers of a cruel and unthinking world (otherwise known as the Meerut Police). The world tries to extinguish the love between the lovers, but even though both lovers die, their love stays alive as the model and inspiration for lovers in centuries to come. And even though the story is set in Northern Arabia, Laila and Majnu have their 'graves' in Northern India, in Binjaur village in the northern part of Rajasthan, close to the border with Pakistan. Indeed, for many years pilgrims from Pakistan were allowed to visit the mazaar for the annual festival in June, during which hopeful as well as newly wed lovers come to be blessed by Laila and Majnu.

In most of its deployments, Operation Majnu has targeted necking couples, as it did in December 2005 in Meerut. With camera crews from news channels in tow, members of the police performed their moral outrage with aplomb. They kicked, slapped, abused and chased couples who had gone to the park. Four police officers were suspended after the event, pending an investigation, but at least one of those officers remained defiant: 'I do not consider that what we did was wrong,' Mamta Gautam asserted. 'If they were not doing anything illegal, then why did they run away?'

Perhaps they ran away because they were nervous about a criminal charge? In this land of Babur's baghs and the mazaar of Laila Majnu, public desire has now been converted into the spectre of public humiliation. The shade afforded by the trees has shaded into the realm of the shady, and the shame of desire has trumped its spectacle. One of the tales that makes up the 1927 short-story collection *Chocolate* by the Hindi writer Ugra observes: 'There are all kinds of places in this country where boys can get ruined. Most of the efforts to mislead boys occur at boarding schools, Brahmacharya ashrams, Company gardens, fairs and festivals.' All these locations, and especially the last three identified in the story—parks, fairs and festivals—are newly suspect. Can you imagine the Mughals instructing their armies to conduct raids in the charbagh surrounding the Taj Mahal? Indeed, Pandey Bechan Sharma Ugra's short story seems to point to a turning point in the history of public sex in India, when gardens start being viewed with an eye of suspicion *because* they provide pleasure.

Insisting that parks, fairs and festivals all conduce to the production of vice, or 'chocolate', the early 20th-century slang term for homosexuality, Ugra refers to parks as 'Company gardens' because the East India Company built parks in several parts of the country during its reign. Despite their sexual prudery, the British extended the topography of the charbagh in their gardens with a layout that very much conduced to covert sexual activity. The trouble with parks, of course, lies in their topography, which blurs the line between public and private. Typically, a park will have both big bushes and trees as well as tame paths and pavements; both undergrowth and pruned plants. Parks have one foot in the wildness of the jungles from which they have been culled, and one foot in the structures of the cities in which they are settled. What goes on in these parks is both hidden from sight behind bushes and visible to everyone who knows what is going on behind the bushes.

A park is public when people go for a walk or a jog in it, when they go with a group of friends and sit on the benches and chat in the open. But a park seems to be private when people lurk behind bushes or in the shadows of buildings, having sex. Even more, a park is both public and private because it can absorb elements of public parade and private pleasure, hurried encounter and lengthy leisure. And therein lies the rub. How can sex, considered by both the moral police and their opponents as something that should be 'private', be seen in 'public'? Parks bring us face to face with that which we do not want to see, especially when we have legislated that it should not be seen. It brings us face to face with desire, with sex, with everything that we obsess about but do not want to be seen as obsessing about. In a country that flaunts its 'public-private partnerships' in the economic sphere, there is horror at the public sight of partnerships that are deemed private. Unlike playgrounds, in which all is visible to the naked eye, and unlike forests which are understood to be spaces of danger, parks bring 'danger' into the middle of transparency. Parks are both safe and not safe because they contain in their undergrowth the smell of sex. Even though public sex in India is not limited to parks, parks pose the biggest challenge to the line dividing the public from the private. Is sex private or public? *Should* sex be public or private?

Both the law and public opinion seem confused about this question. Legal teams arguing the case against Section 377 in India have borrowed from arguments about homosexuality in the US Supreme Court. These arguments state that sexual preference is an innate characteristic of an individual and defines the individual most intimately. Sexuality as a private truth—the most intimate and private truth there is—won gay rights activists the right to marry in the US in 2015.

The legal challenge to Section 377 in India also based itself on notions of an inherent desire acted out in private, and sought to protect such consensual, privatized sex. But what follows from this notion of an individualized private space for sexuality is that the public space for sex gets demonized even further. If sex and sexuality are private, then, the moral police argue publicly, that's where it should stay. Do not bring it out into the open. Even further, private sex should only take place within the public sanction of marriage (this is why the US Supreme Court has legalized gay marriage), and weddings are the only legal events that can celebrate desire in public.

But it turns out that public expressions of desire cannot be contained quite so easily. Parks are democratic to the extent that anyone who cannot have sex elsewhere for whatever reason will resort to the bushes. No matter what the desiring configuration—prostitute and client, husband and wife, boyfriend and girlfriend, boyfriend and boyfriend, girlfriend and girlfriend—tens of thousands of people in India gratify their desire in public. In parks. We might perhaps call this desire parkophilia. And we might now ask ourselves: are we hetero/homo/bi/trans or parko?

Many of the men who make use of parks are married to women but continue to desire sex with men. Such a resort is commonly seen as the choice of the lower classes. Or rather, the lower classes, regardless of sexuality, are the ones who cannot bribe their way out of a sticky situation, and so get caught having sex in parks. Speaking of the popular gay male haunt of Palika Bazar Park in the heart of New Delhi, one man says dismissively of the other gay men he sees in the park that they 'seemed to be like people who cannot afford to meet men in other places such as parties or saunas. I could tell it from their gaudy appearance and the kind of clothes they were wearing which did not seem like branded ones. Also, the way they were talking to each other in a cheap language, calling each other randi (whore). They had weird hair colour, and didn't seem to pass as straight as many other gay men do. And they were using expressions like chikne (hairless one) and gorey (fair one); they were very expressive, but also very filmy and cheesy.'

A less disdainful account of the Palika Bazar Park suggests that, despite Operation Majnu, even the police don't always bother to police public sex. Many gay men who frequent the park said they had rarely witnessed any police harassment of couples there. A few of them suggested that the police too have sex in the park because a man in uniform is attractive to both men and women. Asked what the environment is like at the Palika Bazar Park, another gay man in his mid-30s said: 'See, I went there even before the 2009 Delhi High Court verdict [that decriminalized homosexuality] was out, so there was fear and inhibition. But the Park is like any usual park. If you went in the early evenings as I did, you would see people walking briskly, which suggests that they are locals and there to exercise. But then there will be other men in sports clothes who would look at you. These men would sometimes touch themselves to show that they are interested in you. They are often in groups. But it is like a public secret there. I think the usual crowd and locals are used to the things that happen in the Park and they don't react. I think shopkeepers from the Palika Market below the Park also know about it, as do the roadside vendors. In fact, I think some of them too were getting sex there. Around 8:30 or 9 pm sometimes, when all the shops are closing for the day, you will see young guys standing close to the metro stations, and their body language will tell you that they are gay. People used to tell you about these codes, such as using a handkerchief to find guys, but I think you can simply make it out by observing their body language. But it is all so normal, unlike Nehru Park where you have even heard of people getting harassed or beaten up for this. This doesn't happen in Palika.'

Even the disdainful man continued to frequent Palika and other parks for sex. In one close shave, he was caught having oral sex in South Delhi's Deer Park. The price of sexual freedom in that instance was a bribe of Rs. 500 paid to the guard who discovered the men in the park.

Parks are sites of illicit sex of all persuasions—they are the great levellers of desire. Public sex in India has a long historical memory that continues to bathe metaphorically in the streams of the charbagh and enjoy the picnics of the *Kamasutra*. From Vatsyayana onwards, parks in India have provided a zone of privacy in public. With the advent of the Company gardens and their shifting moral landscape, the line dividing public and private started to be policed more fully, especially in parks which muddied the distinction between public and private. Sex was made private, and parks were meant only to be public. But even today, what do people—heterosexual, homosexual, bisexual, transgendered, queer—do if they do not want to get married, have no private space in which to have sex, and are interested in causal flings rather than in finding soulmates across births?

They go to parks.

11

ARMY

We lead by example, live by chance, love by choice and kill by profession.

—One of many slogans of the Indian Army

In the 4th century BCE, the Greeks made what we today call illicit desire the *basis* of selection to their armies. The Sacred Band of Thebes, for instance, was an army regiment made up entirely of male lovers and beloveds (150 couples; 300 men in all) in the belief that the erotic bond among soldiers would make them valiant. It was assumed that lovers would more easily lay down their lives for the ones they love. Each lover would want to appear strong in the eyes of his beloved and would thus fight harder in order to defeat the enemy. And indeed, this was the case. The troop of handpicked male lovers rose to the rank of the elite in the Theban army, with the defeat of Sparta in 371 BCE marking their most famous victory.

Plato echoes this belief in the *Symposium* when Alcibiades asserts that his would-be lover Socrates saved his life during a military campaign. The samurai in Japan too were bound together as early as the 11th century CE by sexual relationships between the older and younger members of the warrior class. From the ancient Greeks to the medieval Japanese, war and same-sex desire have been seen as coterminous rather than contradictory. In our own time, however, the relation between war and homosexuality has been considered to be utterly antagonistic. So much so that in the 20th and 21st centuries, most Western countries, and almost all post-colonial countries once ruled by the West, prohibited homosexuals from serving openly in the military. The most well-known example of this prohibition was the infamous 'Don't Ask, Don't Tell' policy in the US Military (repealed in 2011) in which gay soldiers were told they could continue to serve only on condition that they never speak about or act on their desires while in the military. There was a zero-tolerance policy for any gay member of the military who violated this rule. An immediate discharge would be the consequence of any self-disclosure of a homosexual person's sexuality.

What is interesting about these tales spread across space and time is not whether homosexuals or heterosexuals make better soldiers. Rather, what is fascinating is that the military, which for many people represents the antithesis of romance, is actually an organization that thinks deeply about the question of desire. Despite appearing to disavow sex, the army (and navy and air force) actually has to grapple with it not only on a daily basis, but also in the very fabric of its policies and procedures. The army, it would be no exaggeration to say, is built on desire.

Consider, for a moment, the roster for a tour of duty of a soldier in the Indian army. Typically, an officer or soldier is posted for 2 to 3 years to a field station followed by a similar duration of a peace posting. Families cannot be accommodated in postings located in combat zones. However, areas where there is no direct contact with enemy forces have arrangements for temporary family accommodations for a period of 2 to 3 months on a rotational basis. The leave policy allows for an annual leave of 60 days for both officers and soldiers. The 60 days can be used in 2 to 3 instalments through the year. Over and above the annual leave, soldiers and officers get 30 and 20 days of casual leave respectively, which too can be split into 2 to 3 lots. An officer attending a course or programme up to a year in a peacetime location is authorized to bring his or her family along even if the officer's original posting is in a field station.

What even this brief description makes clear is that for long periods of time, soldiers are in their own company, devoid of boyfriends and girlfriends, husbands and wives. And since armies around the world and across time have always had to cater to the reality of hundreds of thousands of people, with bodily needs that have to be met, they have always had to plan for their soldiers' desires. Such planning requires thinking about how soldiers will have sex, with whom and how often. If certain sexual arrangements are considered unsatisfactory, then how are they to be avoided? How to ensure that desire does not get in the way of the discipline required to do battle with an enemy of the state (i.e. how to make sure people don't find love within their own squadron or barracks)? Where to go to have desires met without impeding one's tour of duty? How to retain the bond with loved ones despite being away from them for a long time? This last question was answered by the Greeks by incorporating desire into the army. But now, the army is seen as the opposite of desire, and so the latter must be managed strictly in order to ensure the smooth functioning of the former.

Of all the empires that have made up India, and of all their armies, we have the most exhaustive account of how the British Indian army managed the desires of its soldiers and officers (and like so much else in India, the Army too has inherited many of its military systems and traditions from the British). The problem for the British in India was two-fold. First—and this is a question for armies everywhere and all the time—how to cater to the desires of their troops? But second—and this question was specific to the British presence in India—how to cater to the desires of their troops without jeopardizing the racial hierarchy of the colonial enterprise? This latter question was the tricky one. Clearly, the straightforward way of answering the first question—how to satisfy the desires of British soldiers?—was by importing British women to partner with British soldiers and officers. However, while such imports would satisfy ethnic purity, they were not a widespread or long-term answer. Even accommodating a few British wives was an expensive proposition because they would need to be provided with housing, servants and other amenities.

But not providing heterosexual solutions would encourage the development of homosexual ones, or so the British feared. The British and the Indian soldiers belonged to separate regiments and lived in separated barracks, thus minimizing contact and the possibility of homosexual relations between them. Indeed, as Suparna Bhaskaran has suggested: 'There were concerns that not having wives would encourage the Imperial Army to become "replicas of Sodom and Gomorrah", or, as Viceroy Elgin put it, to pick up "special Oriental vices." The fiscal solution was to turn unofficial, unregulated brothels into officially regulated ones for the Army. The mid 1850s saw the conversion of existing brothels into official ones and the establishment of state-regulated brothels where native women had to register to belong. The women had to undergo regular medical exams to make sure they were not vectors of disease for the soldiers. These regulated brothels or *lal bazaars* [red markets, so called because they catered to the red coats, or soldiers of the British Army] were primarily for white use, although "Indians could use them while whites were on morning parade.'"

Female prostitution, then, to counter the threat of male homosexuality. In the face of economic necessities and sexual pruderies, the army under the British set up government brothels in big cities. Needless to say, these brothels were populated entirely by Indian women. And they were primarily for the use of British men. Wherever possible, the British set up separate brothels for white and brown troops, but sometimes the brothels were for joint use, as was the case in Lucknow in 1857. Some of the women servicing the army alleged they had been kidnapped, some joined out of economic necessity, but all were carefully vetted for attractiveness, on the one hand, and venereal disease on the other. It seems possible that the pejorative Hindustani word for prostitutes, 'randi', which originally referred to a single woman, and then a widow, might also have a connection with the Scottish word 'randy', which implies a condition of being filled with sexual lust.

Armed with the Cantonment Act of 1864, the British administration of the Indian Army forced these prostitutes to undergo regular medical examinations to check the spread of sexually transmitted diseases. These painfully invasive examinations were conducted by male doctors, and the women were confined against their will; such acts of violence against Indian women were rationalized as a necessary means of protecting British soldiers. After all, the ratio of prostitutes to soldiers was dangerously low, and one woman had to service several dozen soldiers. Whether the men spread venereal disease to the women or vice versa was almost immaterial since it was only the women who were checked, treated and confined.

The Indian soldiers of the British Indian Army were largely left to their own devices, their desires unthought of. This meant that some of them would use the prostitutes in the cantonment when they were allowed to. Or else they would venture deeper into the surrounding town and pick up their own prostitutes. The multiple use of female bodies coupled with a lack of basic sanitation ensured the flourishing of venereal disease both among the soldiers and the women hired to cater to their desires. Female prostitution, it turned out, was medically quite dangerous.

This idea of providing female prostitutes for the army, however, did not arrive in India with the British. The 3rd-century BCE *Arthashastra*, the handbook on statecraft attributed to Chandragupta Maurya's mentor, Chanakya (also known as Kautilya), assumes the same set of arrangements. In Chanakya's world, too, courtesans accompanied the army when it went on an expedition, and they were allotted camps along the roads. During times of active battle, the women were confined to the rear of the camp, and were expected to be always available to cheer on the soldiers and minister to them at the end of a weary day. The only difference between Chanakya's plan and that of the British is that for Chanakya, the courtesans are meant to service the entire army without discriminating between native and foreigner (or at least, if there were meant to be discriminations, he does not spell them out). Also, we don't get a sense that the courtesans' tenure with the army was akin to a jail-term with enforced hospitalization, which is what it was with the British.

Often, however, the soldiers of the British Indian Army would not go to prostitutes out of a mixture of sexual squeamishness and religious strictures. At such a point, they only had one another. But even this self-reliance or reliance on one's 'brother soldiers' was fraught with difficulty. In 'A Tradition of Quiet Tolerance', Sudhir Kakar points us to a tale narrated by Richard Burton, the soldier-traveller-adventurer who spearheaded the first translation of the *Kamasutra* into English in 1883. After commenting on the pederasty of the Maharajas of Punjab and Kashmir, Burton notes:

Yet the Hindus, I repeat, hold pederasty in abhorrence and are as much scandalized by being called gand-mara (anus-beater) or Gandu (anuser) as Englishmen would be. During the years 1843-44, my regiment, almost all Hindu Sepoys of the Bombay Presidency, was stationed at a purgatory called Bandar Charra, a sandy flat with a scatter of verdigris-green milk-bush some forty miles north of Karachi, the headquarters. The dirty heap of mud and mat hovels, which represented the adjacent native village, could not supply a single woman: Yet only one case of pederasty came to light and that after a tragic fashion some years afterwards. A young Brahmin had connection with a soldier comrade of low caste and this had continued till, in an unhappy hour, the Pariah patient ventured to become an agent. The latter, in Arab, Al-Fa'il, the 'doer', is not an object of contempt like Al-Maful, the 'done'; and the high-caste Sepoy, stung by remorse and revenge, loaded his musket and deliberately shot the paramour. He was hanged by court-martial at Hyderabad and, when his last wishes were asked, he begged in vain to be suspended by the feet; the idea being that his soul, polluted by 'exiting below the waist', would be doomed to endless transmigrations through the lowest form of life.

An obsession with purity displayed by caste Hinduism here collides with and complicates the alleged impurity of sodomy. And the loss of caste purity is compounded by the fact that the Brahmin has been the bottom in the relationship, surrendering his caste privilege of being the one on top. The Brahmin soldier enjoys sex with a lower-caste man, but both the caste and the sex become problematic in the wake of his lover's official elevation. The setting of the army, in which men are in close quarters with one another, makes both the pull of the pure and the horror of the impure seem larger than life.

Male or female, straight or gay, self or other, the army always has to manage the potential disruptiveness of desire. This is why the laws governing the military keep a close watch on how desire plays out in its ranks. The Army Act of 1950, which is almost a replica of its precursor Act formulated during the British Raj in 1911, provides stringent rules for managing desire. (Similar laws also apply in the case of the navy and air force.) Section 45 of the Army Act on 'Unbecoming conduct' states that: 'Any officer, junior commissioned officer or warrant officer who behaves in a manner unbecoming of his position and the character expected of him shall, on conviction by court martial, be liable to be cashiered.' Section 46, 'Certain forms of disgraceful conduct' notes that 'Any person subject to the Act who is guilty of any disgraceful conduct of a cruel, indecent or unnatural kind...shall, on conviction by court martial, be liable to suffer imprisonment for a term which may extend to seven years.' Section 63, 'Violation of good order and discipline', rules that 'Any person subject to the Act who is guilty of any act or omission which is prejudicial to good order and military discipline shall, on conviction by court martial, be liable to suffer imprisonment for a term which may extend to seven years.' And Section 65, which thwarts even an 'Attempt', states: 'Any person who attempts to commit any of the offences specified in Sections 34 to 64 and in such attempt does any act towards the commission of the offence, shall, on conviction by court martial...suffer imprisonment for a term which may extend to 14 years.' All these sections of the Army Act deal with sexual misdemeanours. However, like Section 377 of the Indian Penal Code, they do not name the misdemeanours so much as repeatedly insist that these acts will violate the discipline that is necessary for the army. Desire is very much seen as the disruptor of discipline.

We have heard stories of such disruptions all through history. Both Alauddin and Qutubuddin Khilji, the second and third rulers of the Khilji dynasty that ruled vast tracts of South Asia in the 13th and 14th centuries, are said to have lost their lives and kingdoms to men with whom they fell in love during war. Introducing Ziauddin Barani's 14th-century account of the fall of the Khilji rulers of Delhi, Saleem Kidwai notes that Alauddin Khilji was hopelessly in love with a eunuch slave during his invasion of Gujarat. This slave, named Malik Kafur (or Malik Naib), is listed by Barani as being the third of four reasons for the decline of the Khilji dynasty: '[T]he Sultan loved the Malik Naib very much. He made him the commander of his Army, a minister. He raised him above all the others. The heart of this sodomite beloved of his was soon corrupted.' Similarly, Qutubuddin

Khilji raised a handsome boy called Hasan to the rank of Khusro Khan and sent him on various military campaigns to the Deccan. Like Malik Naib, Khusro Khan too ended up murdering his benefactor. Desire in these two cases was both born out of the army and succeeded in destroying the institution that had fostered it.

But it is precisely because of the proximity of death that desire in the Army is so intense. For Richard Burton's Brahmin sepoy, no less than the British soldiers visiting lal bazaars, desire is heightened by being constantly in the presence of death. The army fosters a readiness, if not a desire, for death, and this in turn can lead to deathly desire. *The Ballad of Reading Gaol*, Oscar Wilde's breathtaking poem from 1898, notes this connection presciently: 'Yet each man kills the thing he loves / By each let this be heard, / Some do it with a bitter look, / Some with a flattering word, / The coward does it with a kiss, / The brave man with a sword! / Some kill their love when they are young, / And some when they are old; / Some strangle with the hands of Lust, / Some with the hands of Gold: / The kindest use a knife, because / The dead so soon grow cold.'

In the *Arthashastra*, Chanakya advocates the use of both sex and sword by the army. Those in charge of the courtesans were given the authority to use the women to undermine enemy chiefs, presumably by seducing them, and thus breaching the enemy army from within. An extended story of sex and war has also developed around an army of women known as the vishakanyas or poison-maidens. Chanakya mentions them in the *Arthashastra* as a weapon by which to destroy enemies who might prove too strong a match in the field. Indeed, according to the 4th-century BCE Sanskrit play *Mudrarakshasa*, Chanakya himself used a vishakanya to consolidate Chandragupta Maurya's empire in India. Chanakya first allied himself with King Parvata to jointly defeat King Nanda. But when a vishakanya was despatched by Nanda's minister with orders to murder Chandragupta Maurya, Chanakya cleverly rerouted the killer to murder King Parvata instead, thus leaving Chandragupta the sole ruler of all three domains. This army of poison-maidens was allegedly fed on an elaborate course of poison and antidotes from an early age. Many of them died as a result of the poison, but those who survived were immune to the poison and had so much of it flowing in their veins that all sexual contact produced poisonous bodily fluids that would kill the people with whom they had sex. In other words, vishakanyas were a potent form of biological weaponry in the Mauryan army. Mentioned in the same category as spies, vishakanyas would infiltrate enemy ranks and then penetrate enemy bodies to spread their poison. Some people have suggested that this spreading of bodily poison might be read as an early precursor of venereal disease. If that is indeed the case, then it is also true that then as now, the idea of fatal bodies is associated primarily with women. This powerfully misogynistic belief in the fatality of female bodies ties together in different ways the armies of both the Mauryan and British rulers of India. While the bodies of vishakanyas were continually manipulated to achieve the desired poisonous result, the body of the British cantonment prostitute was continually checked for venereal disease.

The idea of untrustworthy female bodies in the army continues to live on in the Indian subcontinent today. Pakistan's *Daily Mail* published an article in September 2009 reporting the deployment of an all-women's Indian Army unit in Kashmir, near India's border with Pakistan. The *Daily Mail* article alleged that the women in the unit were prostitutes engaged to cheer up the troops at the border. It quoted sources who said that 'the decision had been taken by senior Army officers who feared that a number of troop suicides and incidents where soldiers had killed their own comrades were linked to loneliness and the absence of female company'.

In *The Telegraph*'s version (28 September 2009) of the story that appeared in the *Daily Mail*, we are told that:

> ...a major-general was sent to Moscow to research how the Russians had dealt with a similar problem in Afghanistan in the 1980s. The Russian consultants told the Indian Army that since the soldiers in the valley were [starved of women], they should be provided with women to meet their genuine and natural needs. A high-level committee of senior army officers was formed to explore how they could recruit prostitutes and give them basic military training. The newspaper claimed India's intelligence agency, the Research and Analysis Wing, was drafted to screen the prostitutes because, it said, it already had a network of prostitutes in different cities of India.

The Government of India, of course, denied the charge and accused Pakistan of indulging in propaganda to demoralize the troops. But both India and Pakistan are heirs to a legacy in which providing prostitutes to cheer up the soldiers has been standard army practice. And in 2018 as in 1858, the question still remains: what do soldiers do when they are without sexual company for months at a time? That the army has explicit rules outlawing homosexuality suggests one answer to that question. That they may or may not, in time-honoured tradition, have provided female prostitutes for their soldiers, is another response. Either way, the army is the space in which desire needs to be taken seriously. If 'all is fair in love and war', then that suggests both love and war suspend the usual moral laws by which we live. Thus it is that the 'indiscipline' of both prostitution and homosexuality fit snugly in the same bed as the discipline of the army.

12

HAIR

The fair one sleeps on the couch, with dark tresses all
over her face;
Come, Khusro, go home now, for night has fallen over
the world.

—Amir Khusro[3]

The urbane young man at the heart of the *Kamasutra* is
told early on in the book to take good care of his hair. This
includes removing the hair from his body and maintaining
well the hair on his head. Such a man would not be considered
heterosexual today; instead he would be termed 'metrosexual'
because he is not quite straight. His bodily hairlessness
will be cause for suspicion because men are thought to be
sexually virile if they have lots of hair on their bodies, and
unmanly if they do not. The *Kamasutra*'s hero would also be
termed 'effeminate' for the attention he pays to the lustrous
locks on his head. Today, long hair in India has become
the provenance of femininity, while masculinity is tied to
short hair. Long hair for men is considered a rebellious style
restricted to the entertainment industry, whose members also
sport gleamingly waxed chests. For the rest of the Indian
masculine world, it is acceptable for heterosexual men to
have a hairy body and a bald head.

---

3. According to Saleem Kidwai, '[t]his famous couplet is generally
considered an epitaph Khusro wrote for himself on hearing of his master's
death. It is exceptional in that the beloved here is gendered female.'

In stark contrast to these men, Indian women are expected to have plentiful hair on the head. Labouring under this same burden, I go once a week to a place in Delhi renowned for herbal oils and tonics and shampoos and conditioners for the hair. The clientele there is a slice of Delhi life—from the bossy brassy Punjabis to the sweet smiling Bengalis to the inquisitive impatient Marwaris. They are all women, though a few—very few—men are catered to in a separate room. Many of the customers have been coming here for well over a decade. But what is particularly interesting are the younger and newer customers who inevitably arrive here as a short-term lead-up to their marriage, either by themselves or chaperoned by their mothers. They bemoan their hair loss, connect it to evil procedures to which they have subjected their hair in the past, and beg the proprietor to please please please fix their hair in time for their weddings, which always seem to be imminent. When I ask some of these young women why they connect having lustrous hair with getting married, they inevitably say it is because they want to look good. I point out that if they are only worried about one day (or five, depending on how extensive their wedding ceremonies are), then there are several procedures by which their hair, no matter how scant, can be made to look plentiful—blow-drying, extensions, wigs. But they say they want to embark on their married lives with a stamp of *authentic* femininity. Since long hair is now the sign of female respectability in India, women getting married want to feel like 'real' women. Glossy hair is the face (as it were) of female desirability in India.

These cascading locks on a woman's head are expected to be in inverse relation to the amount of hair on her body. In following these strictures, women today have taken on the mantle of the *Kamasutra*'s male protagonist. Historically, though, the burden was shared more equitably.

In *Muraqqa-e-Dehli*, a travelogue about his sojourn in Delhi, an 18th-century Hyderabadi noble carefully recorded the male-male desire that was everywhere on display in the city. One of his best-known examples involves the Sufi saint Chiragh Dehlavi talking about his disciple Bandanawaz Gesudaraz. Seeing Gesudaraz playing with his lustrous locks (in Farsi, gesu is hair and daraz is long), the master exclaims, 'If you really want to understand the essence of true love, try to get entangled in the tassels of Gesudaraz.' The hair of the male lover is the most vivid mark of beauty in Persian poetry. Arthur Dudney narrates the passionate way in which even so seemingly fearsome a conqueror as Mahmud of Ghazni is himself conquered by the beautiful hair of his slave, Ayaz. Legend has it that in a drunken stupor one night, Mahmud tells Ayaz to cut off his hair lest it prove too sexually tempting. When Ayaz does so, Mahmud falls even more hopelessly in love with his slave because of this proof of his devotion. Mahmud and Ayaz have almost equal legendary lovers' status as Laila-Majnun and Heer-Ranjha. What is notable is that historically in India, *hair* rather than gender seems to have been the marker of passionate desire. In every case, and regardless of whether s/he is female or male, the beloved is the one with the long and lustrous locks.

Mir Taqi Mir extends this love of hair on the head to a disquisition about hair on the face. Usually, the growth of facial and bodily hair for both men and women marks the onset of puberty. This also marks boys and girls as young men and women, and therefore as people who are ready to have sex. Even those communities that practice child marriage in India will keep the child bride and bridegroom apart until they both start sprouting hair on their genitals and the rest of their bodies. However, when boys in Persian poetry start growing bodily and facial hair, they become *less* rather than more sexually attractive: young men with beards are considered lost to the register of attraction. This attitude invokes yet another historical disjunction: after all, facial and bodily hair on men today is taken as a sign of virility rather than unattractiveness.

But Mir makes his dismissive attitude to facial hair very clear across the course of his couplets. Addressing a 'newly bearded one', Mir proclaims: 'Your face with down on it, is our Quran—/ What if we kiss it—it is a part of our faith.' Here the facial hair being praised is nascent rather than developed, and so the boy may still be considered an attractively hairless boy rather than an unattractively hairy man. In a later couplet, once the down has grown into a beard, Mir expostulates that 'His beard has appeared, but his indifference survives—/ My messenger still wanders, waiting for an answer.' Mir is stunned that the boy's arrogance has survived into manhood. He has a beard, so how can he continue to think of himself as being so attractive as to spurn prospective lovers, the poet asks. The onset of puberty is understood widely in Persian poetry as marking the turning-point of attractiveness in young men. Mir wrote quite openly about the beauties of smooth skin—'These pert smooth-faced boys of the city, / What cruelty they inflict on young men.' Hairless youth is beautiful; hairy adulthood less so. Persian and Urdu poetry associates bodily and facial hairlessness with male attractiveness. In this, they join Vatsyayana who extols exactly this ideal of beauty for men in the *Kamasutra*.

Such an approach to beauty has led to the criticism that Persian and Urdu poetry is pederastic in nature. Praise of the hairless might well suggest that the object of attraction has to be young. But, as women around the world can testify all-too painfully, hairless faces and bodies can also be *created* at any age. In their fetishization of hairlessness, the refined male poets who love hairless boys are joined by heterosexual men who insist that their female objects of desire be depilated to within an inch of their lives. This explains the rich industry in hair-waxing and threading in India. As soon as they enter their teens, urban Indian women are encouraged to remove all traces of hair from their legs, arms and underarms, not to mention their chin (threading or waxing) and sideburns (usually by bleaching). Objects of desire are encouraged to be child-like by being hairless. In urban heterosexual relationships, this is true across the board—women are meant not to have hair on their bodies and faces if they are to be considered attractive. Unlike the parameters sketched by the Persian and Urdu poets, many homosexual subcultures globally revel in bodily and facial hair. But heterosexuality around the world seems fairly united in its insistence that women as objects of desire must have plenty of hair on their heads, and none at all on their faces and bodies. Women must look like pre-pubescent children. This is why they are so often referred to as 'baby'. What passes as a term of endearment is really an insistence that women stay infantile in body and spirit.

So the emphasis on hairless chins need not suggest only young boys or grown women who look like young girls. Historically speaking, hairless male bodies in India have been perfectly compatible with sexual virility. The Hindu gods, for instance, look androgynous precisely because they have long hair on their head and no bodily hair. Long hair—sported by Shiva, Vishnu, Brahma—sits happily alongside masculine virility. Indeed, classical Indian texts seem incapable of imagining desire—for *both* men and women—without sumptuous descriptions of their hair. The kamashastra literature mentions keshagrahana (or the holding of hair) as an essential part of sexual foreplay. In Kalidasa's *Kumarasambhava*, Parvati in the throes of desire pulls Shiva's hair so hard that the crescent moon in his locks feels pain. In Allasani Peddana's 16th-century Telugu classic, *The Story of Manu*, the poet narrates the story of an immortal nymph, Varuthini, who falls in love with a human ascetic by the name of Pravara. When Pravara rejects her, a semi-divine Gandharva in love with Varuthini assumes the shape of Pravara and makes love to her. Varuthini is aware of the deception, but wants to inhabit the illusion of having sex with Pravara. Her descriptions of this pseudo-Pravara make clear the extent of her sexual longing:

> And there he was...
> ...his glistening body, like molten gold,
> lit up the whole garden, and his long hair,
> which could have reached his thighs,
> tied into a knot, was dark as a snake, so dark
> the bees could borrow its hue
> on interest.

Hair has been a marker of sexual attractiveness in India across gender. And across religions. If anything, hair has functioned in all the major religions of the world as the most potent symbol of desire. The adjectives we use to describe hair—luxurious, abundant, plentiful, cascading—all point to something sumptuous about hair that slips out of the band of restraint. Perhaps it is the fear of such abandon that makes religions clamp down on stray hair. On a recent visit accompanying my aunt to the Madurai Meenakshi temple, the security guard disapproved of the fact that my hair was not tied up. 'No free hair,' she shouted at me. I wanted to say that my hair was not free at all, that in fact I spend a lot of money on it. But of course what she objected to in my 'free hair' was sexual licentiousness rather than a possible economic bargain.

Orthodox Jewish women shave their heads after getting married in order to preserve their modesty and show that their desire now belongs only to their husbands. In this they join their Muslim counterparts who cover their hair as a sign of gendered and sexual modesty. Buddhists shave their hair as a sign of renunciation of desire. (Some Hindu and Jain ascetics, however, grow their hair as a sign that they no longer care about the ways of the world.) Hindus also shave their hair as an intimate and inexpensive offering to the gods. At the opposite end of the deprivation spectrum, Sikh men and women grow their hair as a sign of virility and religious fidelity. With every religion in this polyphonous country, hair is multivalently linked to desire. But by and large, plentiful hair on the head for women signifies sexual availability and activity, while its absence signals sexual abstinence and deprivation. Hindu widows, we remember, are made to shave their heads in many parts of the country to signify the end of carnal desire after the death of their husbands. This forced shaving of the head is testimony also to the violence that attends the politics of hair.

Perhaps the most famous tale about this complex knot

of hair, desire and violence is to be found in the story of Draupadi from the *Mahabharata*. Even before the account of Draupadi's hair comes up in the narrative, she is presented to us as a character with an interesting relation to desire. She is married to one of the Pandavas—Arjuna—but then, owing to a miscommunication, she is parcelled out among all five of the Pandava brothers as their joint wife. The *Kamasutra* tells us that any woman who is not a courtesan and who has had sex with five men is to be considered a loose woman with whom any man can have sexual intercourse. By this yardstick alone, Draupadi's sex life is to be looked upon in the annals of Hindu mythology as 'loose'. But despite these parameters, Draupadi is one of the few women in the history of desire in India who is *not* condemned for having multiple sexual partners. Indeed, having sex with five men is considered her dharma, and she is even allowed to have one child with each man.

Sometime after she is married to the five Pandava brothers, the Pandavas invite their cousins, the Kauravas, to admire their new palace in Indraprastha (later to become a part of Delhi). One of the chief attractions of this palace is the Hall of Illusions, in which nothing is as it seems. The Kauravas are depicted in this tale as the country bumpkins, at sea in the home of the urbane Pandavas. They cannot navigate their way around the Hall of Illusions—they assume a crystal floor is a pool of water, and a pool of water is a crystal floor, with the result that they fall into the pool, much to their consternation, and Draupadi's amusement. Draupadi and Bhima laugh uproariously at the uncouth Kauravas, who understandably get upset at thus being the source of their host's amusement. They leave in a rage. And when they come back, they return to take revenge. Duryodhana invites Yudhishthira, the eldest Pandava, to a game of dice, which the latter loses. Among the things he stakes on this game are his kingdom, his brothers, himself, and finally Draupadi. All the Pandavas and Draupadi now become slaves of the Kauravas, and Duryodhana's brother Dushasana is sent to bring Draupadi into the court so she can be taunted with news of her new station in life.

Draupadi turns out to be a recalcitrant subject and refuses to come into the court. Dushasana then drags her in by the hair. Duryodhana gestures to his thigh as the seat on which Draupadi should perch, and Dushasana starts to disrobe her in an attempt to dishonour her fully. The legend goes that Draupadi prays to Krishna to protect her honour, and lo and behold, it seems like Dushasana can never get to the bottom of her attire—the saree simply keeps coming. Exhausted, he gives up, and Draupadi's clothes stay on her body. This episode is commonly referred to as Draupadi's 'cheer-haran' or 'vastra-haran', which means the episode in which Draupadi's clothes are stripped off her. But it should more properly be termed the 'Hairy Tale' since what happens to Draupadi's hair is of more import in deciding the course of the *Mahabharata* and the ruinous war in which the cousins get embroiled.

Draupadi gets dragged into the public court by her hair, which cascades as a sign of sexual availability. After narrowly escaping being disrobed, she vows never again to tie up her hair unless she is first able to bathe it in Dushasana's blood. She prophesies that Bhima, one of her five husbands, will tear open Dushasana's chest and she will bathe her hair in the gore. Until she is able to have that blood bath, however,

she will not tie up her hair. Draupadi's loose hair becomes
the central concern in this entire episode. It is both the
marker of her sexual humiliation, and the indicator of when
that humiliation will end. Her hair becomes an actor in the
theatre of the Great Indian War, the war of Kurukshetra that
is central to the *Mahabharata*. Draupadi's hair is a mighty
weapon, and dance enactments of this episode, for instance,
present it in all its gruesomeness. In a Kathakali version
I once saw, Bhima rips apart Dushasana's chest and, with
his victim still twitching in the throes of agony, tears out

'Draupadi' by Raja Ravi Varma.
Source: www.ravivarma.org

his entrails from deep within the bowels. The entrails that
emerge themselves look like long braids of hair, writhing in
pain and dripping in blood. Draupadi is summoned, her hair
washed in the blood so that there is little to distinguish her
matted hair from the bloody entrails, and finally, her hair is
tied up by a triumphant Bhima. This curtailed hair restores
to Draupadi her chastity and modesty.

Raja Ravi Varma's early 20th-century paintings of
Draupadi reinforce the difference that hair makes. In one,
she sits on a throne with her oldest husband, Yudhishthira,
and surrounded by her other four husbands. Here her hair
is pulled back demurely, perhaps even tied up. This is in
direct observance of the image of the good Hindu wife, even
though this good wife has five husbands, and therefore has
sex with five different men. In another painting, this time
of Draupadi in exile with the Pandavas at the court of King
Virata, Draupadi has been painted with her hair flowing
over one shoulder. This is in obvious response to the plot
of the *Mahabharata*, and Draupadi's vow not to tie up her
hair until it has been washed in Dushasana's blood. But the
loose hair is also a symbol of sexual licentiousness, which is
perhaps the way in which King Virata's commander, Kichaka,
too reads the situation. Kichaka's advances on Draupadi take
place in the 13th year of the Pandavas' exile (the Pandavas
need to spend the 13th year of their exile incognito in
order to avoid a 2nd 12-year term of exile) and they lead
to the death of the commander. Draupadi's hair becomes a
matter of life and death in the *Mahabharata*, as well as in its
reimagination by artists after the fact. Hair is a major pawn
in the battlefield of desire—people live and die according to
whether a woman's hair is tied up or left loose. Entire epics

change course and acquire shape depending on what is going on with a woman's hair.

This is the case again in *The Story of Manu*, when Varuthini is heartbroken after being rejected by Pravara. The force of her sexual ardour is made clear by the fact that her hair is not tied up, and is left to cascade down her entire body: 'She rested her thick hair on her wrists, fragrant as lotus stems, and flowers were scattered everywhere as the hair came loose and, since it had grown so long, darkened her whole body as if the sky with its planets had fallen over her and made her still more beautiful.' This thick hair makes desire beautiful, sexy, dangerous and sensual; it evokes the animal kingdom, the plant world, and the celestial stars. Her scattered hair leads to the plot developing in the way that it does, and Varuthini eventually has sex with the pseudo Pravara to produce a son who goes on to become the father of Manu, the hero of the epic. Hair is here all-encompassing and universal in its desirability.

So much so that even the stones cannot do without it. Erotic sculptures in India, from the 11th-century Khajuraho temples to the 16th-century bronze and ivory statues in the Nayaka kingdom of South India, display abundant hair as a part of their sexual package. Men as much as women pile up hair on their heads, and there is inevitably an equivalence of scale between the bun on the head and the breast of the woman. Male kings and courtiers have hair piled on top of their heads—hair here seems to be a mark as much of sexuality as of power. This intertwining of power and desire is familiar to us from centuries ago: when the male city-dweller in the *Kamasutra* is taught the modes of acquiring power through sex, one of the first steps he has to take is to oil and comb and groom the hair on his head. The history of desire in India grows out of this long Indian obsession with hair and sexuality. Hair is the universal signifier of desire, power, exultation, loss and mourning. For both men and women.

Amir Khusro brings out the poignancy of this desire beautifully when he narrates his shock at hearing of his beloved Nizamuddin's death. With his master gone, Khusro is utterly bereft, his desire no longer has an anchor. Historically, Khusro followed Nizamuddin Auliya to the grave a few months after the pir's death, and he is buried near him. In his immediate poetic outpouring of grief, Khusro feels his hair is disoriented and aimless: 'The fair one sleeps on the couch, with dark tresses all over her face; / Come, Khusro, go home now, for night has fallen over the world.'

So rich is this history of hairy desire in India, that it comes as no surprise to find out that India is the most desirable supplier of hair to the rest of the world. Indian hair is valued so highly on the international market that it makes up wigs and hair extensions at the best beauty salons globally. For his 2009 documentary *Good Hair*, American star Chris Rock travelled to India to get at the root of what makes good hair. Much of the hair for sale in high-end hair salons in the US comes from Indian temples that have turned into tonsure factories. Rock follows the journey of this hair from India to tens of thousands of happy customers abroad. Most suppliers specialize in a product called 'Remy hair', which is the generic name for a bunch of hair in which all the strands grow in the same direction. 'Virgin Indian Remy Hair' is considered the gold standard of Remy hair; it is the most highly priced product on the hair market internationally. The name itself—its virginal quality—suggests the impossibility of thinking of hair separate from desire. As though aware of this sumptuous cultural history, one of the top suppliers of Indian hair is called Desire Inc.

13

MAKE-UP

Tere naina tere naina tere naina main chhupke rehna
Kajra re kajra re tere kaare kaare naina
Kaare kaare kaare kaare kaare kaare kaare kaare naina

(Your eyes, your eyes, I want to hide myself in your eyes
Your kohl-lined eyes, your intensely black eyes...
Black, black, black, black, black, black, black, black eyes.)

—Gulzar; lyrics from *Bunty aur Babli* (2005)

In the *Kamasutra*, Vatsyayana recommends that the following set of daily practices be observed by the man who is the protagonist of his book:

> He gets up in the morning, relieves himself, cleans his teeth, applies fragrant oils in small quantities, as well as incense, garlands, beeswax and red lac, looks at his face in a mirror, takes some mouthwash and betel, and attends to the things that need to be done. He bathes every day, has his limbs rubbed with oil every second day, a foam bath every third day, his face shaved every fourth day, and his body hair removed every fifth or tenth day. All this is done without fail.

These instructions set the scene for the text's protagonist as he goes through his daily life. Vatsyayana insists that the man use a ball of red lac with which to put on his lipstick, and then a ball of beeswax to fix the lipstick in place. The beauty of the outside is meant to complement the betel-inspired fresh breath of the inside of the mouth. In the book at large, both men and women are instructed to use sandalwood paste on their skin, and both use lipstick and eye-shadow to enhance their lips and eyes—the two facial features most associated with erotic desire. The use of lipstick and eye-shadow extended across social classes—it was the idealized aesthetic mode for both men and women, rich and poor. While poor men and women might not have been able to afford the sandalwood paste required to soften their skin and impart to it a golden glow, the red lac required for lipstick and the soot required for kaajal and eyeshadow was freely and plentifully available.

The remarkably 'modern' devices in this passage for fixing one's make-up and appearance include the use of a 'foam bath' and razors for removing body hair. Other texts on bodily aesthetics point to the use of wooden picks to clean the teeth and ears, and brush- and paddle-like instruments to apply make-up on the face. In addition to the lipstick for men advocated by Vatsyayana, wealthy men were also encouraged to paint designs on their arms—sometimes with henna. They also wore a thousand years ago what many Hindu men continue to wear in India today—a tikka or red/yellow mark on the forehead that mirrors the bindi worn by women. This is the mark that reflects Shiva's third eye—the one that flutters tantalizingly and dangerously in the centre of the God's forehead. Both men and women, then, used to walk around with red lips, eyes darkened with kohl, hennaed hands and feet, and a red mark on their foreheads. Rather than being the supreme example of the distinction between genders, make-up in ancient India was a mark of their similarity. One can imagine men and women comparing notes with one another about make-up. This is why the Kamasutra recommends that if a woman gets wet in the rain while en route to visiting her paramour, then the man should be the one to change her clothes and touch-up the streaked make-up on her face. Presumably, this is because he already knows how to do her make-up—exactly as his own.

In a far remove from Vatsyayana, make-up in the Western world has historically been used to differentiate rather than unite the sexes. Even though male actors have been using make-up on stage since at least the 12th century in Europe, off the stage, make-up is what separates men from women. So it is that a Hamlet who is sick of women in general, and his mother in particular, can think of no better way to insult them than to say that women wear too much make-up. While examining a skull in the graveyard—this is the iconic figure of Hamlet with the skull that we see on almost all posters of productions of the play—Hamlet meditates on the fact that no matter who we are, we will all be reduced to this skeletal state. In the case of women, 'let her paint an inch thick, to this favour she must come'. Despite the heavy use of make-up to ward off the reality of age and death, women too will not be able to protect their faces from this tragic end. Even more than cosmetic enhancement, this 'paint' is meant to imply a degree of unreliability—women are 'painted over', not real, not genuine, even as plays themselves are often dismissed for being 'artificial'. Women are 'fake' because make-up is not real. From literature to religion to art, make-up in the West has been used to denounce women for being insincere. Concomitantly, men are praised for being 'real' and 'true' because they do not wear make-up. This distinction between the sexes—women wear make-up and men do not—has only persisted and deepened over the centuries. So much so that a recent line of make-up tries to expand its base and sell its products by announcing that men too can wear make-up.

Unfortunately, such an announcement has not gained much traction because in the history of the Western world, only women and male homosexuals are understood to wear the taint of paint.

And this taint is spreading rapidly in India too. The gender equality advocated by the *Kamasutra* in matters of hair and make-up is thus rather astonishing. In ancient India, this equality is maintained, not only in the face of cosmetics, but also with the use of jewellery. Using ornaments in the hair was a feature common to both men and women; both wore elaborate earrings, bracelets and anklets. In sculptures and temple carvings—for example, in Khajuraho—it is almost impossible to tell a man apart from a woman on the basis of ornamentation alone. In terms of facial and bodily make-up, men and women were equally beautified in both official and unofficial representations. One has to look to the voluptuous breasts to be able to separate a man from a woman. Otherwise, they share alike in all matters of aesthetic embodiment.

As Vidya Dehejia notes in *The Body Adorned*, '[T]he term "beautiful" may be applied to the portrayal in art of the Indian male physique, with its gentle oval face, elongated eyes, and full lips, set off by long hair pulled back into an elegant knot. It bears repetition here that the literature of India employed equally for men and women many of the words that connote beauty, such as *sundara*, *charu*, and *kanta*... Men frequently shared with women a set of established poetic tropes, such as faces that put the moon to shame, eyes that outdo the lotus, arched eyebrows, feet and hands like lotuses, full red lips, and gleaming toenails. Like women, men adorned themselves with appropriate ornament (*alankara*).' In an

11th-century Chola bronze sculpture of the androgynous Shiva as Ardhanarishvara—in which one half of the body represents the male Shiva and the other half the female Uma or Parvati—the sculptor leaves intact the jewellery worn by both sides of the gender divide. Subtle differences in the line of the jaw are unimportant compared to the sumptuous necklaces, armlets, and bracelets worn by male and female halves alike.

Not only did classical Indian representational arts, then, make little to no distinction between men and women on the basis of make-up and jewellery, but erotic literature of the period too elevated male make-up to an art form. The 64 fine arts that the *Kamasutra* recommends should be mastered by all men about town (and also some women who study the text), include: the art of colouring the teeth, clothes, and limbs; making garlands and stringing necklaces, making diadems and headbands; making costumes; making various earrings; mixing perfumes; putting on jewellery; needlework; knowledge of the colour and form of jewels; skill at rubbing, massaging and hairdressing; and the art of using clothes for disguise. Many of these art-forms have been gendered beyond Vatsyayana's recognition—no one would say today that knowledge of needlework is an essential part of being a complete man. But the strength of the *Kamasutra* lies in the fact that it allocates to men skills we usually think of as being the sole provenance of women.

And these skills run through centuries of Indian fabric. Advice to a man on how best to adorn his face and body is the subject of Najmuddin Shah Mubarak Abru's witty 18th-century poem on 'Advice for the Adornment of a Beloved'. Eloquently rendered in English by Saleem Kidwai, the poem is an extended meditation on what and how much make-up looks best on a man:

> Remember what I say—a lad like you,
> So uninformed, must mould himself anew
> First let your hair grow out and fall in locks
> Around your face, but not run wild—that shocks
> The connoisseurs of beauty; snip your curls,
> But no shaving, no razors, no sideburns!
> Wash your hair with shampoo every morning,
> Never skip this—oil it, comb it, adorning
> It in braids, in buns, but please don't keep
> Flaunting it to get stared at—that's cheap.
> A bit of oil and turmeric on your skin—
> And when it's sunny, please, please, stay in!
> Saffron and jasmine oil with lemon juice
> Gets rid of blemishes and acne—use
> It each night, and wash it off each morning.
> Whiten your teeth, darken your gums, chewing
> Betel will keep your lips red—smile a lot
> But don't say much, and, my dear, not a jot
> More collyrium than your eyes can take—
> Too much of it looks dreadfully fake.
> Put henna on your fingers, not your palms;
> If you like fingerbands, enhance your charms,
> My beauteous fairy, with an amber ring—
> A shining necklace too is quite the thing.

In India, especially outside the bigger cities, and whether this is acknowledged or not, men still need to be made-up in order to be attractive. And the horizons of their make-up are vast, covering multiple arenas of jewellery, comportment and recommendations on both facial and head hair.

These skills of make-up are recommended for men across texts, religions and centuries. They also come in handy for visual and literary depictions of the erotic shenanigans of Krishna and Radha since their entanglements inevitably involve Krishna dressing up as a woman—complete with make-up and flowers in the hair—in order to meet Radha.

'Krishna and Radha walking by the Jumna by moonlight
after having exchanged clothes' (PD.114-1948)
© The Fitzwilliam Museum, Cambridge.

There are several variations on this theme. Kangra paintings—like the one on page 212 from the 18th century—routinely depict Radha dressed as Krishna, and Krishna made-up as Radha.

As Vidya Dehejia notes, Krishna's erotic potential has iconographically been presented as being coincident with his ability to be in disguise—'the legendary ease with which Krishna, on many an occasion, disguised himself as a woman to get access to his beloved Radha. Seventeenth- and eighteenth-century painted manuscripts all emphasize this artistic ideal, whether they portray Krishna in the guise of a female bangle-seller, as a participant in the all-women's Holi celebrations, or as a beautiful male figure bathing with the gopis in the waters of the Jamuna'. Such disguise was easy to achieve when men and women wore the same make-up and jewellery. The only thing needed to complete the 'disguise', then, would have been an upper cloth with which to create the illusion of voluptuous breasts and cover the head.

Of the many items of make-up used alike by men and women in India from at least the 3rd century onwards, the one that has persisted the longest in terms of being the subject of treatises, is the one we now know as kohl (the word itself is related etymologically to the Arabic kuhl, or powdered antimony, a black powder, and also to the English 'coal'). Indeed, kaajal (the popular vernacular name in India for kohl) was the very first article of make-up I ever bought, and it continued to be the only make-up I owned for many years. For several men and women in India, kaajal is the only make-up they ever wear.

While kaajal is now mass-produced by international brands, there are also persistent, old-world descriptions of how to make kaajal at home, using nothing more than some cotton, a bowl and a flame. Here is a recipe—one of many, found in diverse texts—for making kaajal. This description is part of the narratives in *Almond Eyes, Lotus Feet*, an account by Sharada Dwivedi and Shalini Devi Holkar of the pre-Independence pastimes of Indian royalty, which included embarking on lavish picnics:

> Off to one side of our sumptuous picnic sat big baskets of cotton wool. This nectar-filled cotton that had absorbed the moon's rays would be used to make the wicks for the lamps with which we would then make our kaajal... To the cotton we added powdered dill and bishop's weed or ajwain seeds for their medicinal properties. Then we burned those wicks in clarified butter or mustard oil to make our kaajal for the year.
>
> We turned a little copper or silver cup over the flame to catch the soot, then collected this in a small silver box and mixed it with some clarified butter... But there was an additional, more elaborate procedure, thanks to the good Pandit Dubey. He proclaimed that kaajal was not really beneficial unless it was kept for a few weeks in a Margosa neem tree, tucked into the hollow of a branch. Perhaps he recommended this because the neem is cooling?

Variously known on the Indian subcontinent as kohl, surma, collyrium or kaajal, black eye-liner has been ubiquitous on the Indian face for centuries. Both men and women have over the ages put kaajal in their eyes to make their eyes healthier, more lustrous and cooler. And for generations before the coming of the age of mass production, the method of preparing kaajal followed the general pattern outlined above.

As the royal recipe for kaajal published in a book subtitled *Indian Traditions in Beauty and Health* suggests, an important function of cosmetics in India was hygiene and bodily protection. Dehejia points to a poem from the 9th-century cycle of Tamil devotional poetry, the *Tirukkailaya-nana-ula*, in which the woman, 'as though cooling the passion of her lily-dark eyes / ...quells them with highlights of kohl'. Apart from using it for its alluring and highlighting potential, people in India also wear kaajal to cool their eyes. And these uses applied to both men and women, in both Muslim and Hindu traditions. While Hindus derived their love of kaajal from classical art and literature that depicts kaajal as a feature of health and beauty, Muslims derived their sanction for surma from a divine source. There is a sunnah about the Prophet Muhammad applying—and advising people to apply—surma before going to bed at night, first in the right eye and then in the left, three times on each side. Apparently, when put on at night, surma lasts longer in the eye. The Prophet is narrated as exhorting his followers to 'apply antimony [kuhl] regularly, as it clears the sight, makes the eye lashes grow and is the best of things beautifying the eyes'.

Making up the eyes In India has a long, non-gendered history that is easy to detect. Not only are eyes beautiful objects to be looked at, but they are also beautiful objects through which to look. As Dehejia points out, 'Sanskrit has over a hundred words and phrases to describe beauty, loveliness and attraction, a large proportion of which are connected with the concept of amorous play... The eyes are specially favoured with a range of phrases that include "a drink for one's eyes alone" (*netraika-peya*), "a festival for one's eyes" (*netrotsava*), and "a resting place for one's eyes" (*netra-vishrama-patra*).' The favour bestowed on the eyes by the Sanskrit language is in the service of erotic desire. The

eyes that look are also the eyes that desire. And the eyes
that desire are also the eyes that are represented as desiring
and desirable. Thus the attention paid to the eyes in treatises
on representational art. Of the eight rasas, or emotions—
including anger, shame, desire, joy—Dehejia points out that
'shringara [the erotic rasa] is described as the king of rasas
and has high visibility in visual and literary material'. The
Natyashastra too—the classical text devoted to matters of
dance, drama and music, composed between 200 BCE and
200 CE—idealizes the sringara rasa as the most important
and beautiful of all rasas. It states categorically that the
sambhoga or fulfilled version of the sringara rasa 'must be
expressed by loving looks, lifting eye-brows, side-glances,
graceful steps and gestures'.

These loving looks are most expressively cast by eyes lined
with kohl. It is in this incarnation of erotic allure that kaajal
or surma has existed imaginatively on the Indian scene. In
historical treatises, Urdu and Sanskrit poetry, Hindustani film
songs and everyday speech, kaajal has become the shorthand
indicator of erotic desire and aesthetic pleasure alike. These
pleasures cross genders and religions, languages and regions.
Like the image of the Ardhanarishvara, they combine rather
than differentiate between masculine and feminine.

It is in this combinatory mode that Mirza Asadullah
Khan Ghalib (1797-1869), one of the foremost Indian poets
in Urdu and Farsi, writes the following ghazal featuring the
seductive beauties of surma:

dil-e-naadaan tujhe hua kya hai
aakhir is dard ki davaa kya hai...

Naive heart, what has befallen you,
What is the cure for this pain?

I am eager and they are bored
O lord, what is this matter at hand?

I too am capable of speaking,
I wish you would ask me what the matter is.

When there is no one but you around
Then, O lord, what is this tumult?

What these angel-faced people are like!
What coquetry, what glances, what mannerisms!

Why are these curls in musky tresses,
What is there to compare to the surma in their eyes?

Where have the greenery and the rose come from,
What is this cloud, what is this wind?

We expect fidelity from them
Who do not know what fidelity is.

Do good and good will be done to you
What else is the saint's call?

I sacrifice my life to you
I do not know what else prayer is.

I accept that it may not be anything, Ghalib
But if it comes for free, then what is wrong with that?

Like all ghazals written in Persian and in Urdu after the style of Persian poetry, this ghazal too does not specify the pronoun of its recipient. All that we notice about the beloved is that his or her eyes are described as being beyond compare because they are lined with surma. The scent of amber, the curl of tresses, and the dark-line of the eye, all join forces with the coquettish glances of the beloved to entrance the poet. But what is most intriguing about the lavish attention paid by Ghalib to the beloved's eye make-up is that though this make-up marks the beloved as beloved, it also refuses to tell us if the beloved is male or female. Make-up is not a gendered differentiator.

In the 1968 Hindi film *Kismat*, something similar happens. The film features two songs about kaajal, one of which makes clear the seemingly inseparable link between men and make-up in India. In the song 'Kajra mohabbat wala...' (lyrics by S.H. Bihari, music by O.P. Nayyar and vocals by Asha Bhosle and Shamshad Begum), the protagonists (played by Biswajeet and Babita) dress in drag in order to escape from the goons who are chasing after them for much of the film. The song sequence begins with a series of shots lovingly focussed on the hero-heroine's body, beginning with his anklets and then moving up the entire body. The 'kajra mohabbat wala' or the 'kaajal of love' is a line that is always sung by the heroine dressed as the hero to the hero dressed as the heroine. Even as the lyrics talk about a woman who wears kaajal and a man who admires it, the visuals of the song show us a man who wears kaajal and a woman who admires it. In a song full of erotic desire that evokes Delhi as the setting of that eroticism—an idea that recurs in many Bollywood songs—'kajra mohabbat wala' seems to provide a backward glance at a culture in which both men and women wore make-up freely and frequently, and a glance forward to a situation in which that freedom has all but vanished:

Kajra mohabbat wala, akhiyon mein aisa dala
Kajre ne le lee meri jaan, hai re mai tere qurban

Duniya hai mere peechhe, lekin mai tere peechhe
Apna bana le meri jaan, hai re mai tere qurban...

Aai ho kahan se goree aankhon me pyar leke—(2)
Chadhtee javanee ki yeh pehli bahaar leke

Dilli shaher ka saara Meena Bazar leke—(2)
Jhumka Bareilly wala kaano mein aisa dala
Jhumke ne le lee meri jaan, hai re mai tere qurban.

Duniya hai mere peechhe, lekin main tere peechhe
Apna bana le merijan, hai re mai tere qurban

You have applied the kaajal of love in your eyes with such
  vigour
That it has taken away my life, which I sacrifice to you.

The whole world is chasing me, but I am chasing you
Make me yours, my love; I sacrifice myself for you.

Where have you come from, O Fair One, with love in your
  eyes,
With the first bloom of youth in your body,
With all of Delhi's Meena Bazar in you?
The jhumka from Bareilly you are wearing in your ear
Has taken my breath away; I sacrifice my life to you.

The whole world is chasing me, but I am chasing you
Make me yours, my love; I sacrifice myself for you.

In an age when gendered difference depends increasingly on a difference in one's relation to make-up, it is thrilling to remember texts and times in which kohl, red lips, red and yellow marks on the forehead, necklaces, bracelets, anklets, united both men and women in a joint adoration of the aesthetics of desire. That was a time when 'the whole world' was chasing the pleasures of the made-up face and body.

14

Psychoanalysis

Actually, Hariya's attraction to his mirror had recently
increased a great deal, and it perplexed all of us that Hariya,
who never used to look in a mirror even to comb his hair,
had started studying his reflection so intently.

—Manohar Shyam Joshi, *The Perplexity of Hariya Hercules*
(trans. Robert A. Hueckstedt)

One day, almost a hundred years ago, a significant
disagreement arose between the founder of the Indian
Psychoanalytic Society, Girindrasekhar Bose, and the founder
of psychoanalysis in the West, Sigmund Freud.

In a letter dated 11 April 1929, G. Bose wrote to S. Freud
to point out what he thought was a difference between the
castration threat posed by the Oedipus complex in the West
and in India: 'I do not deny the importance of the castration
threat in European cases: my argument is that the threat owes
its efficiency to its connection with the wish to be female.
The real struggle lies between the desire to be a male and its
opposite, the desire to be a female. I have already referred to
the fact that the castration threat is very common in Indian
society but my Indian patients do not exhibit castration
symptoms to such a marked degree as my European cases.
The desire to be a female is more easily unearthed in Indian
male patients than in European.'

The Oedipus complex, often considered the cornerstone
of Freudian psychoanalysis, describes a scenario in which
the little boy is threatened with serious consequences if

he does not forego sexual interest in his mother. If he disobeys—if he continues to express a sexual interest in his mother—then his punishment is castration. For Freud, the successful negotiation of the Oedipus complex—i.e. giving up sexual interest in the mother—is the pathway to masculine heterosexuality. The child has been warned that if he does not give up the mother, then he will become a woman like the mother. Male heterosexuality will henceforth consider castration as the biggest threat to its masculinity, and accordingly, it will guard its masculinity by attacking femininity with the violence that had once been psychically wielded against it. The move to becoming a man has to take a decisive turn away from the woman. In Freudian psychoanalysis, this complex psychic negotiation takes place in boys between the ages of three and five.

According to Bose, Indian men do not fear becoming women so the threat of the Oedipus complex is not as strong—they do not display the same fear of castration as their Western counterparts. Bose insists that Indian men have a deep psychic memory, reinforced by religion and mythology, of the easy interchangeability of male and female bodies. What's more, these stories about men who become women are often accompanied by narratives of greater rather than diminished sexual prowess. The reduced presence of castration anxiety in Indian men, then, is because there is something attractive rather than threatening for a man about the possibility of becoming a woman.

Freud was clearly curious about Bose's local flavouring of the Oedipus complex, especially because for him too the Oedipus complex is characterized by a boy's attraction towards the possibility of being a woman. It is the sheer attractiveness of being the same as one's mother that needs to be overcome. The trauma of moving away from the desire to be a woman is great precisely *because* the attraction too has been great. But in Freud's world, if a man wants to be a woman after the Oedipus phase is over, then he is greeted with horror and painted with shame. This is why male homosexuality, in its turn away from Oedipal masculinity, has had such a long and troubled reception in the Judeo-Christian world.

Freud was curious but couldn't afford to be too curious about Bose's theory because that would affect the universality he had claimed for his idea of male heterosexual development. Nonetheless, with or without Freud's imprimatur, Bose's ideas about the attractiveness of castration to the grown (and not necessarily homosexual) Indian man is a radical chapter in the history of desire anywhere.

But what was Bose drawing on for his evidence? Perhaps on the *Rig Veda*, the oldest of the Hindu texts, dating from about 1500 BCE and composed in the area that is now Pakistan? In its description of how the cosmos came to be, the Gospel of John in the New Testament says that 'in the beginning was the Word'. In its parallel description about the start of things, the *Rig Veda*, a collection of hymns to Vedic deities, says very clearly that 'in the beginning desire came over That [One], which became the first seed of mind'. As an account of the beginning of the world, the *Rig Veda* places desire at the very centre: all things come out of and are drenched in desire. And this desire does not belong to one person or one god alone. Rather, it is a mobile desire, interacting with sages and gods and natural elements and ideas. There is certainly mention made of one supreme being—'That One'—but no knowledge is attributed to this being: 'This creation, whence it came into being, whether spontaneously or not—he who is its highest overseer in heaven, he surely knows, or perhaps he knows not.' As opposed to Freud's Vienna, in which the Law ('the Word') holds sway over a monotheistic society presided over by one all-knowing Father-God, the world of the *Rig Veda* is ruled by a desire over which no single entity has control.

For the *Rig Veda*, desire is everywhere. It is at the very beginning and it is also in the present. Desire is the all in all, that without which nothing can be. But it is also nowhere because no *one* source for it can be identified. It cannot be reduced to being the product of one body or another. It is within this universe that we see a multitude of desiring positions undercutting the central importance of castration anxiety. Desire might take on the local shape of man and woman. But male and female are not the primary nodes through which desire exists in the universe. Instead, desire is inchoate, which means it is not limited to or defined by gendered bodies and roles.

Perhaps learning from this earliest text, several cults of divine worship in India repeat the *Rig Veda's* hymn of mobile desire. The great devotional movements that arose in homage to both Shiva and Krishna in the 12th century emphasized the necessity of detaching oneself from masculinity in order to experience erotic bliss. In the corpus of Bhakti poetry written in India over the last 900 years, the erotic love of Krishna is narrated from the woman's point of view, especially by male poets. Masculinity in Bhakti poetry recasts itself in the mould of the feminine in order to fully embrace what it is like to worship the god of multiple desires. In the history of his worship, Krishna assumes several different shapes, and so do his devotees. The very form of this Bhakti poetry is transsexual—men become women in order to worship a man, and have to live the erotic experience of being women in order to be able to write their poetry. Many saint-poets have written about this ecstatic state in which they enter into erotic bliss with Krishna. In *Freud along the Ganges*, Sudhir Kakar quotes the 15th-century Gujarati poet-saint, Narasinh Mehta: 'I took the hand of the lover of gopis in loving converse… I forgot all else. Even manhood left me. I began to sing and dance like a woman. My body seemed to change and I became one of the gopis. I acted as go-between like a woman and began to lecture Radha for being too proud… At such times, I experienced moments of incomparable sweetness and joy.'

Femininity here becomes a state of erotic bliss to be experienced with Krishna, the experienced and infinite lover. This state—and this is a fact repeated by several Bhakti poets—demands the embrace of being feminine. Such a movement is problematic because the state of adoration is inevitably conflated with being a woman, while the adored is a man. But equally, it is significant both that it is inevitably the *male* devotee who moves from being male to female. And this movement from male to female enhances rather than reduces his pleasure.

Even more, the migration from male to female does not necessarily entail a genital change in the body. Rather, the change happens in the way in which the body operates. For instance, Krishna is repeatedly described as becoming woman-like in order to experience the depths of bliss. In Jayadeva's 12th-century *Gitagovinda*, Krishna sings to Radha: 'Punish me, lovely fool! / Bite me with your cruel teeth! /

Chain me in your creeper arms! / Crush me with your hard breasts! / Angry goddess, don't weaken with joy! / Let Love's despised arrows / Pierce me to sap my life's power!' Krishna in Jayadeva's imagination attaches great erotic value to being the beloved who is crushed and pierced and bitten. Radha assumes all the typical attributes of a man in the grip of passion—crushing, piercing, sapping the supine Krishna. And this interchange of gendered identity passes without comment in the poem. Krishna becomes a woman and Radha a man: these personae are two among several possibilities. But whether desiring as a man or as a woman, Krishna and Radha's *bodies* do not change. Krishna is not described as a biological woman when he wants Radha to bite him. And Radha is not described as a biological man when she pierces Krishna. There is no physiological change that is needed in order to explain their changed sexual positions. No matter what persona they inhabit, there is no talk of emasculation or castration.

But whether we understand castration as a lopping off of the penis (which is how Freud understood it) or as a removal of the testicles (which is the more accurate definition of the term), the state of being castrated in the European imagination involves a physical and metaphorical change in genital attributes. And because this change is understood as a violent one, its psychological effects are fairly devastating. In Freud's Europe, castrated men are no longer considered men because they have failed the test of heterosexuality. They are 'reduced' to being women because their object choice is not the correct or approved one. In several Indian traditions, however, men become women because it *elevates* them in relation to desire. Their desire as men increases rather than decreases by becoming women. This ability of desire to change the fixity of the gendered self can never be underestimated.

In a different part of India, Ksetrayya in the mid-17th century wrote thousands of Telugu padams, or short classical compositions meant to be sung as an accompaniment to dance. These padams are almost all narrated by a woman to her cosmic lover whose divinity is subservient to his role as a lover. The gods come to earth in order to entangle with the courtesans, and they haggle over the price of amorous encounters. Contrary to what we might expect in such an encounter, it is the courtesan who is given a strong and supple voice. And in addition to giving the women this voice, Ksetrayya also does interesting things to the bodies of the courtesan and her cosmic lover: he makes them undifferentiable from one another. Consider, for example, a padam titled 'A Woman to Her Lover':

> 'Your body is my body,'
> you used to say,
> and it has come true,
> Muvva Gopala.
>
> Though I was with you
> all these days, I wasn't sure.
>
> Some woman has scratched
> nail marks on your chest,
> but I'm the one who feels the hurt.
>
> You go sleepless all night,
> but it's my eyes
> that turn red.
>
> 'Your body is my body,' you used to say.

Even outside the Bhakti traditions devoted to Krishna, Shiva and their various avatars, the erotic interchangeability of bodies was the norm in religious and poetic discourse. Such fecund multiplicity is an obvious extension of Hindu beliefs in multiple gods and goddesses. But even a monotheistic religion like Islam planted a firm root of erotic ecstasy in India. Male poets and their spiritual masters in Sufi poetry, for example, often changed shape with women and femininity. In the 18th century in Punjab, Bulleh Shah's verses addressed to his pir, Shah Inayat, are legendary for their movement between bodies: 'Separation from you has made me mad,' he claims, 'and has labelled / me "crazy girl".' Even more, Bulleh Shah insists that 'You have raised your veil and made me wander, like Zulaikha in Egypt. / With a burqa on his head, lord, Bulla has been made to / dance by your love.'

Who is Bulleh Shah in these lines? Is he the male poet or is he the female lover? Is he a man or a woman? Instead of giving us a clear picture of how his sexuality relates to his gender, the poet talks openly about himself as a man dressed in women's clothes. A man in a burqa caught in the ecstasy of love. A large corpus of poetry and devotional songs from all around the country—from Gujarat in the West to Punjab in the North to Tamil Nadu in the South, from the 12th to the 18th centuries, and continuing to this day—unabashedly praises men who become women in the throes of desire. As Indrani Chatterjee notes in 'When "Sexuality" Floated Free of Histories in South Asia,' this corpus 'spoke of adulterous erotic yearnings of mutably gendered beings, of gods who came as ordinary customers to haggle over a courtesan's fees, of the enjoined feminization of all biologically male devotees of Krsna or Siva. Themes of sexual indeterminacy bound eastern Indian Vaisnava poetics from the sixteenth century to their Sufi counterparts in the Panjab and the Deccan well into the late eighteenth century.' One can get some sense, therefore, that the prospect of becoming a woman does not quite carry the same sexually threatening charge in India as it might have done in Freud's Vienna.

But it is not only the difference between levels of castration anxiety felt by the European and Indian man that marks the distinctiveness of desire in India for Bose's psychoanalysis. It is also the relation between erotic desire and the status of the body. Krishna, Bulleh Shah, Ksetrayya do not change their bodies in order to become women. They assume they are women and announce their desires accordingly. Thousands of gods and poets change their gender, sliding from masculine to feminine, and the devotees who adore them follow suit. In these religious, cultural and poetic traditions, bodies are not permanent biological indicators of any particular desire.

As Bhaskar Sripada points out in *Freud along the Ganges*: 'The fact is that in...India there is a general acceptance of psychic bisexuality and delinkage between gender identity and sexual object choice. A god with male and female attributes is intended to convey this essential bisexuality and not intended to imply the worship of some genetically or biologically hermaphroditic or intersexed being. Western notions... confuse psychic bisexuality with bisexual behaviour.' In other words, sexuality in India seems historically and religiously to be migratory rather than a biological pre-given. Sexuality does not imply a fixed personhood; gender does not fully determine desire. One does not become less of a man for being a woman. And one can often become more of a woman after taking a temporary detour through masculinity. This idea of a psychic bisexuality formed the basis also of the recent Supreme Court NALSA judgement on transgendered people in 2014.

Indeed, this rich and varied history of desire is one of the many reasons why modern categories of sexuality—hetero-, homo-, bi-—are of relatively recent provenance in India. Their success as identities is to make us believe that the body is a single category and that its desire too is singular. In such a worldview, desire, body, dress, behaviour, object-choice are all expected to line up neatly behind one or other of these categorical doors. But what if one's desire is *expected* to change and fluctuate during one's lifetime, and one's appearance not necessarily so? Krishna does not start looking like a different person when he merges into Radha. What Bhaskar Sripada calls 'psychic bisexuality' refers precisely to this fluidity. Not that sexuality lies only in the mind. But rather, that multiple desires can be held together in the same body. A change in desire is expected rather than apocalyptic.

This is what Mirabai in the 16th century reminds the male priest at Mathura about when he refuses her permission to enter the temple because she is a woman. Looking at him with pity, she says that *all* of Krishna's devotees are gopis or cowherdesses in their ecstatic devotion, and this is a fact he must never forget. Astonished, the priest repents of his mistake, and not only allows her in to the temple, but also becomes her ardent follower.

For thousands of years in Indian history, across religions, there have been narratives that allow men to be women in a state of desire. Being 'castrated', then, does not carry the same charge among Indian patients and practitioners of psychoanalysis as it does in the West. As Sudhir Kakar notes in *Freud along the Ganges,* in relation to his patients: 'for most of the worshippers and the saints, as for the rest of us, the wish to be a woman is not a later distortion of phallic strivings but rather another legacy from our prehistoric experience.' After all, the Indus civilizations have for long considered auspicious an entire group of people called hijras. Their auspiciousness lies precisely in their non-attachment to masculinity and their comfort with male bodies that dress and act like women. Many hijras never undergo the nirvana operation of castrating themselves to become women. Their male bodies become female without necessarily losing their penis. As Indrani Chatterjee notes in a remark that brings together grammar, sexuality and psychoanalysis: 'Like every other European language, English has no room for the "it-ness" once valorized by Tantric Buddhists, Saiva and Sufi-Baul alike.' The psychoanalytic grammar of desire manifests in multiple accents in the Indian subcontinent.

Indeed, Girindrasekhar Bose was categorical about this difference. He said in yet another paper that during 'my analysis of Indian patients I have never come across a case of castration complex in the form in which it has been described by European observers'. This is not to say that in psychoanalytic terms, Indian men and women do not undergo castration anxiety—they worry about losing control over their bodies, and they worry about not having social acceptability. Most perniciously, Indian men persecute women as much as their counterparts in the West do. But the cause of their misogyny might lie less in a renounced fear of being a woman and might owe instead to other factors like class disparity and aspirational power games. In historical terms, the sexual possibility of a man becoming a woman—

and therefore the violent warding off of that possibility—has not emerged with quite the same force in India. For complex historical reasons, there is instead a more willing acceptance of the migrations of desire regardless of bodies.

India proved to be a fertile ground for Freudian psychoanalysis because both Islam and Hinduism already had thriving systems of dream interpretation. But when Girindrasekhar Bose founded the Indian Psychoanalytic Society in Calcutta in 1922, what was even more significant was the way in which psychoanalysis in India laid bare sexual possibilities that were part of people's everyday realities. Desire was the central focus of both religious and literary life. Moveable genders were a recognizable part of the cultural and historical landscape. Men became women to experience erotic bliss. Men announced themselves as women without having to undergo surgical reassignment surgery. These histories of desire in India challenge the Oedipal focus of Freudian psychoanalysis. And these are the histories on which Bose drew while arguing his case with Freud.

But something was also beginning to change as Bose was trying to rewrite the impact of castration anxiety among Indian men. Under the weight of a colonial morality, hijras were criminalized, Hindu gods were shunned as effeminate, and Muslim rulers who dressed as women during saints' festivals were defined as perverse. As Ruth Vanita and Saleem Kidwai tell us in *Same-Sex Love in India*: 'The kingdom of Avadh…was simultaneously the last hold-out against the British, and the one that the British narrated as being the most sexually deviant.' Its nawab, Nasiruddin Haider, would on 'the birth date of each Imam…pretend to be a woman in childbirth. Other men imitated him, dressing and behaving like women during that period. British Victorian men viewed this kind of transgendered masculinity as unmanly decadence.' Fairly rapidly, British morality insisted that body and gender and desire should all line up neatly behind one another. There began a strong and concerted effort to erase the multiple histories of desire in India. And even though the subcontinent's messy histories of changeable bodies have not disappeared, they are being recognized less readily as *our* histories. In other words, Girindrasekhar Bose's Indian rewriting of the 'universal' Freudian doctrine of castration anxiety might not be as recognizable today as Indian.

Thus, the high status accorded to hijras is fast diminishing, and they are increasingly being forced to beg for a living. The new Bill passed in the Lok Sabha in 2016 'protecting' the rights of transgender people in India has, as we've already seen, insisted that trans-people be identified biologically rather than desirously and psychically. India seems to be moving further away from the Bhakti and Sufi poets who 'became' women because they desired to do so. Today, those poets, and even the gods, would need to have a sex-change operation in order to align their body with their gender and with their sexuality. If one were to do a survey among psychoanalysts in India today, chances are high that the number of their patients suffering from castration anxiety will have increased at a faster clip than could ever have been predicted by Girindrasekhar Bose.

15

BHABHIS

Woh Teri Bhabhi Hai, Pagle (Madman, She's Your Sister-
in-law)
Bhabhiji Ghar Par Hain? (Is Bhabhiji at Home?)
Hum Aapke Hain Kaun (Who am I of Yours?)
—(Titles of two Hindi TV soap operas and
a Bollywood film)

Prashant and Rakesh have been friends since their days
together in college. Prashant is now married to Sunita, while
Rakesh is unmarried. For Rakesh, Sunita is his bhabhi, or
sister-in-law, even though they are not related by blood or
law. All three characters star in a hugely popular Youtube
video that has gathered over 27 million views so far.[4] Titled
'Lunch with my Friend's Wife', this video charts the course
of a lazy Sunday morning. Rakesh is on his way to Prashant's
house for lunch. He is in a good mood, humming old Hindi
romantic songs. Then he gets a call from Prashant, which
causes him some annoyance. Prashant says he has had to go
out on an urgent matter and will not be back for another
two hours. Rakesh says he will go ahead to Prashant's house
anyway. When Prashant tells Rakesh to wait for him at a
coffee shop instead, Rakesh guffaws that he will do nothing
of the kind. 'Silly fellow,' he says a minute later, 'suspects me
of flirting with his wife.'

---

4. This video is based on a true story: https://www.youtube.com/
watch?v=rEm-w5WPH58

Rakesh reaches Prashant's house soon enough and is greeted by his Sunita bhabhi, who seems to be a bit out of sorts. Over lunch, Rakesh asks her why she is looking upset. Sunita then embarks on a tale of marital woe in which Prashant, though a loving and attentive husband, is no longer sexually attracted to his wife. The couple does not have sex, Sunita complains, unless she complies with Prashant's 'weird' desires. When Rakesh asks her what those desires are, she refuses to answer, and runs off sobbing into the bedroom, where she flings herself on her bed. After a couple of perplexed moments, Rakesh follows Sunita into the bedroom, starts to wipe away her tears, and then the inevitable happens. The only word that can be heard as they get hot and heavy is 'Bhabhi, oh Bhabhi' repeated many times over. The next scene focuses on the post-coital moment—Sunita is patting her hair back in place, Rakesh wakes up and starts smoking a cigarette. The atmosphere between them seems strained. Then Sunita looks at Rakesh in the mirror and says, 'For how long will all this continue, Prashant?'

The entire film then plays out in flashback: 'Rakesh' gets Sunita to call him in the guise of Prashant to say he will not be at home. This puts Rakesh and his 'bhabhi' in a potentially compromising situation, flagged by Rakesh's laughing comment about flirting with Prashant's wife. Sunita bhabhi then talks about Prashant's weird desires, followed by Rakesh trying to comfort his bhabhi by having sex with her. The film pivots on and leads up to the fact that Prashant can only have sex with his wife if he is 'Rakesh' and sees her as his bhabhi. This is the 'weird' desire to which Sunita refers early on in the film. The desire that desexualizes wives, and hyper-sexualizes sisters-in-law.

Prashant desires Sunita sexually only when he can see her as his sister-in-law rather than as his wife. In much of the post-Freudian West, the cult of the desirable older woman has been cast in the mould of the mother figure (displayed powerfully in a film like *The Graduate*). But in India, illicit male desire tends to be focussed on an older female figure who is *not* the mother while still being a relative in the family.

This older female relative is the 'bhabhijaan' of Vishal Bhardwaj's 2014 film *Haider*. Based on William Shakespeare's *Hamlet*, *Haider* is the third in Bhardwaj's Shakespeare trilogy, after *Maqbool* (Macbeth) and *Omkara* (Othello). In Shakespeare's play, the protagonist is gutted because his father has been murdered by his uncle, Claudius, who has also married Hamlet's mother Gertrude. In the Shakespearean family tree, Gertrude is, of course, Claudius's bhabhi. Sigmund Freud famously used Hamlet as an example of the Oedipus complex—where the son is jealous of the father and sexually possessive about the mother. For Freud, 'Hamlet is able to do anything—except take vengeance on the man who did away with his father and took that father's place with his mother, the man who shows him the repressed wishes of his own childhood realized. Thus the loathing, which should drive him on to revenge, is replaced in him by self-reproaches, by scruples of conscience, which remind him that he himself is literally no better than the sinner whom he is to punish.' Freud discusses Hamlet in relation to his theory of the Oedipus complex, and most commentators have understood this to mean that Hamlet is the son who wants to sleep with Gertrude, the mother. But what if Hamlet is reacting badly not because of the thwarted desire of a son for his mother, but because of the fulfilled desire of a brother-in-law for his sister-in-law? Is he furious with Claudius because Claudius is the brother-in-law who now has sexual access to his bhabhi? Does Hamlet's dilemma in the play owe to the fact that the brother-in-law's sexual interest in the bhabhi is socially accepted as being next only to the husband's while the son's desire is not accepted at all? After all, marrying a husband's younger brother was quite a widely accepted practice even in England. Henry VIII, father of the Queen of England in Shakespeare's time, married Katherine of Aragon, his older brother Arthur's widow.

Hamlet's Hindustani rendition in *Haider* thus points to a more widespread and acceptable version of male desire—that of a man's for his older brother's wife.

The character of Gertrude is central to Shakespeare's play, but Vishal Bhardwaj makes her even more central to his film. *Haider's* Gertrude and Claudius are Ghazala and Khurram. In response to Ghazala's question about why he is not married, Khurram says he will only marry someone as wonderful as his bhabhijaan. And so it comes to pass. Khurram arranges for his brother's death, and marries Ghazala, who is shown to reciprocate his desire for her. In fact, Ghazala's desire is so obvious in the film that it becomes hard to ignore. Married to a man who puts duty above love, Ghazala is no longer sexually attractive to her husband. And she has always been sexually desirable for her devar, or younger brother-in-law. Ghazala seeks and accepts emotional and sexual sustenance from Khurram rather than from her son, Haider. Nor does this seem unusual. Even as they are publicly mourning his dead brother, Khurram asks the gathered community for permission to marry his bhabhijaan in order to look after her welfare. The members of the community are unfazed. Of course the younger brother 'looks after' the older brother's wife—this has long been a tradition in India.

After all, the etymology of devar is doosra var—or second husband. In the conservative book of laws, the *Manusmriti*, this tradition of marrying a dead brother's wife is known as niyoga, or delegation. It describes a practice common in Vedic times in which the brother-in-law is allowed to have sexual relations with, and even marry, his bhabhi for the sake of her welfare and in order to produce offspring. As Sudhir Kakar describes it in *Intimate Relations*, 'the psychological core of niyoga [is] the mutual awareness of a married woman and her younger brother-in-law as potential or actual sex partners'. In fact, so common does niyoga seem to have been that Chapter IX of the *Manusmriti* lays out in great detail the protocols by which it should be governed:

1. It can only happen when the husband is impotent or infertile or has died without producing an offspring
2. It can take place only with the consent of the woman, and only for the purpose of having a child, not for pleasure
3. The man picked for the task should ideally be an immediate family member. The *Manusmriti* names only the husband's brother as a familial candidate; other contenders are gods or venerable sages
4. One man can perform niyoga only three times in his lifetime (lest he get addicted to having sex with his brother's wife)
5. The child born of this union would be considered to belong to the woman and her deceased/infertile husband rather than to the sexual partner, who is not allowed to make any paternal claim

6. Both sexual partners need to cover their bodies in ghee so that they cannot linger on the contours of the body for pleasure and will focus only on the acts required for reproduction.

Niyoga delegates have had a long and hoary history in Hindu tradition. Without them, for instance, the *Mahabharata* would not have had a story worth telling. Both patriarchs of the warring factions, Dhritarashtra (father of the Kauravas) and Pandu (sire of the Pandavas), were born only because Queen Satyavati forces her son, the sage Vyasa, to have sex with his dead brother Vichitravirya's widows, Ambika and Ambalika. (Vyasa also fathers a son with Ambika and Ambalika's maid, who is the first woman to be sent in to Vyasa because the two sisters were terrified by his fierce appearance.) King Pandu, one of the products of this niyoga, in turn has his wives impregnated by several gods because he is cursed to die if he ever approaches a woman with amorous intent. And thus are born the Pandavas. When the *Mahabharata* enters the epic stage, then, all its main actors are in place thanks to the fact that women have had sex with men who are not their husbands, and in the case of Vyasa, the sisters-in-law have had sex with their brother-in-law.

While Vyasa is the older brother of Vichitravirya, and dominates his sisters-in-law, such a structure of patriarchal sexual privilege is the exception in cases of bhabhi desire. Definitionally, bhabhis are older and more sexually experienced than the brothers-in-law; in the bhabhi-devar configuration of desire, the man is the dependent one. Sometimes, though, the desire between the bhabhi and the devar can highlight how both are lower in a pecking order that is dominated by the older man—the bhabhi's husband, and the devar's brother. The two get up to mischief because they are both consigned to a place of frivolity. This is certainly the treatment that Rabindranath Tagore gives to the bhabhi (or boudhan in Bengali)-devar romance in his short novella *Nashtanir,* which was later turned into an acclaimed film and named *Charulata* after its female protagonist. In the novella, Charu and her loving-yet-distant husband Bhupati's younger cousin, Amal, build a bond over a shared love of literature. The intensity of their emotional interactions, the quality of their literary encounters, their moments and months of privacy, rise to a crescendo that is breathtaking in its intimation of a love that dare not speak its name. Charu does not realize what Amal means to her until he leaves her to get married to someone else. But when she does realize the extent of her loss, that fact is not lost on her husband, who then leaves her to take up a job in Mysore. Scholars and biographers have speculated that *Nashtanir* is based on Tagore's real-life interactions with his boudhan, Kadambari Devi, wife of his older brother Jyotirindranath Tagore. Like Amal in the novel, Rabindranath too starts developing his love of literature alongside his sister-in-law; like Amal, he too leaves his love to get married and then go to England to study. But while the novella only hints at the disaster lying in store for Charulata, in real life, Kadambari Devi committed suicide within months of Rabindranath's marriage.

For many young men in India, bhabhis fill the socio-sexual gap with which they have grown up. Reporting from the ground in Banaras, Steve Derné notes that 'Indian men have little opportunity to interact with women outside their immediate families. In Banaras, men do not usually attend schools or universities with women, and even in places where coeducation is common, a man usually has little experience interacting with women since parents try to limit daughters' contacts with young men. For younger sons, the often sexually charged relationship with their bhabhis—women who are defined as sexual creatures—is an important experience that may lead them to desire similarly close relationships with their own wives.' For the bhabhi, like for Kadambari Devi and Charulata, the presence of the devar fills a gap of emotional loneliness and physical longing.

This comfortable co-existence can be shattered for the bhabhi by the impending marriage of the devar since that takes him away both sexually and emotionally. This was the subject of a bold soap opera on Indian television that ran from December 2015 to April 2016. *Aadhe Adhoore* had as its protagonist Jassi, whose husband is working in the Middle East, and who lives with her mother-in-law and devar. In the very first episode we are told that Jassi and her brother-in-law are in an emotional and sexual relationship with one another. Jassi even gets pregnant during this affair and has an abortion. In order to provide a veneer for her relationship, she arranges a marriage for her devar, but predictably, everything goes wrong after that. In the case of *Aadhe Adhoore*, what also went wrong was a moralistic viewership, which wrote in frequently to demand that the 'characterless' Jassi be punished in the show. And so she was—made to fall to her death. Her devar's wife stands triumphant and pregnant over her corpse. Like Charu and Kadambari, Jassi too succumbs to the intolerable pressure exerted by the departure of the devar from her love life.

Even Sita in the *Ramayana* seems to be aware of this

dynamic of desire in India. Devdutt Pattanaik points to an episode in the Valmiki *Ramayana* (dated between 200 BCE and CE) that makes such sexual tension clear: 'This episode is fairly well known yet few people like to talk about it. It happens in the forest in the final year of Rama's 14-year exile. Sita is so smitten by a golden deer that she begs her husband, Rama, to get it for her. After a long chase, Rama manages to shoot it down only to discover that it is no deer but a shape shifting demon who before dying mimics Rama's voice and shouts, "Help, Sita! Help, Laxman!" Hearing this cry, Sita begs Laxman to go to Rama's rescue. Laxman refuses since his brother had ordered him to protect Sita and not leave her side under any circumstances. Annoyed by his reticence, Sita says, "You wish his death in order to secure me. It is clear to me that just for me you have refrained from going to your brother..." These are the exact words of Makhan Lal Sen who translated the *Ramayana* of Valmiki in 1927... Laxman responds to the accusation with horror and to prove Sita wrong goes in search of Rama, leaving Sita unguarded. Shortly thereafter Sita is abducted by Ravana, the demon-king of Lanka.' And thereby hangs a tale.

Elsewhere, in literature and life, the physical absence of the husband creates the necessary conditions for bhabhi-devar romance. An anthropological study in Kerala, which is the cradle of Indian migration to the Gulf, bears this out. 'When men reach their late 20s or early 30s without being married (recently, relatively common because of Gulf migration), they are said to be "desperate" for a woman, and dangerously over-heated. These unmarried men can constitute a direct danger to the community, as they might start illicit sexual relations with married women (brother's wives in most common cases), note Filippo and Caroline Osella in 'Migration, Money and Masculinity in Kerala'. They even give as an example a case that was recorded in North Kerala: 'While elder brothers Joyson and Joey worked away in the Gulf, their wives stayed back in Valiyagramam with their children, their husbands' parents, and the youngest (unmarried) brother, Jojan, then in his late teens. When Joyson came home on leave, his wife appeared around the village with a black eye, while Jojan was extremely subdued: it was rumoured that Joyson had found evidence of an affair between his wife and Jojan and had beaten the pair of them. One year later, Joey came home unexpectedly, having received a letter from his mother informing him that Jojan had this time been found with his second sister-in-law. A public scene ensued, in which Joey openly beat his wife in the compound outside his house; she was later rushed to hospital, having drunk poison in a suicide attempt. When Joey returned to the Gulf, he took his wife and children with him.'

But most tales of bhabhi-devar romance are not tragic. In fact, extending the historical legacy of niyoga, bhabhis are very much in the realm of sexual fantasy in India. According to PornHub, one of the world's most popular adult websites, India pushed Canada aside to become the world's third largest online consumer of porn in 2015. Indians visited the site 21.2 billion times; of that number, 30% identified themselves as women. In 'The Top 10 Searches of 2015 in India', PornHub lists 'Indian' as the top keyword search and 'Indian Bhabhi' as the second most frequently searched keyword. Fascinatingly, there was a 222% increase in the search for the phrase 'Indian bhabhi devar'. The Indian obsession with bhabhis is now measurable on international websites, and in comparison with the rest of the world.

http://www.newindianexpress.com/lifestyle/books/2009/jun
/06/savita-bhabhi-is-the-new-face-of-freedom-55291.html

Savita bhabhi, of course, epitomizes this obsession. India's first and perhaps most famous porn icon, Savita bhabhi started life in 2008 (and was banned by the Indian government in 2009) as the star of a pornographic online cartoon series about a 'bored Indian housewife'. She fulfils the two considerations for bhabhi desire in India—her husband is not sexually interested in her, and she is sexually fascinating to younger men who call her bhabhi. Even more interestingly, and perhaps reflecting the increased percentage of female Indian visitors to porn websites, Savita bhabhi slakes her desire with devars of various stripes, from salesmen to enemies of the state. With her voluptuous figure, Savita bhabhi looks like a Barbie-Bhabhi. She is a fantasy of Indian male desire for bhabhis but she is also an expression of the sexually curious and bold Indian bhabhi herself who wants to be desired. Savita bhabhi could be the aspirational ideal for the Indian woman who visits PornHub in the dead of night. Or perhaps even in the broad light of day.

This modern-day bhabhi comes in multiple guises, and in Deepa Mehta's 1998 film, *Fire*, she finds herself in an interesting situation. *Fire* was not only passed by the Censor Board of India, but also commended by them as an important film for Indian women. Nonetheless, the censors asked for one fairly significant cut to be made before the film was released. This involved changing the name of one of the protagonists from Sita to Nita so as to avoid hurting religious sentiments. The change was in effect only in Maharashtra; all other places in India saw and heard Sita on screen.

The other protagonist—and Sita's love interest in the film—is named Radha, who too has an illustrious presence in Hindu mythology. But perhaps her name bothered the Censor Board less since Radha is already known as the extra-marital lover of a younger man who happens also to be the god Krishna. Thus, the name of Sita, the model of dutiful and self-sacrificing Indian womanhood, needed to be protected more than that of Radha.

In the film, both Radha and Sita/Nita occupy the position that bhabhis often do both in fantasies like *Savita Bhabhi* and also in real life: they are stuck in loveless marriages. One's husband prefers chastity to his wife while the other husband prefers a Chinese girlfriend. The women are drawn together because they lack both emotional and sexual sustenance in their marriages. This is the second staple of a classic bhabhi-devar romance, except that in this film the romance is between two sisters-in-law. Predictably, all hell breaks loose when their relationship is discovered. The film ends in a utopian manner, with Radha and Sita escaping the bounds of a patriarchal household to a dargah in which they seek refuge. But what is even more startling than the lesbian desire openly depicted in the film is the fact that such desire remains within the bhabhi romance genre. Sita's husband, Jatin, calls Radha bhabhi because he is her husband's younger brother, and the usual suspect for an illicit romance with her. But this time, it is the brother-in-law's wife who runs away with the bhabhi.

Bhabi-love from *Fire*. *Source:* Hamilton-Mehta Productions

Fire was ground-breaking in several ways, but one of the most significant was that it provided a variation on the theme of the bhabhi-devar romance. By making the brother-in-law a sister-in-law instead, the film points to the pervasiveness of certain lines of attraction in the Indian family. Radha and Jatin get set aside in favour of Radha and Sita, but they continue to occupy the positions of desire that have been familiar to Indians from even before the writing of the *Manusmriti*.

16

GRANDPARENTS

'A 55-year-old widow making dirty phone calls to a young boy. You should be ashamed.'
—from *Lipstick Under My Burkha*
(2016; trans. Manjari Sahay)

In the *Mahabharata*, Vyasa is the grandparent for whom desire exists only in the line of duty. He is a celibate sage who has sex with his dead brother's wives in order to continue the family line. The children born of this sexual union in turn give birth to the Pandavas and the Kauravas, who are the *Mahabharata's* protagonists. In his epic role as grandfather, Vyasa exemplifies the fantasy frequently associated with grandparents in the Indian subcontinent: selfless service to the family, and no desire for the self. Grandparents are thought of as members of a sedate older generation who have always lived straight and narrow lives, utterly obedient to their parents' wishes, and devoted to upholding social norms. After all, Vyasa impregnates his sisters-in-law only because his mother insists that he do so for the benefit of family and society. Grandparents are also imagined to be the repositories of indignation should any member of their lineage not uphold those same social norms. In such situations, they embody fire and brimstone, tears and threats, thunder and drama. But whether they are noble, sacrificing and silent, or thunderous, punitive and vocal, grandparents in India are seen as having a distant personal relation to desire. They are typically the ones with whom you would never discuss sex.

So even though we know that grandparents have had sex in order for their children and grandchildren to be alive, we tend not to think about them in relation to desire. How did they desire when they were younger? What do they desire now? Have their desires changed over time? Do they regret what they once desired and wish they could do it differently? Was their desire rebellious rather than dutiful? Did anyone ask them earlier what their desires were? Do we ask them now? What if grandparents had desires that would shock us?

The two stories that follow—one in the past tense about a grandmother who is no longer alive, and another in the present tense about a grandfather who is alive and well—give us a glimpse into lives that we tend not to associate with the viccisitudes of desire.

These tales reconstruct the youthful sexual histories of people who have aged. Both stories challenge the notions of sexual propriety we retrospectively assume our grandparents always possessed. In these narratives, people who are now grandparents reveal histories that differ widely in scope from Vyasa's.

* * *

STORY 1: ULLATTIL KALYANIKUTTYAMMA AND CHINGACHAMVEETIL KUNHIRAMAN

(The source is my family, and the protagonists, my maternal grandparents.)

Ammamma (my mother's mother) was very particular about her appearance. She was always well dressed and had a high opinion of her good looks. In the Victorian English she was fond of speaking, she termed herself 'handsome'. She liked dressing up and smelling nice. But she was equally invested in studying and being professionally independent. In the Kerala Nair milieu in which she was raised, even though women inherited the family name and property, they were not encouraged to attend college, let alone work for a living. As with so many matrilineal societies, real power resided with the women's brothers, and such was also the case in Ammamma's family.

Ammamma was the brightest and most ambitious child in a family of nine siblings—three brothers and six sisters. Some of these siblings were half-siblings who had the same father and whose mothers were twins, one of whom died early. (This practice of marrying sisters- and brothers-in-law is, of course, a common practice all over the subcontinent. In Kerala, there was also a specialized version called the 'exchange marriage' in which one brother and sister married a sister and brother from another family in order to minimize expenses.) She completed her schooling at Moyan Girls High School and her intermediate at Victoria College in Palghat, where she was only one of two girls in her class of 100 students (the boys would block the door in order to tease the girls, who could only enter the classroom along with the teacher). After that, Ammamma persuaded her mother to send her to college in Madras. Ammamma wanted to study medicine—she had her heart set on it. But there was a lot of objection to this course of action, especially from Ammamma's brother, Narayan, who seems to have had the power to sit in judgment on all the actions that his sisters were and were not allowed to perform. 'There is no need for girls to study further,' Narayan insisted, basing his remarks on what, we do not quite know. But Ammamma was the rebel.

Even as her mother was being swayed by Narayan's strongly stated objections, Ammamma mounted an equally fierce case for being allowed to study further, even going so far as to approach her father (fathers were distant, unapproachable figures at the time) to speak on her behalf. This determined resistance was but a template for what was to follow later on. It was also the reason that Ammamma was a committed member of the freedom struggle against the British and donated her gold jewellery to the nationalist cause when Gandhi asked his fellow-countrypeople to give their all.

Finally—whether from sheer exhaustion or the prevailing of better sense—Narayan was won over, but only to a compromise position. Ammamma was still not allowed to study medicine, but was allowed to study Chemistry instead. Ammamma's mother acquiesced to this compromise position, and so Ammamma moved to Madras to study at Queen Mary's College. She was a good student and won many prizes for both academic achievements and co-curricular activities. She also continued to dress well; so much so that her friends called her 'the princess'.

During the week, Ammamma stayed in the hostel on the Queen Mary's College campus. But on weekends, she would take a break and go to her step-sister's home. This was Kunhimalu, whose mother had been the twin of Ammamma's mother, and who was now married to Rao Bahadur C.B. Nair, who worked with Indian Railways.

Also staying in the house at this time was C.B. Nair's nephew, Kunhiraman, who had finished his education and was in Madras to look for a job. Kunhiraman was Ammamma's nephew—her father's older sister's grandson, so he was someone she had known all her life.

When it was time for Ammamma to return to college after the weekend, it was often Kunhiraman who borrowed a motorbike and dropped her back at the campus.

Romance blossomed between aunt and nephew, and bloomed for many years. Through Ammamma's BA degree at Queen Mary's College, then her lecturer training (the degree now known as a B.Ed) at Lady Willingdon Training College, and then her job as the headmistress of a school in Kannur, just outside Calicut, they were were romantically involved for about 4-5 years before Ammamma told her mother that she would marry none other than Kunhiraman.

This announcement caused a great deal of consternation, as we might imagine, and created scenes similar to the ones we see in Indian movies. Parents promising to have heart-attacks on demand, the family honour being called into question, the woman being forbidden to leave the house ever again. Ammamma's brother Narayan (yes, the same one), even picked up a knife and went after my grandfather-elect. Luckily for us all, he was stopped in time. Finding his physical violence thus thwarted, Narayan then turned his wrath onto Ammamma and her helpless mother and said that Ammamma was not to step out of the house.

In fairness, there were objections to this marriage from both families. Kunhiraman's family said that their clan had already married three women from Ammamma's clan, and they did not want to add to that number, especially given that they were closely related. Ammamma's family countered this social slight with an intellectual attack. According to them, Kunhiraman was not academically as highly qualified as Ammamma (he studied at Madras Christian College, but did not complete his BA), and did not have a 'proper' job yet.

What was even more shocking was that he was also younger than Ammamma by one whole month!

And so it went—punch and counter-punch—until Ammamma's older (step) sister from Madras, Kunhimalu, came visiting to the family house in Kavallapara, Kerala. Sensing an opportunity (after all, her romance with Kunhiraman was hatched under Kunhimalu's roof), Ammamma pleaded with her sister to intervene on her behalf. For added dramatic effect, she locked herself in a room and refused to come out until she had everyone's permission to marry Kunhiraman. So Kunhimalu spoke to her anxious step-mother and her angry step-brother and managed to convince them that if marrying Kunhiraman was what Ammamma wanted, then it should be allowed forthwith.

And so, defying family, custom and propriety, Ammamma followed her desire. She travelled on her own, lived on her own, thought for herself, fought with her family, and married the man she picked for herself. Kunhiraman—my Ammachan—meanwhile, followed his own desire, defied his family's wishes (the women of his clan did not attend the wedding), and married the woman he had picked for himself. Ammamma married Ammachan in Palghat in 1937. My mother was born in 1942, 5 years after their marriage. Ammamma and Ammachan lived together (mostly happily, as far as I could tell) for 59 years until Ammachan's death in 1996.

* * *

STORY 2: 'PETE'

(The source is a lightly edited transcript of an email exchange I had with a grandfather named 'Pete'. He wrote to me after being contacted by my research assistant, Shilpa, and asked if I would be comfortable with an email exchange.)

1 November 2015

Dear Pete:

Thanks for your reply. And yes, we can certainly start over email!

This chapter for which I wanted to find queer grandparents is born directly of one of the premises of my book (called *A History of Desire in India*). We are often told in India, at the first sign of sexually untoward behaviour, that 'your grandparents would never have done such a thing' or 'your grandparents would be horrified if they ever found out' or 'wait till your grandparents hear about this'! By finding grandparents who have themselves been sexually untoward, I'd like to showcase the hollowness of such a claim of familial propriety. I also hope this will allow people to feel more easy in relation to such manufactured family strictures. An additional goal is to suggest that sexual desires can change: most gay people around the world start out as straight, even if only in accordance with family wishes, and then somehow figure out what it is that they want. Desires exist multiply and differentially in all of us.

I am thinking of desire as a universal term but trying to find landing points for it in India. Rather than a history that starts with the *Kamasutra*, however, I am focussing on somewhat eccentric subjects, like grandparents!

Could we start with a broad and general conversation about your story: how would you narrate the trajectory of your desire?

With many thanks,
Madhavi

24 November 2015

Dear Madhavi,

I started writing in reply to your mail but the process ended up being part catharsis. I've cut back a lot but I suspect it is still much more than what you neeed or want.

I'm afraid that I don't fit your image of an Indian grandfather. My children certainly couldn't use the expression 'What would your grandparents say?' (at least about same sex desire) since both my wife and I made it clear to them that whatever their sexual orientation turned out to be, we would be accepting of it.

I also question your premise that most gay people start out straight. Though sexuality can be fluid and not just evolve but oscillate over time, I suspect that most of us are kind of hardwired one way or the other. In a heteronormative world, however, it might take a homosexual some time to recognize and acknowledge his orientation and, just as there is satisfying M2M sex between heterosexual urban migrants, I suspect many homosexual men are capable of heterosexual relations.

In my case, I should have known from the beginning that I was homosexual even though I had sexual relations with a number of women. It somehow never occurred to me to reflect on why none of my heterosexual couplings (I really can't call them affairs) ever kindled the kind of passion I felt while in the arms of another man.

Regards,

Pete

I am interpolating a later email exchange here since it is on the same subject—of how this chapter is to be framed:

30 August 2016

Dear Madhavi,

While beginning to write my next bit to you, I went over our previous mails.

When I re-read the premise of your chapter on grandparents, I felt it rang a little hollow in how an Indian parent would address 'sexually untoward behaviour' with a child. Feedback from me might not be appropriate and I would take no offence if you chose to ignore it. However, if you are so inclined, I'd like to hear of how you arrived at that premise.

Either way, I've decided to share as much of my life and its context as you wish to hear and let you figure out how relevant it is to your chapter.

I will try to tell my story with candour and honesty because of your commitment not to share my identity with anyone.

Pete

PS: I was at the 50th reunion of my High School class this February and was thinking what fertile ground it might have been for you. :-)

Dear Pete:

I haven't yet got to the chapter on grandparents, but I think my premise remains largely the same: to see desires where we might not think to look for them. By and large people don't think of 'older' people as having desires, and certainly not as having 'deviant' desires. What happens, then, when we tell stories of people about whom we did not think 'in that way'? The basic mandate of this book is to enlarge the horizons of desiring possibilities, and that is the framework within which I also see this chapter.

I will only use what you send me if I feel it fits this mandate. And of course, your identity is completely safe with me!

With warm wishes,
Madhavi

Dear Madhavi,
It makes perfect sense as you put it now.

I find that the very notion of Sex/Desire is taboo here. Never to be discussed. Certainly not with your parents or in turn your parents with theirs.
Pete

And here, in his own words, is Pete's story:

THE TRAJECTORY OF DESIRE

Long before I had actual sexual desire I was fascinated by the shape of the young male body and had a deep interest in its genitalia. My first experiences were with older cousins when I was seven. They were probably preteens but if I recall correctly, it was I who seduced them. Not the other way around.

When I turned eight my family moved to the US for some four years. American schools in the 50s had a very casual attitude toward same-sex nudity and boys were exposed to each others' naked bodies during showers after gym and swim classes in the nude. With my Indian shyness, I was embarrassed to be naked but I can't say that proximity to so many naked boys didn't excite me. Though I still knew nothing about sex, let alone homophobia, some sixth sense kept me from openly displaying my interest. I missed my vacations with my cousins at my ancestral home and looked forward to returning and resuming our play. I did not anticipate that by then their interests would have changed.

Almost twelve, I still had no clue about sex but that soon changed with my enrolment in an all-boys' boarding school. A senior boy coerced me into my first 'French' kiss but I never needed to be coerced again and the next four years were bliss. Pretty much everyone slept with everyone but we all assumed that it was a phase and that we would 'straighten' out once we had access to girls.

In my case that never happened.

I attended college in Delhi in the late 60s and was a member of the Westernized 'hep' set influenced by the hippie invasion. We thought it was cool to partake in drugs and espouse free love and liked to think of ourselves as the trendsetters of Delhi University. Somewhere along the way, unbeknownst to me, I'd also turned into a swan and the girls were plentiful and available. However, I evaded addressing my lack of desire by convincing myself that I was behaving like a 'gentleman'. Despite my occasional anonymous nighttime encounters in the dark verandahs of Connaught Place, it never struck me that I might not be the only one for whom same-sex attraction was not just a phase. More difficult to explain is how I could have overlooked the passion in the relationship I had with my one true love. The one who was in my mind when I posted a poem on the Orinam website which led Shilpa to write me.

At 24, I went back to New York for graduate school—and finally lost my virginity. It was almost by accident. Unplanned, unwanted (certainly by me) and unemotional. But she was a gorgeous blonde diva from the entertainment world who made the move on me. How could I say no? I then slept with many other women in quick succession. Blonde, Brunette, Ethnic Chinese, Jewish, Black American, Black African, you name it. Maybe I was trying to find the same degree of passion that I had with men or maybe I was trying to convince myself that my 'phase' had passed? Anyway, I put out of my mind the parade of men who were also simultaneously sharing my bed.

Convinced of my 'manhood', I proposed to an Indian woman of the appropriate community, caste and class. A Fulbright scholar with a PhD, she was not just any ordinary woman but an intelligent, good-looking academic with a sense of style that her students tried to ape. She was also the object of many a man's heart but with my still youthful good looks, the beginnings of a successful career and a family background of note, I was the one who won her hand. I must say that we made quite a striking couple. I entered the union fully convinced that I would be able to fulfil the implicit vow of fidelity that marriage entails. After all, I had never lusted after any woman. What should have been a curious lack of desire I once again explained away as a product of my upbringing as a gentleman.

THE AFTERMATH

My wife and I had successful careers and are blessed with great children. Though no angels, they've given us much joy and filled us with pride as they've become adults and parents themselves. To the world at large we're an ideal family and our luck is enviable.

As for fidelity, I started straying soon after marriage and have strayed ever since. But discreetly. My wife and I have many openly gay friends but not to even one of those friends have I ever come 'out'. I remain deeply closeted and it's a role to which I have become accustomed.

Am I ashamed of being gay? Not one bit. If being 'out' only affected myself I probably wouldn't hide. But my sexual orientation is only one aspect of me as a person and my coming out now would devastate my wife. The rest of my world I could handle. My guilt is entering into a contract that I should have known I could not keep. My wife deserved better, even though I did tell her as I proposed that I was attracted to men and had had homosexual relationships in the past.

Retired now and with time to reflect, I realize that while my duplicity was expedient, it came at a terrible price.

Pete

26 November 2015

Dear Pete:

Thanks also for your account of the trajectory of your desire. I will return to some details in it at a later stage, but for now, could you tell me, please, what the socio-historical setting was for that trajectory? Were there people around you, in college, in New York, your friends, who were out? If so, then why, do you think, were you not able to come out? What was the narrative of your friends who did come out? Was there ever conversation in your family about homosexuals or homosexuality? If so, then what role did you play in those conversations? And what do you think of the very idea of 'coming out'? What would it mean for you to 'come out'?

As always, thanks! Please take your time, and please also ask me if you need any clarifications.

With warm wishes,

Madhavi

After several months of silence, I heard back again from Pete, but this time, under his real name (which I have rendered below as 'No Name'), in an email titled 'Come from the Shadows':

18 August 2016

Hi Madhavi

This is [No Name]. Pete is a nickname from school that I use (less and less with each passing day) for anonymity. I'd intended to send you a longish note I'd written a while back but it seems to have vanished into the ether as I switched mail accounts.

Cheers

[No Name]

21 August 2016

Thanks, Pete. When you sit down to recreate your email, do see if you can also extend the narrative to your current position, in which you very bravely seem to be, in your words, coming from the shadows. Please also be assured that I am not going to share your real identity with anyone, until and unless you'd like me to.

With warm wishes,

Madhavi

22 August 2016

Oh Madhavi. It's nothing to do with bravery. I'm not 'coming out' or doing anything dramatic. I just succumb more easily these days to the fatigue of leading a duplicitous life.

I generally tend to be open—with one obvious major exception.

The constant lying and paranoia involved in leading parallel lives takes its toll and I find as I age that I'm less willing to pay that price.

I don't believe I'm being rash. My trust is not blind. However, somewhere inside me I've decided that, should that trust be misplaced, I will live with the consequences.

[No Name]

* * *

Thinking about desire in relation to older people in India is difficult because there are very few venues in which to do so—theirs is not a desire that is discussed openly. Quite apart from this external taboo, older people I have spoken to seem conflicted within themselves about what their desire is: do they want continued sexual engagement or do they prefer the shade of detachment? This is a genuine conflict for older people (perhaps for some younger ones too?), and it is a difficult one to resolve. Not only because the number of viable social outlets for older people's desire are limited, but also because these outlets tend to be tainted by guilt and shame. For instance, there is actually an active online world that caters to the desire of and for older gay men—websites like Silverdaddies and apps like Daddyhunt. But even those who are on these sites are often not on them openly. It's the Pete syndrome in which the older man—sometimes married—uses a pseudonym, and does not know if he will ever be able to act on his desires. Perhaps needless to say, I have not found any online site that caters to the desires of older heterosexual women.

Indeed, 'shame' becomes the overwhelming emotion associated with such desire—witness the scorn heaped on the character of 'Buaji' (aunt) in *Lipstick Under My Burkha* that provides the epigraph to this chapter. Perhaps older people here join younger ones in being told that sexual desire outside a heterosexual marriage, before and beyond a certain age, is a taboo to be shunned?

17

SAMBANDHAM

'I was married at your age. You don't even want to learn how
to cook daal. No more studies now. Ab only shaadi (now
only marriage).'

—from *Bend It Like Beckham* (2002)

Many years ago, I met my partner. A few months later, my
parents met my partner. And some time after that, my father
took me aside for a téte-a-téte.

During the course of that short conversation, he asked me
if I was going to get married. (My mother knew better than
to ask.) I said no, and he asked me why not. I trotted out my
political objections about not wanting the State to regulate
my desire. I said I should be free to choose who to love and
when and for how long. My father looked unconvinced and
even quite worried about his wayward daughter. I knew I had
to come up with another answer quickly since he was now
clearing his throat in preparation for making a Significant
Pronouncement: 'You are asking me to move away from my
traditions,' he thundered. 'No, no,' I protested, casting about
for what to say next. And then a dim memory of an ancestral
narrative entered my flailing mind. Snatches of tales from a
long time ago. Echoes of women's voices that were related to
me. I looked at my father and said with renewed confidence:
'I'm not asking you to move away from your traditions—I am
asking you to go back to them, to get closer to your roots.'
This flummoxed him entirely, and I knew I had won the day.

What did I mean by what I had said?

Arguably, marriage is the single biggest obsession among middle-class Indian families. Weddings are big business on the subcontinent, as they seem to be everywhere in the world. All masala Bollywood films tend to feature a wedding scene, and some films are plotted entirely around the preparations for, and lead-up to, the wedding. Clothes, jewellery, astrology, singing, dancing, eating, drinking, travelling, fighting—these are some of the many ingredients that go into the making of an Indian wedding. Some add more exotic flavours like elephants and forts; others tone it down to three- rather than ten-day-long celebrations. There are tales of female-female weddings from small-town India, often performed by priests. Techincally, there is nothing in India's marriage laws that specifies the two people getting married have to be one man and one woman. The Hindu Marriage Act of 1955, for instance, says that the two parties to a marriage have to be Hindus, without specifying their gender. One or two mothers have asked me to find brides for their daughters—whether seriously or not, I do not know. And countless parents have asked me if I know of 'nice' boys and girls with whom to hitch their daughters and sons. Everyone always wants to get married. Or so it seems.

But it turns out that marriage in India has a history. Here is a tale that the *Mahabharata* narrates: Svetaketu was a sage whose name was associated with specific sexual techniques (his father Uddalaka had been taught deep lessons of sexual mysticism by his guru, Dhaumya, and he passed those lessons on to his son). Svetaketu was also the author of a treatise on the kamashastra or arts of love that was a precursor to Vatsyayana's *Kamasutra*. The sage lived during a time of uninhibited sexual union when people studied the arts of sex and practised them at will and without fetters. Despite this deep immersion in the realm of the sexual, however, the tale told by the *Mahabharata* is of a sage who put an end to what he saw as the sexual licence of women by creating the institution of marriage. And this happened, or so it seems, because of a fight that Svetaketu had with his parents.

One day, he saw his mother walking off with a Brahmin man other than his father in order to have sex. Outraged, he turned to his father, who did not seem in the least bit upset. Instead, the father explained to the son that this had always been the practice because 'female beings of all kinds are unhindered'. There was, the father Uddalaka continued, no cause at all for offence. But here was a case of the younger generation being more conservative than the older one. Svetaketu would have none of his father's explanation, and according to the legend, went on to impose strict monoandry on women (the legend says nothing about his attitude towards men or even why his edict was obeyed). In addition, he insisted that such a monoandrous union between a man and a woman should be for this life and the next.

And so, according to the tale and seemingly overnight, 'Indian' society moved from being an advocate of free love to an enforcer of restricted desire. 'Hindu' traditions, broadly defined, developed eight different kinds of marriages, each of which subjugated women's desires to various degrees, and many of which reflect the continued and deep-rooted misogyny in India today. The worst among the eight kinds of marriage was the paisacha, where a raped woman was made to marry her molestor in order to be granted the social status of a wife. Then there was the rakshasa marriage in which a woman is carried off as the spoils of war; the daiva, in which the woman is given as a sacrificial fee to a priest; and the brahmya marriage in which a woman, bedecked in jewels and carrying a hefty dowry, is given to a Brahmin. (Two other forms of marriage, now largely obsolete, are the prajapatya marriage, in which the man and woman are supposed jointly to perform their civil and religious duties; and the arsha marriage, where the Brahmin father of the bride receives two heads of cattle in order to perform the sacrifices necessary to solemnize the marriage.)

The remaining two of the eight versions of marriage are interesting because they give us a glimpse into what once was and what could be once again. The first is the gandharva marriage, in which a man and woman are understood to have developed affections for one another, and where their sexual consummation does not require the enactment of any rites. This seems to be a throwback to the kind of sexual union that Svetaketu was opposing. But the gandharva union qualifies as the best type of marriage only when it is accompanied by religious rites. It is the equivalent of what we would today call a 'love marriage'—not arranged by one's parents, but enacted nonetheless along prescribed legal and social norms.

And then there is the asura marriage in which the woman is 'sold' to the highest bidder. The man pays a dowry, but what is interesting is that this money is retained by the woman herself rather than given to her father. This version of marriage too strains against Svetaketu's edict reining in women's agency because it gives the woman some financial heft. It is telling, however, that the money that used to be paid to a woman has been completely reversed in our own times and has now become the often crippling dowry paid in marriage by a woman's family to a man in a Hindu wedding.

This privileging of the Hindu man's share in marriage is a legacy also of the European tradition which, from the 12th century onwards, has used marriage as a means for men to access the property of women, including their bodies, estates and children. To ensure that a man's property was recognizable as his, the woman had to change her name after marriage, and the children too took on their father's name. This name was legally recognized as the name of the unit of property headed by the father.

Despite Svetaketu's fondness for the subjugation of women's agency, however, the role of the husband and father in India is not always recognizable as that of the property owner. Not only does India have matrilineal societies—in the south-west and in the north-east—but it also has a variety of social and religious microcosms—the joint family, for one—in which the caste name for Hindus rather than an individual's name is predominant. The family thus has a caste identifier rather than an identity based on one man's name, though this too is fast changing, especially in South India, where men are starting to use their first names as their children's last names. Among Muslims, the practice of meher—in which it is the woman who receives the dowry from the man; money or goods that become her property for life—also disrupts the idea that women are no more than the property of an individual man. And among the Khasi tribes of what is now the north-eastern state of Meghalaya, the youngest daughter rather than the eldest son traditionally inherits the family property.

A history of desire in India thus offers several alternative practices by which people can exercise agency over their bodies and their properties outside the patriarchal frameworks within which marriage has developed. Among the Nairs of Kerala, for instance, that alternative practice until the early parts of the 20th century was the ritual of sambandham.

Dating back at least to the 9th century if not earlier, the practice of sambandham—or 'relationship'—governed the sexual and property relations of all Nair women. In its current version, marriage is a State-approved set of communal rituals and practices in which the man is dominant in terms of both name and property. Even in secular 'resgistered marriages', what is being registered is the status of a relationship so that it can be overseen by the State. This was all quite alien to the Nair women of Kerala.

A matrilineal community in which the family name and property passes down through the female line, the Nair women already had possession of name and property, so they felt no need for the formal presence of a man in their lives. Instead, in a sambandham, a Nair woman picked a man with whom she wanted to have sex or towards whom she was romantically inclined. There were no term-limits on this relationship. There was no ceiling on the number of such relationships a woman could have. And there was no moral outrage surrounding the sambandhams. In many ways, this sounds like the system that Uddalaka described to his son—the system against which Svetaketu militated when he instituted marital monoandry for women. All the children born to the woman belonged to her family and carried the family name. And all property passed through the woman to her daughters, regardless of fathers and sons.

Some scholars have rightly pointed out that the system of sambandham had its exploitative side as well because it allowed a man from the landowning namboodiri upper caste to have a sexual liaison with a Nair woman who was a tenant on the land, without ascertaining her desire and only for the satisfaction of his. Since the fathers bore no responsibility for the children born of such relationships, the Namboodiri men had no strings attached to their desires. Several such cases have been known, but they were certainly neither the intended nor dominant form in which sambandham was practised. Ideally, the woman was free to take on the partner of her choice. And she even devised a sign with which to signal her choice to the world, and warn other men to keep away. This sign consisted inevitably of the man's umbrella (it rains a lot in Kerala) and his slippers left outside the woman's house to signify that she was otherwise occupied.

What separated sambandham from other notions of marriage was that there was no binding contract between the two partners. Nothing was promised other than a night of pleasure that was extendable according to the woman's will for however long she decreed. Many sambandhams lasted a lifetime, others a shorter duration. But what was remarkable was that the termination of the relationship was built into its founding. There was no expectation of the 'happily ever after' narrative that so strongly marks our belief about marriage today. This is also the narrative that puts pressure on both partners to stay in a relationship that either might have outgrown. As Praveena Kodoth points out in 'Courting Legitimacy', Western feminism won a major victory when divorce was officially made available to either party in a marriage. But divorce is the recent equivalent in the West of what has been in practice among Kerala Nair women for centuries: the socially recognized possibility, even in the moment of instituting a relationship, of its dissolution. The Matrimonial Causes Act allowing divorce was enacted in England in 1857, but it was not until the 1937 revision of that Act that women were able to get a divorce easily. And in the US, it was not till 1969 that the courts passed a no-fault law that enabled women to file for divorce freely. In Kerala, Nair women have been able to walk away at will from a relationship with a man from the 9th century onwards. The woman not only had agency, but she was also allowed to take her pleasure seriously. And she did not need to account for her choice because she had the full sanction of her extended clan.

Indeed, what propped up sambandham among the matrilineal Nairs of Kerala was also what made the British and Indian reformers look down upon it: the fact that the woman had agency without having to subjugate her body or her property to a man. Like Svetaketu, the British too did not like this system. Not only was their idea of marriage very different—it involved the supremacy of the father and husband—but perhaps more importantly, their idea of sex too was very different. In the British moral universe, sex was to be had only with one partner (this rule applied especially in the case of women), and for the duration of one's adult life. Monoandry was the rule, and all the power to choose was given to the man. In sambandham relationships, polyandry was the rule, and the term of each liaison undertaken by the woman was unfixed.

Despite their avowed intention of not interfering in the personal laws of Indians, the British were so deeply unsettled by this practice that they issued several pejorative statements about sambandham. A Madras High Court ruling in 1869 stated that sambandham is 'in truth not marriage, but a state of concubinage into which a woman enters of her own choice and is at liberty when and as often as she pleases'. Under the shrinking sexual horizons of British morality, temple dancers in the south of India and courtesans in the north of India had become prostitutes, and Malayalee women who entered into sambandham were labelled concubines. The British legal and administrative apparatus did not recognize Nair relationships as 'marriage' because they could be dissolved so easily, and because they did not affect property rights—the woman and her daughters always inherited the family property. Married or not, men had no rights to that property.

Such a system was starkly opposed both to British legality and Indian moralities. Almost as though they were trying to finish the job started by Svetaketu, the colonial powers mounted an assault against sambandham through their education system. English-educated Nair men like Sir C. Sankaran Nair—the only Malayalee to become President of the Indian National Congress—internalized British mores about the need to 'reform' the idea of marriage in India, and undertook to change precisely what was most liberating for women about the practice of sambandham. Fully taking on board the language of the Madras High Court ruling, Sankaran Nair noted that 'our wives are concubines, our children are bastards in a court of law and there is a necessity therefore for a bill to legalize marriage and provide for the issue of such marriages'. Sir Sankaran Nair spearheaded the Malabar Marriage Act of 1896, which was based on the recommendations ofthe Malabar Marriage Commission of 1891, to 'reform' the behaviours associated with Kerala Nair sambandhams.

This Act was intended by its principal sponsors to be a permissive rather than a restrictive one. People could choose whether or not to register their sambandham relationships as marriage. But they had no choice but to do so if they wanted recognition for their relationships in the civil courts. What is interesting is that despite being seen as benign by its sponsors, the Malabar Marriage Act was roundly rejected by the Nair community it was meant to govern. Both men and women were outraged that they were being asked to 'prove' the marriage-worthiness of the sambandhams in which they had been involved for centuries. They refused to accept the implicit and explicit hierarchy in which a European notion of marriage was placed above the Malayalee Nair version of a sexual and familial relationship. And so the Act failed to garner support, and sambandham stayed on as a widespread practice among Kerala Nairs until well after Indian Independence in 1947.

Unfortunately, the new Indian State—governed largely by British-educated lawyers and reformists—had internalized a sexual prudery that made them rationalize and homogenize marriage practices. The Hindu Marriage Act of 1955 put in place the frameworks within which a contract of marriage could be entered into. Nothing would be recognized as marriage outside this contract. Marriage not only became legally binding but it could also only be dissolved by the legal act of divorce. The Hindu Succession Act of 1956 laid down the law about how and to whom family property could be passed on. (This law was meant to ensure that women too receive an inheritance, but such protection was required mostly in North India. In Kerala, it meant putting an end to the financial autonomy that had been enjoyed by Nair women for centuries.)

More recent Supreme Court judgements have granted legal protections to live-in heterosexual relationships. The 2015 judgement by Justices M.Y. Eqbal and Amitava Roy notes that couples living together under the same roof should be considered husband and wife in the case of property and inheritance. But despite seeming to side-step the institution of marriage in matters of property for women, as sambandham does, these laws continue to presume that women need to be protected by a paternalistic State. The judgements 'allow' the woman to be given the status of a wife in matters of inheritance if the man and the woman are living under the same roof. Children born of such live-in relationships will only inherit if they bear their father's name. Not only does the Supreme Court not say anything about sexual pleasure and the woman's right to choose her partners at will, but it also insists that couples have to be living together in the same household, and that children have to bear the father's name. By entirely ignoring the question of why couples might choose not to get married, these post-colonial laws continue to bear the trace of Svetaketu's ancient Indian horror at women's sexual agency. And they continue to emphasize the colonial insistence that desire should be domesticated in its household arrangements. These notions of masculine naming, sexual monoandry, and financial dependence, were all alien to the practice of sambandham among Kerala Nairs.

All my female ancestors practised, and were a product of, sambandham arrangements. Not a single one of them was legally married. They had their own name, their own money, and their own desires. My family name belongs to my mother's clan. And this is why I told my father that I was going back to my roots in not wanting to get married. He is still mulling over my argument.

18

PAAN

Paan khaye saiyan hamaro. (My lover eats paan.)
—Shailendra; lyrics from *Teesri Kasam* (1966)

Paan stands at the opposite end of the Indian desire spectrum from yoga: it is understood only and always as a luscious and fleshly delight. Not only does no one question its erotic appeal, but the *Kamasutra* also sprinkles flecks of paan throughout its instructions for seduction. In fact, paan's erotic prowess can be so fearsome that it is historically forbidden for use by celibate ascetics and students. Here is a recipe for paan: do try it at home.

STEP 1: PREPARE THE BETEL LEAF

Cultivating betel leaves is almost as ritualistic as worshipping in a temple. The soil needs to be loamy and the weather must be tropical and wet. Betel leaves grow as vines, and they are often shaded to protect them from the sun, much like grape vines are when grown for wine. Since they are consumed raw, no pesticides are used to farm betel; their yield is therefore rather fragile, and increasingly expensive. In keeping with ritual notions of cleanliness and purity, menstruating women have historically not been allowed to cultivate betel vines. The ostensible reason—as always—is fear of infection. Some farmers in Odisha are challenging this stigma, and now allow women to farm betel vines. But by and large, the bastion of betel farming is preserved for

men. These are the men—'naked and manure-coloured' as
he describes them in his essay on 'Pan'—that E.M. Forster
saw when he first encountered betel vines: '...aromatic and
lush, with heart-shaped leaves that yearn towards the sun and
thrive in the twilight of their aspirations, trained across lateral
strings into a subtle and complicated symphony.' Noting the
solemnity of their ritualistic tending of the vines, Forster asks
about the men: 'What acolytes, serving what nameless deity?'

The heart-shaped betel leaves have often invited
comparisons with desire. Indeed, food and erotic desire have
a close relation in Indian history. As A.K. Ramanujan notes
in his essay on 'Hanchi: A Kannada Cinderella', the Sanskrit
terms for eating and sexual enjoyment have a common root
in the word bhuj. As the *Kamasutra* instructs us, paan is to
be consumed before and after lovemaking: 'As for the end
of sex, when their passion has ebbed, the man and woman
go out separately to the bathing place, embarrassed, not
looking at one another. When they return, they sit down
in their usual places without embarrassment, and chew
some betel.' Bhakti and Sufi poetry routinely enlists paan as
a token of love. In one of Ksetrayya's 17th-century erotic-
devotional songs to Krishna, the protagonist highlights the
use of betel leaves during the act of sex. Complaining about
the fickleness of her 'husband'—Muuvagopala, or Krishna—
the dutiful 'wife' says: '...as I offer him folded betel leaves /
suddenly covering my eyes for a fleeting moment, offering
her slyly his own chewing paan / if he went on pressing his
lips on to her mouth / Who will bear [it]?' In some South
Indian Hindu traditions, Kama, the god of Love, is himself
said to reside on the outside of the betel leaf. Forster found
the intensity of the betel leaf unbearable at first—'I stretch

out my hand, I pluck a leaf and eat. My tongue is stabbed by a hot and angry orange in alliance with pepper. I am in the presence of Pan.'

The betel leaf must be trimmed before eating: cut off the stalk, trim the edges, and scrape the veins of the leaf to make it as smooth as possible.

STEP 2: APPLY CHUNA AND KATTHA

The next step is to make this hot leaf even hotter by applying chuna—a mixture of lime powder and water—and kattha—a paste made by mixing catechu and water—to the trimmed leaf. Lime powder (calcium carbonate) is considered highly efficacious as a cure for male and female impotence, as well as menstrual cramps (which is ironic, given that menstruating women are usually not allowed near betel leaves). Catechu (or kattha) is an extract of the acacia tree and is rich in vegetable tannins. These seem to be rather unpromising ingredients to produce effects that are 'unattainable anywhere else, even in heaven', as described by one of the characters in *Almond Eyes, Lotus Feet: Indian Traditions in Beauty and Health* (by Shalini Holkar and Sharada Dwivedi). According to him, the combination of these three ingredients produces a paan that 'sweetens the breath, aids digestion, reddens the lips, and tastes divine'.

It is the chemical interaction of chuna and kattha that forms the trademark red colour associated with paan. The betel leaves themselves—which grow in various shades of lighter or darker green—do not contribute to the red colour except as the vehicle for mastication. Indeed, the deep rust-red colour caused by the combination of lime and tannin is extremely attractive to paan-chewers. A historically documented fan of such paan-created red lips is the Empress Nur Jahan (1577-1645), the most beloved wife of the Mughal Emperor Jahangir. She apparently loved her paan-stained red lips to such an extent that she initiated the fashion for elaborate paandaans or paan containers so the ingredients for paan could always be at hand for a touch-up of her red 'lipstick'. If you are rich, then these paandaans are in intricately-worked silver with compartments to house all the separate ingredients. But if you are poor, then any container will do.

Among the British colonizers, though, the redness of paan inspired outrage. Mocking their reaction, Forster says of the typical specimen: 'Another shock has to be borne: golly, I am bright red! Why this happens, when the betel was green, the areca brown, and the lime white, I do not know. It is easily rinsed away, but there is always a danger that one may forget, go to play bridge at the Club with vermilion jaws, and be ruined forever.' The British response is quite the opposite of the Indian one, where the red-staining chuna and kattha are desired as great aphrodisiacs. In fact, one of the many varieties of paan available in India today is the palang-tod paan, or the bed-breaking paan, also known as the Honeymoon paan—its name clearly outlines the sexually vigorous virtues contained within its leaves.

In popular legend in Kerala, yakshis—female earth spirits associated with sex and fertility—are said to haunt forests in the form of beautiful, seductive women. The yakshis ask men for chunnambu (the lime used to turn betel leaves into paan) and, driven to a sexual frenzy on consuming the chuna, proceed to kill the men and drink their blood. The yakshis make clear the link between betel juice, passion and blood. The 17th-century Italian traveller Niccolao Manucci, too, makes this connection in his *Storia do Mogor*. Shocked at the ubiquitous sight of blood-red lips on men and women in the western port city of Surat, he notes: 'I was much surprised to see that almost everybody was spitting something as red as blood. I imagined it must be due to some complaint of the country. I asked an English lady what was the matter... she answered that it was not any disease, but due to a certain aromatic leaf, called in the language of the country, pān.' Manucci goes on to note the addictive nature of paan: 'It happens with the eaters of betel, as to those accustomed to take tobacco, that they are unable to refrain from taking it many times a day. Thus the women of India, whose principal business it is to tell stories and eat betel, are unable to remain many minutes without having it in their mouths.' Perhaps

'Cold Sweet Paan' by Biswarup Ganguly.
Source: Wikimedia Commons

fittingly, 'katha' (pronounced the same way as kattha) is the Hindustani word both for an essential ingredient of paan, and for story itself.

Apply the chuna and kattha onto the betel leaf with a stick or the back of a spoon or a washed, damp, betel leaf.

A silver paandaan. Photo courtesy Jonathan Gil Harris; Location: Lucknow Mahindra Sanatkada Festival, 2018

Empress Nur Jahan eating Paan.
Source: http://www.vimlapatil.com/vimlablog/
wp-content/uploads/2012/01/6.-Noor-Jehan-
eating-paan.jpg

Step 3: Mix It Up

Once the chuna and kattha have been applied, the two have
to be carefully mixed together so that they sink rapturously
into the dampness of the betel leaf. This intermingling of
the chuna and kattha into the betel leaf is essential to laying
the ground for all paan, no matter what one adds to it later

on. It also symbolizes the multiple ways in which paan has resonated across the centuries in India, mixing together borders of region, religion, caste, gender, language, taste and sexuality. Everyone in India, or so it seems, has always eaten paan. It is first mentioned in classical Sanskrit erotic and medical texts, and later taken up enthusiastically by Muslim texts and practices. In the *Kamasutra*, courtesans are advised to lace their cultured conversations with lashings of betel leaves and betel nuts. In tawaif or courtesan culture, the serving of paan plays a crucial role in setting the stage for the erotic arts. No matter what else they might or might not have, every market, every village, every city and town in India and Pakistan will have two shops, often joined together: one selling sweets and the other selling paan.

Ruth Vanita points also to the sexual varieties of paan eroticism in her translation of *Chocolate*, by Pandey Bechan Sharma Ugra. In these short stories, the homosexual protagonists tend to place their desire in relation to paan: 'The groups of urban young men who are his protagonists eat both in public and private. They give parties where they consume sweets and other delicacies. They also court their beloveds at pān stalls, which even today are public places where men hang out together. In Ugra's stories, feeding pān to the beloved is a prelude to kissing him. In one story, the protagonist insists on feeding a beautiful boy pān with his own hand and then kisses him just before putting the pān in his mouth.' In Bankim Chandra's 19th-century tale *Indira*, paan is repeatedly evoked as a symbol for erotic beauty and desire. Mixing up hetero- and homo-sexual desire, Subho, Indira's female friend, teaches Indira how to seduce her husband by feeding him paan. By way of example, Subho feeds Indira paan before kissing her. For Indira, this kiss resonates excitingly for the rest of the tale, even as she is trying to woo the husband who does not recognize her. Among Bengali Hindus, the bride covers her eyes with two betel leaves that she removes only to look at her husband; in Maharashtra, the impending sexual consummation of the newly married couple is signalled by the bride biting off half the paan that the groom holds in his mouth. In nikah ceremonies, the bride is given paan as a symbol of auspiciousness and guests are always served both paan and sharbat. When Ksetrayya's female protagonist is shunned by a Krishna who has moved on to another lover, she knows she has been rejected because 'When I say, without thinking, / "Give me a bit of that betel in your mouth," / he yells at me and says "No!"' The betel leaves that signal the beginning of a sexual liaison also signal its ending: 'He vows never to speak / nicely to me again. / Arguing, he says / "I want nothing to do with you"—/ and gives me the betel—/ this same Muvva Gopala / who once so lustily / made love to me.'

Paan is eaten both at the beginning and at the end of transactions. It is popular among both Hindus and Muslims. It is eaten by rich and poor alike—from the refined tawaif to the quotidian maid. It is both a sacred and an erotic object, offered to gods and lovers, especially in erotic poetry that blurs the boundary between the two categories. Paan is prosaic and poetic. It is the least expensive and the most exalted of aphrodisiacs in India.

The best instrument with which to mix the chuna and the kattha is the index finger.

STEP 4: ADD SUPARI

Supari is the final basic ingredient necessary to making a paan. It is the term used to describe the areca nut, which is a hard berry rather than a nut. When fully ripe, this offspring of the areca palm has a consistency as hard as wood, and can only be sliced with special cutters that are often as elaborately designed as the paandaans themselves. Sometimes called betel nut because it is eaten most often in India along with the betel leaf, supari is not to be confused with the betel leaf, though, which is the product of a vine rather than a palm. The supari is the most stimulating of the four basic ingredients that go into a paan. Taken in small quantities, its effects are similar to that of nicotine and caffeine. And taken in larger doses, the impact can be as strong as that of cocaine. Supari heats up the blood. According to Forster—who describes the nut as 'fabulously hard, darkling without, and radiat[ing] spokes within'—'To have even a fragment of areca in the mouth is alarming.' In his description of the first-time user's response to paan, Forster notes that 'the leaf is mild enough, the crisis coming when its fibres tear and the iron pyrites [his term for the sharp heat of the supari] fall about and get under the tongue. Now the novice rises in disorder, rushes in panic to the courtyard, and spatters shrapnel over the bystanders; it is as if the whole mineral kingdom has invaded him under a vegetable veil, for simultaneously the lime starts stinging. If he can sit still through this a heavenly peace ensues; the ingredients salute each other, a single sensation is established, and Pan, without ceasing to be a problem, becomes a pleasure…the formidable areca yields, splinters, vainly takes refuge in the interstices of the gums, and is gone.'

The heat generated by supari makes it the ideal substance to incite a passionate encounter. Neurological studies explain the science behind the symptoms that mimic the body's state during euphoria and stimulation: an increase in heart rate, and heightened alertness. Keeping these effects in mind, the *Kamasutra* repeatedly invokes betel nuts as both a prelude to and a marker of lovemaking: 'When the woman has accepted his embrace, he gives her betel with his mouth. If she does not accept it, he gets her to take it through conciliating words, oaths, repeated requests, and falling at her feet. (Even a bashful or very angry woman cannot resist a man falling at her feet; this is a universal rule.) While giving her the betel, he kisses her softly, calmly, without a sound.' In the section on 'Making Advances', Vatsyayana again resorts to the betel nut: 'When he has understood her signals and uncovered her favourable feelings for him, he uses her possessions as they share one another's objects of enjoyment... When she takes betel from his hand as he prepares to go to a social gathering, he asks for a flower from her hair... By degrees, he goes with her to a place where they are alone together, embraces her, kisses her, takes betel from her, and after giving it to her exchanges things with her and caresses her in her hidden places. Those are the advances.'

The areca nut makes amorous advances possible. It is also the most essential stage in the production of the paan. Supari is the hard core—it is the part that lasts the longest and is the most resistant to being owned by the eater. One has to coax the supari in much the same way as Vatsyayana teaches us to coax a lover. The final submission of the supari marks what Forster—himself a paan aficionado—describes as both a problematic pleasure and a pleasurable problem. Supari is the staunchest ingredient in the paan.

Areca nut has to be boiled and then dried in the sun for several days before being diced in preparation for its journey as supari into the heart of a paan.

STEP 5: EMBELLISH, FOLD AND SERVE

Several other ingredients can be added to the paan after this stage—tobacco for the more addictive personalities (or a tobacco and spice mix called kimaam), dried dates, cardamom, ginger, cloves, saffron, preserved rose petals, saffron, grated coconut, dried fruit, nutmeg; edible silver foil is often placed on the outside of the paan to give it a shimmering finish. A paan leaf is capacious enough to accommodate several ingredients, and finished paans can be quite plump. But there is an etiquette—a tehzeeb—to eating paans both plump and skinny. And the first rule of this etiquette is that one has to put the entire paan in one's mouth rather than biting off a part of it. In order to secure all the ingredients within the paan, then, artistes need to learn the arts of folding the paan skilfully and using a clove to secure the end product in place. As Dwivedi and Holkar describe it: 'We folded all the various ingredients into these leaves. The whole thing was an art and a solemn ritual; we took the eating and offering of paan very seriously in the palace.' In fact, the folding of the paan—what Forster calls 'a gracious and exquisite performance'—is important primarily in the erotic sphere. All religious uses of betel leaves and supari tend to serve the leaves open-faced rather than folded. It is in the sphere of eros that paans enclose the secret of desire. *Almond Eyes, Lotus Feet* goes on to lay bare the intricacies of the folded paan: 'On festive occasions, it was the task of the zenana women to prepare the paans that were offered to the guests after the banquet. We had a lot of fun. We sat in a large circle, laughing, gossiping and teasing each other as we worked. We washed the betel leaves, snipped off the stems, and laid out the leaves in rows. We piled on the various ingredients and finally folded them in different shapes: cones or triangles or little squares held together with a clove. In the old days even the way a paan leaf was folded could convey a message such as, "He's away, so I'm free tonight!"'

Eating paan is not for the faint-hearted—it is for the erotically and adventurously inclined. Do not be put off by Manucci's account of his first encounter with paan, which echoes Forster's description of the first effects that eating paan had on him: 'Having taken some betel leaves, my head swam to such an extent that I feared I was dying. It caused me to fall down, I lost my colour and endured agonies, but she poured into my mouth a little salt, and brought me to my senses. The lady assured me that everyone who ate it for the first time felt the same effects.' After going through that trial by fire, paan becomes addictive, with or without the tobacco. A 13th-century short poem by the great Amir Khusro wryly notes: 'Last night my paan-seller was up to his tricks / as he slowly prepared paan leaves in his shop. / As he gave the people in his shop their leaves, / in return they surrendered to him their lives.' An erotically charged set of lyrics from the 1966 Hindi film *Teesri Kasam* describes the heroine's lover as a paan-eating saiyan (lover)—an extended song sequence details the kimaam-breath, the red lips and the intoxicated pleasures induced by eating paan as marks of the true lover. No paan without a lover, and no lover without a paan: such is the story of paan in the history of desire in India.

Eat, faint, enjoy, and repeat.

19

DATING

Wherever I find love, I will accept it.
                    —Quote attributed to M.F. Husain

This could well have been a chapter about dating. Until recently, the romantic Western idea of 'going on a date' was unheard of in the subcontinent of arranged marriages. There was little to no expectation that partners will go on dates and get to know each other before deciding to spend their lives together. But now, with the Americanization of the world, going on a 'date' has become the thing to do for lovers in India. International dating apps like Tinder are all the rage, and many urban young people with smartphones are on it. These dating apps blur the line between a sexual liaison and marriage, which is exciting for some and shocking for others. Where once swans and pigeons and sahelis (female friends) and eunuch harem guards were the messengers of love, now we have the internet and the smartphone as the organizer of dates.

But despite being understood as symbols of sexual freedom—spontaneous, irreverent, romantic—dates abide by a more rigid set of conventions. Contrary to our commonplace understanding of romance, there is very little about dating that is spontaneous and uncalculated. Instead, it follows the dictates of the fixed calendar dates of the work week. Thus 'dates' are usually scheduled outside working hours—in the evenings or on weekends. Romantic dates abide carefully by calendar dates in their planning and execution, and calendrical dates sustain the rhythm of romantic dates.

This is a chapter about that more literal understanding of 'dating' in which calendars divide time into days and weeks and months and years in order to regulate time in a productive and standardized manner. Even more, it is about the rich overlap between calendrical dates and visual representations of desire, a phenomenon that takes on unique shape in the Indian subcontinent, where dates accompanied by prominent visual designs hang in every household, shop and office in the form of a calendar.

The calendar widely followed around the world is the solar, Gregorian calendar, which remains unchanging from year to year (except minutely for the leap year). This is the gold standard of dating and provides the template for most economic, and many romantic and sexual, transactions. It is set in its ways and cannot be changed, no matter what the exigencies of a particular date might be. With the Gregorian calendar, we cannot suddenly wish that March 24, for example, could be a Saturday rather than a Monday.

But historically, such flexible dating has been possible with other calendars around the world, and certainly with various Indian calendars—Muslim, Hindu, Zoroastrian—that are based on the lunar or lunisolar cycle and change from month to month and year to year. Dates vary annually, and festivals fall on different days each year. This means that every Indian has access to multiple forms of dating depending on the lunar, lunisolar and solar calendars. Such access exists in combinations rather than singly: many Indians will have two birthdays, for instance, one according to the solar calendar and the other according to the lunar calendar. Two dates for the 'same' day. Of these, the lunar and lunisolar calendars, governed by the moon, are the ones that keep changing. Because of this changeability, the lunar is linked etymologically to the lunatic, which brings lunar dating closer to the Sufi qalandars (ecstatic dervishes in the grip of desire) than the Gregorian calendars.

Can we draw a correlation between cultures that have multiple modes of calendrical dating and multiple modes of desire? Can we say that the same cultures have multiple calendars and desires? Might a more elastic, changeable set of calendrical 'dates' suggest also a more flexible attitude to desire? Is there a correlation between a single mode of calendrical dating and a single way of doing desire? Does a standardization of calendar dates also control desire in a more rigid manner? It is impossible to answer these questions definitively. In an India governed by multiple calendars, people's attitude to dating too is multiple.

The mass production of calendars in India started only under the British in the 19th and 20th centuries. Colonial markets had allowed objects to reach far and wide. Catering to this expanded market, calendars used artwork as advertisements for products and shops. The dates on these calendars are most often in keeping with the fixed Gregorian system of dating. But the artwork tells more fluid tales of desire. Calendar art often provides a visual battle between the standardization of the sun and the messiness of the moon, between the strictness and moodiness of dates.

The most recognizable form of this calendar art was pioneered by Raja Ravi Varma, the painter-cum-businessman, who set up the first lithographic press outside Bombay in 1894 to mass produce his artwork. Indeed, paintings and

sketches by famous Indian artists—from Mario Miranda
to M.F. Husain (whose quote provides the epigraph to this
chapter)—continue to be used on many sets of calendars.

Ravi Varma's paintings were mostly of gods and goddesses
from Hindu epics, but there were also paintings of stand-
alone women. He was praised both for producing Indian
erotic masterpieces and high European naturalistic art.
With mass printing, this high art also became 'low' and
was adapted to calendars that were produced in the tens
of thousands for distribution across regions, classes and
religions. These calendars sometimes listed their dates in

Figure 1 (*All calendar art images courtesy of
the Priya Paul Collection*)

three different formats—the Gregorian, the Hijri and one or other regional version of a Hindu calendar. Prior to Independence in 1947, firms advertising on these calendars list offices in Lahore and Karachi as well as Delhi and Bombay. Pre-Independence calendars use several European models, for example, to sell beedis (Figure 1). Post-Independence calendars move to Indian models and the socialist principles of the newly-independent State. Many of the women models personify Nehruvian ideals of agriculture and innovation, while continuing the Ravi Varma tradition of being painted as sexual beings (Figure 2).

Figure 2

This use of human models expands later to include film stars and politicians. But by far the largest number of images on calendars, both before and after Independence, are those of gods and goddesses (Figures 3 and 4). Not only did this calendrical investment bring together business and religion, but also its use of gods and goddesses tells us a lot about the visual histories of desire in India. Reproduced below are calendars that I have slotted into two categories, each of which tells us something about a history of desire in India. The first deals primarily with goddesses, and the second with gods who are also sometimes goddesses.

I—Baby Boom

One of the most striking sets of images in calendar art is the use of goddesses to promote baby products. Both the Saraswati and Lakshmi figures above are taken from famous Raja Ravi Varma paintings, and are enlisted on these calendars to sell Vinolia Baby Soap and Glaxo baby products respectively. 'Glaxo Builds Bonnie Babies' announces the 1930 advertisement for the company's famous dried milk. And it probably did, given what an immensely successful business

Figure 3   Figure 4

Glaxo-Smith-Kline continues to be. But the only discordant note in these otherwise striking advertisements is the oddity of having a Hindu goddess endorse baby products. Because the thing about Hindu goddesses is that they specifically do not produce babies. Goddesses are goddesses by virtue of the fact that they are not involved in the messy business of reproduction.

Take Shiva and Parvati, for example, widely considered in all their avatars to be the First Couple among the gods. Shiva and Parvati have four children, but none of them is produced biologically by Parvati. The eldest child, Kartikeya, is produced when Shiva's semen is incubated by the River Ganga. The second son, Ganesha, is produced by a bored Parvati out of the earth that she fashions into the shape of a boy. (As the legend goes, Shiva does not recognize his 'son', and lops off his head when Ganesha—who too does not recognize his 'father'—prevents Shiva's entry into his home. Berated by Parvati for this act of filial violence, Shiva then cuts off an elephant's head to breathe life into his decapitated 'son' and create the icon we now recognize as Ganesha.) Of their two daughters, Ashokasundari was created by Parvati out of a tree, and Manasa was formed when Shiva's semen touched a statue carved by Kadru, mother of the snakes.

So Kartikeya is Shiva's child but not Parvati's; Ganesha is Parvati's creation but not Shiva's; Ashokasundari is Parvati's heir but not Shiva's, while Manasa is Shiva's offspring but not Parvati's. No matter how one counts, though, the Goddess Parvati does not bear any children.

Which makes the connection forged by calendar artists between goddesses and children an actual forgery, a distillation of non-reproductive desires into reproductive ones. Popular nomenclature takes this one step further, attaching the prefix of 'ma'—mother—to various avatars of Parvati, like Durga and Kali, none of whom actually has any children.

In fact, across the ancient Hindu texts, it is commonplace that gods and goddesses will not produce children. As M. Marglin notes in *The Divine Consort*, 'In this world, the world of *samskara*, pleasure is brief and one begets children, whereas in the divine play of Krishna there is continuous (*nitya*) pleasure and no children. The gopis are not impregnated…Krishna's erotic dalliance with the gopis has no ulterior purpose or consequence. It exists for itself, in itself.' Many Hindu gods have an untold number of sexual encounters to their credit, but their liaisons do not result in either pregnancy or biological birth. None of the Hindu goddesses gives birth to a child. Even though in some cases they do, like the Glaxo ad, 'build' one.

II—Divine Desires

Shiva is repeatedly represented by calendar artists as a sensual man rather than as a celibate god. And even as he is sometimes flanked by one or more child, it is his sensuality that seems most fascinating for calendar art. It is easy to see why this might be the case considering that the Shiva lingam—understood commonly as Shiva's phallus, emblematizing his potential—stands in for the God himself. The word lingam derives from the Sanskrit for mark or symbol (this is the same word that defines the various genders in Sanskrit) and is usually understood to describe gendered identity both linguistically and physiologically. However, the lingam is also related in the *Shiva Purana* to the Sanskrit word for a cosmic pillar (sthamba). This might suggest the shape of the lingam and can refer metaphorically not only to the vast divine powers endowed in Shiva, but also to the tantric practice of ascension up a series of rigorous meditations.

But the renowned 14th-century Telugu poet, Srinatha, makes it clear that the primary association of Shiva's lingam is with the God's phallus. In 'Śiva in the Forest of Pines', he provides a somewhat humorous description of how the lingam came to be Shiva's chosen symbol of devotion. The poem recounts the story of Shiva, in which the god leaves his father-in-law's house after being berated for his rude and sensual ways. He wanders into the Forest of Pines, which is inhabited by ascetic Brahmins and their beautiful wives, and proceeds to seduce every one of the women during their husbands' absence. When the Brahmins find out what has been happening behind their backs, they gang up against Shiva and attack him:

> Now, while eight-formed Śiva was playing these rowdy games, the heads of houses were manhandling him; so he threw off his loincloth and made his linga—long as the trunk of Airāvata, Indra's elephant—stand up erect, and with that powerful weapon hit those Brahmins on the head, nape, earlobes, faces, noses, bruising them...He extended his linga up to the sky.

When Brahma sees that Shiva's lingam is threatening to engulf the world, he begs the God:

> 'Withdraw it before the cosmos cracks,
> Relax it before the path of stars is disturbed.
> Make it soft, lest the Seven Winds are blocked,
> Let go of your power, lest the ends of space crumble.

Pull it back, stop this defiance, let it become supple,
leave it, your ever-so lovable linga.'

Śhiva listened well, laughed a wild laugh, and said,
so that all the world could hear:
'You sages, gods, demons,
my incomparable linga is worthy of worship
from now on.

I will happily bring into my company
whoever worships the linga
with a good heart...'

And thus it is that Shiva devotees worship his cosmic form
as it is manifested in the phallic lingam. In Figure 5, Nandi's

Figure 5

Figure 6

hump too is suggestively shaped as a phallus, perhaps to describe the extent of his devotion to Shiva. And in Figure 6, a devotee drapes herself seductively across the lingam itself.

But as much as it extols Shiva's phallic sensuality, calendar art also highlights the difference in attitude between various other gods to the question of erotic desire. These differences are most stark between Rama and Krishna, even though both are avatars of Vishnu. If you look at Rama—for instance, in Figure 7—then what is immediately obvious is his marital chastity rather than his sensual desires. In fact, even though Rama is inevitably painted/printed alongside Sita, Rama and Sita are never cavorting by themselves—there is always Lakshmana and often Hanuman by their side. These images tend to be extremely hierarchical, with Hanuman bowing at the feet of a seated Rama who is flanked on both sides by the standing Sita and Lakshmana. There is not a whisper of desire that emanates from this image other than a desire not to desire; to have order in all aspects of life; to endorse a feudal-patriarchal view of the world in which the man is in front, with a wife behind, and a servant below.

What is interesting, though, about the figures of Rama and Lakshmana on this calendar is how fragile they are: slender, slim-waisted, hairless. Quite unlike our current depictions

Figure 7

of a muscular Rama after whom vigilante armies spewing violence are named. As Kajri Jain points out in *Gods in the Bazaar*, there were specific iconographic restrictions in place *against* showing the musculature in a god's body. She quotes calendar artist Indra Sharma's instructions against the use of musculature: 'Now the body is very strong, but we will not show the anatomy. For god's body, the description is of a gentle, beautiful (*sukomal*) body... There won't be any muscles, we people avoid muscles.' Rama's body tends to be soft and graceful, at least till the 1990s, after which it was replaced by the 'muscular' body of the icon of the Ayodhya movement.

Figure 8

Figure 9

Compare this slender and constrained image of Rama and Sita with the plump and voluptuous abandon that is visible in calendar art depicting Krishna and Radha—see Figures 8 and 9.

There is a mutuality of desire in these images that is premised on the breaking of boundaries. After all, Krishna and Radha are not husband and wife, nor do they uphold the social traditions of being upper-caste rulers. There are no rules; Krishna even advertises 'Shiva Pen House' (Figure 9). Unlike Rama and Sita's iconography, which is geared towards maintaining the status quo in matters of desire, Radha and Krishna spread out with abandon. The sense of desire

captured by these images reflects also the followers of Rama
and Krishna respectively. Over the last century, the most
vocal and visible followers of Rama have tended to become
increasingly militant, patriarchal and casteist, in keeping
with the Rama legend of a man who suspects his pregnant
wife's sexual purity and consigns her to the flames in order
to test it. Followers of Krishna, meanwhile, not only retain
a sense of abandon, but actively cross boundaries in their
expressions of desire. And this has been the case historically.
In fact, as Sudhir Kakar points out in *Tales of Love, Sex, and
Danger*, '...in the *bhakti* cults, where the worshipper must
create an erotic relationship with Krishna, the transcendence
of boundaries of gender becomes imperative for the male
devotee, who endeavours to become a woman in relation to
the Lord. In his case, the violation of the biblical injunction
"The woman shall not wear that which pertaineth unto a man,
neither shall a man put on a woman's garments" is far from
being an "abomination unto the Lord thy God". In *bhakti*
Krishna not only demands such a willing reversal from his
male worshipers but is himself the compelling exemplar.'

The worship of Radha is central to the cult of Krishna. So
much so, that desiring Krishna *while taking* on the form of
Radha becomes the fundamental duty of all Krishna devotees.
And concomitantly, Krishna himself is often represented
iconographically in sakhivesh—dressed as one of Radha's
female companions, longing for himself. As Kajri Jain
notes, 'Pushtimarg priests identifying with Radha reported
intense sexual experiences before the image of Krishna. An
account of the Sakhibhava sect of Mathura and Brindavan,
written behind an eighteenth-century painting of one of
its members, describes how male devotees wore red loin

cloths every month to simulate menstruation, and after this period was over: "In the manner of married women, anxious to be physically united with their husbands...they take to themselves... a painting of Shri Krishna, and stretch themselves, raising both their legs, utter "ahs" and "ohs", adopt woman-like coy manners, and cry aloud: "Ah, Lalji, I die! Oh Lalji, I die'!"

Calendars of Rama and Krishna thus encode very different messages of desire. While the one is highly gendered and ordered, the other is messy and openly sensual. These mixed messages of desire drawn from India's mythological past also make the dating of desire difficult in India. Is desire puritanical or permissive? Repressed or expressive?

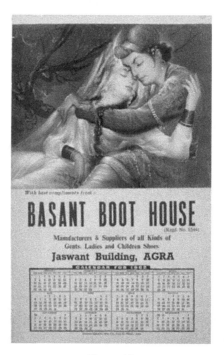

Figure 10

Restricted or expansive? And when was it all or any of these things? If the evidence of calendar art is anything to go by, then desire in India is a mix of things, and has always been so. Indeed, mixture seems to be central to the iconography of calendar art, as is visible in different ways in Figures 10 and 11.

The Heer-Ranjha/Salim-Anarkali/Romeo-Juliet-type iconography of the calendar from 1962 (Figure 10; advertising shoes despite using models who are cut off at the calves!) incorporates the ecstasy of the Radha-Krishna and Shiva-Parvati calendars. It has none of the Rama-Sita hierarchical purity, and in fact, by casting Muslim protagonists in the mould of Krishna and Radha, it adds another violated boundary to the heap already accumulated by the transgressive lovers. Is the desire in the 1962 calendar Hindu or Muslim, chaste or promiscuous, familiar or strange? It's hard to tell.

Equally difficult is it to tell who is desiring whom, who is male and who is female, in the calendar from 1960 (Figure 11). The most mythologically dense of all the images in this chapter, the 1960 calendar visually narrates the churning of the ocean for the nectar of immortality. This mythological tale is narrated first in the *Mahabharata*, and is a classic for its account of the wickedness of the gods. In the story, the gods (the devas) and the demons (the asuras) have fought to gain control of the world, and the asuras have won. The devas turn out to be bad losers and appeal to Vishnu the Preserver to help them regain control of the world, which Vishnu promises to do. The asuras and devas then come together in order to churn the ocean for the nectar that will make them all immortal. But Vishnu has secretly promised

Figure 11

the devas that they alone will be given the nectar, never mind the earlier promise of immortality extended also to the asuras or the labour expended by them in the actual churning. Once the nectar has been extracted, Vishnu takes on the form of Mohini and distracts the asuras with his/her seductive charm. Mohini channels the nectar away from the demons and starts distributing it to the gods, which is the scene pictured in the 1960 calendar. In this calendrical version, the image next in importance to that of the foregrounded Mohini is a vision of Shiva emerging in a blaze of glory from the heavens and the ocean. But what precisely is Shiva doing on the scene?

This legend has it that after Mohini has cheated the asuras of the nectar and distributed it to the devas, Shiva begs Vishnu to take on the form of Mohini once again. When he sees the beautiful form before him, Shiva is overcome by desire and chases after Mohini in order to consummate his passion. And he does this despite Parvati being around as a witness—there is a mural in Kochi's Mattancherry Palace of Parvati looking away in shame at her husband's open infidelity. And Raja Ravi Varma has a painting of Mohini on a swing, with a bit of her torso showing to suggest sexual attractiveness. There are several versions of this encounter between Shiva and Vishnu, many of which involve intense and instantaneous attraction on Shiva's part. In fact, so violent is Shiva's desire that he is described as spilling his seed just by looking at Mohini. His spilled seed in turn gives rise both to lingams and to other gods like Ayyappan.

This entire mythological landscape of desire is on a calendar advertising cotton yarn. Greed, lust, betrayal, gods, cross-dressing—all part of the history of desire in India. In terms of dates, the calendar brings together on one page the present—which at the time is 1960; the past—the myths it embodies date from centuries ago; and the future—the cotton it advertises extends well into the decades to come. The histories of colonialism and post-colonialism too are engraved on the calendar—A&F Harvey Ltd. gives way to Madura Mills Co. Ltd. And the cloud of desire in which Shiva is enveloped looks like a map of India itself. Far from providing strict rules for every day of the week, telling us which dates are for work and which for romance, calendars in India represent the traditions of dual and multiple dating, where desires cannot be measured quite so precisely.

The Rama and Sita calendars seem to be in line with the constrictions on desire imposed by the global practice of romantic dating. Within these constrictions, the seeming efflorescence of desire is squeezed into the moulds of capitalism (no romance within working hours), patriarchy (all desire should lead to marriage) and nationalism (containing the borders of desire also protects the borders of the country). But the non-reproductive goddesses, Radha, Parvati and Mohini/Vishnu, all paint alternative and messy pictures of desire in India. A changeable desire for every lunatic date. Different gods for different desires. No wonder, then, that India has more than 330 million of them.

20

SEXOLOGY

2. Get children into the habit of sleeping alone on their beds.
3. Young girls should not be allowed to sleep together on the
same bed. 4. Boys and girls should be stopped from sleeping
on the same bed. 5. Boys and girls should be watched so that
they do not go to the bathroom together and do not stay there
alone for too long…6. Young boys should not be allowed to
sit in a room alone. Privacy is destructive for the young…
12. When you are awake after the young boys and girls have
gone to sleep, you should have a look at them. If, in the
morning, the young stay tucked in their quilts for a long time,
then trouble is possible. Therefore they should be awoken
early and made to rise from bed.

—*Ways of Protecting Young Boys and Girls*,
edited by Hakim Muhammad Yusuf Hasan
(trans. Saleem Kidwai in *Same-Sex Love in India*)

I need a title for this book.

'What should it be called?' I ask Ravi Singh, my editor.

'How about *A History of Desire in India*?' he says right
away.

'No,' I say, petulantly, 'why should it be restricted to India?
After all, Michel Foucault's famous book with a similar title
is called *The History of Sexuality* (in three volumes, no less,
and intended to be *five*), and it does not locate itself with
any geographical specificity. So why should I?'

'Because as far as I can tell, you are not writing *the* history
of anything! And while the title would say "India", you're
complicating our sense of "Indianness", aren't you? Besides,

no one in India would buy your book if it didn't announce itself as being about India.'

'I suppose so,' I say ungraciously. 'Foucault simply assumed that he would be talking about everyone everywhere all the time, and no one had a problem buying *his* book!'

'Well, what does Foucault have to say about desire, anyway?' Ravi asks reasonably, trying to change the subject a little bit.

'Not much,' say I.

* * *

Michel Foucault (1926-1984), famous philosopher and brilliant theorist, has a lot to say about sexuality. For him, sexuality—by which he means bodily desires, orientations, practices—is not natural but created. It is fomented within power structures that reward certain orientations and punish others. Far from being a cause of anything (of how we feel, for instance), sexuality is an effect of power (how we are made to feel). For Foucault, sexuality is a thing that can be assessed, dissected, categorized. He does not have much to say about desires that *escape* categorization. Desires that might not be physical. Or desires that challenge the very regime of categories.

And what does Foucault have to say about desire in India? Surprisingly, despite having lived in France and the US and never even having visited India, Foucault has nonetheless written about India in a way that is both important and problematic. In the first of his three-volume book, *The History of Sexuality*, published in 1976, Foucault notes that historically, there are two modes in which sex has been encountered. The first mode he terms the ars erotica, or the erotic art, in which sex is based on pleasure rather than utility. In such a scheme, sex is an artistic secret into which a disciple is initiated through a series of lessons. The second mode he terms scientia sexualis, or the science of sexuality, in which sex becomes a thing to be categorized and used in the service of power. Sex here is treated as something that can be studied scientifically, and discourses are developed in order to understand sex.

According to Foucault, ars erotica was practised in 'China, Japan, India, Rome and the Arabo-Moslem societies', while scientia sexualis is a feature of 'our civilization', by which he means Europe. In such a division, India has apparently cultivated and followed pleasure in sex, while Europe has been busy monitoring and classifying it. His description of the ars erotica notes that:

In the erotic art, truth is drawn from pleasure itself, understood as a practice and accumulated as experience; pleasure is not considered in relation to an absolute law of the permitted and the forbidden, nor by reference to a criterion of utility, but first and foremost in relation to itself... Moreover, this knowledge must be deflected back into the sexual practice itself, in order to shape it as though from within and amplify its effects. In this way, there is formed a knowledge that must remain secret, not because of an element of infamy that might attach to its object, but because of the need to hold it in the greatest reserve, since, according to tradition, it would lose its effectiveness and its virtue by being divulged. Consequently, the relationship to the master who holds the secrets is of paramount importance; only he, working alone, can transmit this art in an esoteric manner and as the culmination of an initiation in which he guides the disciple's progress with unfailing skill and severity.

The early chapters of the *Kamasutra* play straight into this mould of the ars erotica by suggesting that eroticism is to be learned from masters adept in these arts. Foucault's observation that in such societies erotic pleasure was not considered taboo seems to be true of India, where temple sculptures from the 10th century are so sexually explicit as to make Madonna seem like a nun. It is also true that the *Kamasutra* advises us that a list of 64 arts—including 'putting on jewellery', 'practicing sorcery', and 'skill at rubbing, massaging and hairdressing'—should be learned alongside the arts of wooing and sexual aptitude taught in the text. Erotic pleasure is an art that requires many skills to make it bloom.

Unlike the scientia sexualis, which Foucault puts in direct opposition to the ars erotica:

> Let us consider things in broad historical perspective: breaking with the traditions of the ars erotica, our society has equipped itself with a scientia sexualis. To be more precise, it has pursued the task of producing true discourses concerning sex, and this by adapting—not without difficulty—the ancient procedure of confession to the rules of scientific discourse... Nearly one hundred and fifty years have gone into the making of a complex machinery for producing true discourses on sex: a deployment that spans a wide segment of history in that it connects the ancient injunction of confession to clinical listening methods. It is this deployment that enables something called 'sexuality' to embody the truth of sex and its pleasures.

Foucault draws several distinctions between the ars erotica and scientia sexualis. The first one hinges on the question of time. On the one hand, scientia sexualis can be traced all the way from the medieval Christian practice of confession to the present moment in Europe, where it has been most fully visible since the middle of the 19th century. On the other hand, and in contrast to this fairly precise swathe of time, the ars erotica seems to be suspended in the swirling mists of a timeless past.

In addition to this temporal difference, there is also a geographical division between ars and scientia. Art belongs to 'the East' while science is the province of 'the West'. There are thus three sets of distinctions that Foucault draws between the ars erotica and the scientia sexualis: the ars is mystically ancient, Eastern and one half of a binary. The scientia is temporally mappable, Western and the other half of a binary. Temporal segregation is mapped onto geographical division and made worse by an absolute binary distinction between categories. Drawing these distinctions is very much in keeping with Foucault's project in *The History of Sexuality*.

Reading this outline of sexual regimes presents a complication for the reader of texts like the *Kamasutra*. I read *The History of Sexuality* several decades before I ever laid eyes on the *Kamasutra*. I had been steeped in a milieu in which Foucault's divisions of sexuality were unquestioningly accepted as the truth. But even then, without knowing quite why, I had a sneaking suspicion that things could not be this cut and dried in matters of desire. And when I read the *Kamasutra*, my suspicions were confirmed many times over.

If the difference between East and West for Foucault depends on whether cultures treat sex as an art or a science, then a text like the *Kamasutra* frustrates the drawing of such distinctions. And indeed, it frustrates the drawing of all hard and fast distinctions in matters of desire. It is a pleasure text that slots into Foucault's description of an 'Eastern' celebration of eroticism, but it is also a sexological treatise that participates in the classification of sexual behaviour. It talks about desires that escape categorization, but it also gives us schemas within which bodies can be organized. The *Kamasutra* makes clear that the ancient tradition of the ars erotica in India was no stranger to the attractions of the scientia sexualis.

Contrary to popular belief, the *Kamasutra* can for large portions read like an utterly dry sexological treatise, citing authorities with whom Vatsyayana either agrees or disagrees. Suvarnanabha, Gonikaputra, Auddalaki and Gonardiya are some of the many authorities to whom he refers while laying bare his ideas about kama. Arguments are arranged rather tediously with pros and cons from various authorities gathered, sifted and analysed. In turn, Vatsyayana becomes an authority for subsequent sexological treatises like the 11th-century *Kokashastra*, and Kalyanmalla's 15th-century *Ananga Ranga*. From this evidence, the scientific study of sex in ancient India led a flourishing existence in the folds of what was known as the kamashastra, or the science of desire. Along with the science of religious law (dharma shastra) and the science of material power (artha shastra), the kamashastra formed the three great fields of scientific endeavour in classical Sanskrit writing.

For Foucault's distinction between ars erotica and scientia sexualis to hold, then, Indian understandings of sex must have had nothing to do with sexual classifications. But as all the kama-shastra texts reveal—and there are plenty of them—the fabric of desire in India is woven with threads drawn from both the more liberal erotic arts and the more confining scientific temperament. To pretend otherwise seems to partake of a colonial mindset that relegates 'the East' to a backward moment in relation to the developed 'West' whose development is measured in terms of scientistic categorization. Equally, it refuses to recognize that permissiveness in matters of sex can also be accompanied by strictures against it. Certainly it is not true that 'Eastern' societies did not punish sexual deviance. If Foucault's basis for distinguishing between art and science rests on the idea that science conduces to discipline while art fosters a more liberal attitude, then texts like the *Manusmriti*—the book of social rules as formulated by Manu—more than belong in the former camp. Manu's text provides punishments for various forms of pre- and non-marital sexual deflowering, as well as homosexual sex. The fact that these punishments are fairly mild does not mean that the *idea* of discipline itself is absent from the consideration of sex.

Foucault might be correct to suggest that India, and the Far East (and South America, and Africa, and Melanesia, and Polynesia too, for that matter) smiled more appreciatively at a multitude of desires. But it seems incorrect to argue that there is an absolute distinction between the art and science of sex or that this difference can be mapped spatially onto East and West or that it can be divided temporally into the past and the present.

For example, here is what the first chapter of the *Kamasutra* tells us by way of a summary of the rest of the book:

The second book, on Sex, has seventeen sections in ten chapters: sexual typology according to size, endurance and temperament, types of love, ways of embracing, procedures of kissing, types of scratching with the nails, ways of biting, customs of women from different regions, varieties of sexual positions, unusual sexual acts, modes of slapping and the accompanying moaning, the woman playing the man's part, a man's sexual strokes, oral sex, the start and finish of sex, different kinds of sex, and lovers' quarrels.

The very first of these chapters in the section on Sex is an exercise in scientific classification: 'Sexual Typology according to Size, Endurance and Temperament'. This chapter classifies the male partner in a heterosexual act as 'a hare, bull, or stallion, according to the size of his sexual organ', while a woman is termed 'a doe, mare, or elephant cow'. There are thus 'three equal couplings' between heterosexual partners of commensurate size, and 'six unequal ones' between partners of different sizes. According to Vatsyayana, there are 'nine sorts of couplings according to size'.

These are not the esoteric observations of a secret society. The *Kamasutra* was a widely disseminated text (among the upper classes), and it does not treat sex as a secret to be taught in person by a single master. Instead, it is the mass-produced sex manual of its time. Foucault is partly right to note that in ars erotica societies there is no shame attached to talking about and teaching sex. But rather than learning from a master, the *Kamasutra* presents sex as something to be studied from a sexological textbook of rules and recommendations. And like these other textbooks, the *Kamasutra* too has classified sex into knowable categories.

What happens, then, if we think about desire as both art

and science: ars erotica *and* scientia sexualis? The *Kamasutra* in fact describes itself using both terms. An early chapter is titled 'Exposition of the Arts', thus situating the text firmly within an ars erotica that will outline the artistry of sex. But the opening sentence in that chapter describes itself in terms of a science. Laying down the ideal conditions under which one should embark on reading the *Kamasutra*, Vatsyayana writes that 'a man should study the *Kamasutra* and its subsidiary sciences as long as this does not interfere with the time devoted to religion and power and their subsidiary sciences'. Despite the use of different words (science is vidya and art is kala), both art and science exist side-by-side to form a bond between pleasure and practice, curiosity and classification. Towards the end of that same chapter, Vatsyayana refers again to the 'sixty-four *arts* of love' that he extols in a poem immediately following:

> The daughter of a king or of a minister of state,
> if she knows the techniques,
> can keep her husband in her power
> even if he has a thousand women in his harem.
> And if she is separated from her husband
> and in dire straits, even in a foreign land,
> by means of these sciences
> she can live quite happily.

The technique of science cohabits happily here with the art of eros, which is more than one can say about the 'thousand women' in the poem's harem.

What is fascinating about this history of desire in India is that it endlessly complicates Foucault's distinction between an ars erotica and a scientia sexualis. Foucault's compulsion to divide and separate is met here by an equally compulsive desire to mingle and complicate. Desire in India dips into traditions of both ecstatic sensuality and stern asceticism; both an embrace and a shunning of sexuality; both pleasure and punishment. The ascetic tradition in India was judgmental about the 'excesses' of desire, and based its philosophy entirely on renunciation. But equally, the renunciates and the sensualists were not so far apart that they could never meet. Instead, as Vatsyayana himself points out, he remained chaste during the entire period of writing the *Kamasutra*: 'Vatsyayana...made this work in chastity and in the highest meditation, / for the sake of worldly life; / he did not compose it / for the sake of passion.' The taxonomy of sexual types and positions is placed within a larger framework of aesthetics from which renunciation is not absent. In fact, Vatsyayana here highlights what was later to become a commonplace even for Foucault: that disciplining sex might itself be a pleasure rather than its opposite.

This coming together of different strands of being, thought and desire is evident in every chapter of the *Kamasutra*. It is perhaps most distinctive in the final verse, when the text circumscribes the pleasures it has itself delineated in the rest of the text: 'The unusual techniques employed to increase passion, / which have been described as this particular book required, / are strongly restricted right here in this verse, / right after it.' As Wendy Doniger and Sudhir Kakar note in their translation of the *Kamasutra*: '...the *Kamasutra* has characteristics of both "procedures", thus posing a challenge to Foucault's taxonomy.' Both permission and restriction, exuberance and repression, art and science.

In India, desire has never easily been recognizable as one thing in opposition to another. But for Foucault, the project of separating East from West seems to acquire more importance than the challenge of studying the complications of desire. Some awareness of the fact that he was flattening desire seems to have crept in at a later stage when he admitted that European scientia sexualis did not in fact banish ars erotica altogether, and that the disciplinary project of classification has its own erotic pleasures. But even as he noted that pleasure might exist in science—the ars in the scientia—he was never able to move his thinking in the other direction to note the many echoes within the ars erotica of the scientia sexualis.

Perhaps the reason why the ars erotica seems to be different from the scientia sexualis for Foucault—though he has never said so in these terms—is because the former deals with capacious desire while the latter focuses on restrictive sexuality. The *Kamasutra* is able to give us classifications *and* exceptions to classification; sexual orientations *and* desires; recognizable identities *and* mobilities. These realms are not opposed to one another even as they mess up the neatness of distinctions.

Despite pronouncing on India, then, *The History of Sexuality* does not grapple with the messy histories of desire that are to be found all over the Indian subcontinent across different periods of time. Indian sexology has always refused to draw the line between art and science, desire and sexuality. This refusal of categorical clarity extends also to a refusal to separate the here from there, the now from then. If the kama-shastra texts in India provide the starting point of this categorical confusion among Indian sexologists, then the present-day hakim, or 'native' doctor, straddles the same divides. The hakims use patently unscientific cures for sexual diseases that have nonetheless been classified scientifically. From the famous Sablok Clinic in Delhi's Daryaganj to Dr. Promodu's Institute for Sexual and Marital Health in Edappally in Kerala, the hakim draws from both art and science. Autorickshaws advertise hakim's remedies for lost 'vigour' and 'strength', while clinics promise to cure everything from homosexuality to erectile dysfunction. All cures offered are for 'gupt rog' or secret maladies. Such a secret sounds like Foucault's idea of the ars erotica—an art into which the disciple has to be initiated. But the category of gupt rog also partakes of the scientia sexualis in which

An autorickshaw in Delhi advertising products that will 'increase your youth and strength' or will give you 'your money back'.
Photo courtesy the author

sex is shrouded in secrecy and becomes a thing to be cured rather than celebrated. From Vatsyayana to the hakim, then, Indian sexology has been steeped in categorical multiplicity.

And as the hakim, so the general breed of Indian sexologists. The late 19th and early 20th century saw the feverish rise of sexology as a science around the world, thanks in large part to European colonial expansion. Indeed, it is against this rise of sex as a science that Foucault writes in *The History of Sexuality*. But his desire to separate both chronological periods and geographical spaces blinds him to the fact that 20th-century Indian sexology bears the mark not only of Enlightenment rationalism and British colonialism, but also of ancient Sanskrit sexological treatises and medieval Persian poems. In fact, modern-day sexologists in India— the practitioners of what Foucault calls scientia sexualis— saw themselves as an utterly international, intertemporal, intercategorical species.

The embodiment of such a multi-layered sexologist in India is someone called Nalapat Narayana Menon. Grand-uncle of renowned novelist and poet Kamala Das, Menon wrote the first sexology treatise in Malayalam in 1934. Menon is also related to me, as the last name suggests, though like Foucault, he too is a writer I have never met. He and my paternal grandmother belong to the same matrilineal clan. Born in the late 19th century, Menon was an Indian sexologist who rubs against the grain of Foucault's theory of segregated lands and times. His book is called *Rathi Samrajyam* (*The Empire of Sex*, now in its 10th edition) and is written entirely in conversation with the ideas of English sexologist Havelock Ellis. Well, perhaps not *entirely*. Menon is very indebted to the Western sexological tradition, and so his list of references at the end of the book (reproduced below) is almost entirely from Europe. However, he also includes Indian books in his list, including the *Manusmriti* and some works in Malayalam:

ഈ ഗ്രന്ഥത്തെ സഹായിച്ചിട്ടുള്ള പ്രമാണഗ്രന്ഥങ്ങൾ

1. *Studies in the psychology of sex* -7 vols. by Havelock Ellis
2. *Man and woman*   "
3. *Psychology of sex*   "
4. *The Mind of woman*   "
5. *The Study of Phallicism* -by Alexander Stone
6. *A Research in Marriage* -by G.V. Hamilton
7. *Psychopathia Sexualis* -by Krafft -Ebbing
8. *The Sexual Question* -by August Forel
9. *The Intermediate Sex* -By Edward Carpenter
10. *Love's Coming of Age-*   "
11. *My days and Dreams*   "
12. *The Drama of Love and Death*   "
13. *Factors in the Sex Life of Twenty-two Hundred women* -by Katherine B. Davis
14. *The History of Marriage* (Ist Volume) by Westermarck
15. *The Natural Philosophy of Love*-by Remy de Gourmont
16. *The Sexual life of our time* -by Iwan Block
17. *Sex Worship and symbolism*- by Sanger Brown
18. *The Science of New life*-by John Cowan
19. *Zoology* -by Parker and Haswell
20. *Outlines of Zoology* -by J. Arthur Thompson
21. *Sex* -by F.A.E Crew
22. *Sexual Ethics* -by Robert Michels
23. *Sex and character* -by Otto weininger
24. *The Women of the Renaissance* -by Maulde La Glaviere
25. *Marriage, Children and God* -by Cland Mullins
26. *The Riddle of The Universe* -by Ernest Heckel
27. *Insects* -by Frank Balfow Browne
28. *An introduction to Biology*-by William j. wakin
29. *Sin and Sex* -by Robert Briffault
30. *Heredity* -by F.A.E. Crew
31. *Origin of Life* -by Dr. Hollick
32. *Womanhood and Marriage* -by Bernard Macfodden
33. *Preparing for mother* - hood
34. *The Confessions* -by J.J. Rousseau
35. *Youth and Sex* -by Scharlier and Sibly
36. *Problems of Sex* -by Arthur Thompson and Patrick Geddes

37. *Disorders of the Sexual Function in the male and Female* -by Max Hulner
38. *Married Love* -by Marie Stopes
39. *Sex* - by Henry Staunton
40. *Prostitution in Ancient World* -by Leo Markun
41. *Sex Problems in India* - by N.S. Phadke
42. *Young Men's Guide* - by Dr. Gangadin
43. *Sexual Life of Women* - by E.H. Kinch
44. *Love and Marriage* - by Ellen Key
45. *Evolution* - by Thomas Geddes
46. *The Secret of Sex* - by S.H. Terry
47. *Sex knowledge for women* - by W.J. Robinson
48. *Parenthood* - by Micheal Fielding
49. *Modern Problems in Biology* - by William J. Dakin
50. *Theories of Psycho-Analysis* - by Pro. J.C. Flugel
51. *The New World of Thought* - by Sir James Jeans
52. *Origin of Species* - by Charles Darwin
53. *Civilization: Its Cause and Cure* - by Edward Carpenter
54. *Sex Problems in Woman* - by A.C. Magian
55. *The Geneology of Love* - by C. Thessing
56. *Papers in Psycho-Analysis* - by Ernest Jones
57. *Kama Sutra of Vatsyayana* - by Prof. Gambers
58. സസ്യശാസ്ത്രം – മഞ്ചേരി രാമകൃഷ്ണയ്യർ
59. മനുസ്മൃതി
60. കുചിമാരതന്ത്രം
61. അനംഗരംഗം
62. രതിരഹസ്യം
63. രതിരത്നപ്രദീപിക

Despite the disparity in numbers, this set of readings points to a *conversation* between East and West, old and new, art and science, out of which Menon's book emerges. Menon works with the assumption that sexology has never been only one thing or another: it has always been complicated and various and multilingual. The book—written in Malayalam and based on texts written in English—is as much a mixture as the traditions out of which it is written. In India, the *Kamasutra* translated a variety of earlier sources; it was in turn reconceived in the *Kokashastra*, which was translated into Persian as the *Laddat-al-Nisa*, which was then unseated by the British Penal Code. All of these texts then produced a 20th-century sexologist in India writing a Malayalam text titled *The Empire of Sex*. And, as we know, the sun never sets on this particular empire.

While *The History of Sexuality* deals only with the geographical West, including classical Greece and Rome, the title of the book suggests a universality: it calls itself *the* history of sexuality. When I was thinking about a title for this book, I wanted both to speak about desire in Foucault's tongue *and* write back to him in Menon's voice. I too would plot a history, but it would be a history of desire over time and space and category rather than *the* history of sexuality within segregated periods and times and classifications. Equally, it would locate itself in a land that has no fixed location. What counts as 'India' now was not 'India' when Vatsyayana wrote the *Kamasutra*. 'India' under the 11th-century Cholas included Sri Lanka but not present-day North India; British India included Pakistan, Bangladesh and Afghanistan. Desire in India has always been cast in a mix of languages, arts, sciences and even countries. 'Desire' and 'India' are thus two endlessly unstable terms. A history of desire written by multiple Menons, then, rather than *the* history of sexuality, seems like the best way to tackle the subject at hand.

For, in matters of desire, East or West, rigid distinctions cannot hold.

ACKNOWLEDGEMENTS

With passionate thanks:

For Research Assistance: Aanchal Vij, Shilpa Menon, Ishanika Sharma, Shiv Datt Sharma, Manjari Sahay, Kaagni Harekal, Ayesha Verma, Saumya Bhandari, Alishya Almeida, Shubhangi Karia, Pia Bakshi, Shreyashee Roy.

For Material Help: Anupama Chandra, Gayathri Prabhu, Pratyay Nath, Kaushik Roy, Saikat Majumdar, Ranjit Rai, Nivedita Sen, Sambudha Sen, Nirmala Jairaj, Navtej Johar, Asha Jain, Vidya Dehejia, Malvika Maheshwari.

For Love and Support: Mohan and Indira Menon, Manju and Bugsy, Nandini Gopinadh, Bill Cohen, Poonam Saxena, T.R. Arun Kumar, Ritin Rai, Asma Barlas, Ulises Mejias, Lavanya Rajamani, Rahul Govind, Sanghamitra Mishra, Joseph Litvak, Elizabeth Wilson, Maya Gopinadh, Gita Muralidharan, Himani Verma, Nuriya Ansari, Vikram Menon, Ramya Subrahmanian, Javed Sayed, Shally Bhasin, Deepshikha Bahl, Shweta Kumar, Norman and Stella Harris, Miriam Harris, Sarah Schieff, Alex Calder, Freyan Panthaki; all my fabulous students at Ashoka University.

Above and Beyond:

Lee Edelman for love and brilliance;

Sudhir Kakar, Ruth Vanita, Saleem Kidwai, for their incredible work on Indian sexualities;

Justin McCarthy, Alex Watson, Vasuman Khandelwal, for answering all my questions all the time;

Judith Brown, dear friend, rigorous reader, fellow Indian;

Nadhra Shahbaz Khan, for artistic splendour;

Shohini Ghosh for *dhai akshar prem ke*;

Ashley T. Shelden, Nur-jahan;

Priya Paul for generously allowing me to delve into her archive of calendar art; Pratima Arora for facilitating access to the archive; Hemant Chawla for photographing the calendars;

Ravi Singh: fabulous and iconoclastic editor;

Mera yaar, Gil Shaandaar.

Bibliography

Works on Desire I Have Consulted and Quoted From:

1. 'Accidental Deaths and Suicides in India.' *National Crime Records Bureau.* 2015.

2. Aczel, Amir D. *Finding Zero: A Mathematician's Odyssey to Uncover the Origins of Numbers.* New York: St. Martin's Press, 2015.

3. Aczel, Amir. 'The Origin of the Number Zero.' *Smithsonian Magazine,* Dec. 2014, http://www.smithsonianmag.com/history/origin-number-zero-180953392/

4. Ahluwalia, Sanjam. 'Controlling Births, Policing Sexualities: A History of Birth Control in Colonial India, 1877-1946.' *Electronic Theses and Dissertations Center,* 2001, https://etd.ohiolink.edu/pg_10?0::NO:10:P10_ACCESSION_NUM:ucin980270900

5. Ahmad, Omair. *The Storyteller's Tale.* New Delhi: Speaking Tiger, 2015.

6. Ahuja, Naman P. *Rupa-Pratirupa: The Body in Indian Art.* National Museum, New Delhi, 2014.

7. Aijaz, S. 'Birth to Re-birth: The Man Who Made Savita Bhabhi.' *YourStory,* Feb. 2015, https://yourstory.com/2015/02/savita-bhabhi/

8. Akhtar, Salman. *Freud along the Ganges: Psychoanalytic Reflections on the People and Culture of India.* New York: Other Press, 2005.

9. Alter, Joseph S. *The Wrestler's Body: Identity and Ideology in North India.* Berkeley: University of California Press, 1992.

10. Amnesty International India. 'Briefing: The Armed Forces Special Powers Act: A Renewed Debate in India on Human Rights and National Security.' *Amnesty USA*, Sept. 2013, https://www.amnestyusa.org/reports/the-armed-forces-special-powers-act-a-renewed-debate-in-india-on-human-rights-and-national-security/

11. Anand, Mulk Raj, and Krishna Nehru Hutheesing. *The Book of Indian Beauty*. Vermont: C.E. Tuttle Co.,1981.

12. Aranyani. *A Pleasant Kind of Heavy and Other Erotic Stories*. New Delhi: Aleph Book Company, 2013.

13. Arondekar, Anjali R. *For the Record: On Sexuality and the Colonial Archive in India*. Durham: Duke University Press, 2010.

14. Badiou, Alain. *Saint Paul: The Foundation of Universalism*. Trans. Ray Brassier. California: Stanford University Press, 2009.

15. Berlant, Lauren. *Desire/Love*. New York: Punctum, 2012.

16. Bersani, Leo. *Is the Rectum a Grave and Other Essays*. Chicago: University of Chicago Press, 2010.

17. 'Betel Leaves in Hindu Rituals—Importance of Betel Leaves in Hindu Pujas.' *Facebook*, Sept. 2010, www.facebook.com/notes/mantra-shlokas/betel-leaves-in-hindu-rituals-importance-of-betel-leaves-in-hindu-pujas/161637570515742/

18. Betts, Vanessa, Victoria MuCulloch. *India—Forts, Palaces, the Himalaya*. Bath, UK: Footprint Travel Guides, 2013.

19. Bhandar, Sudhanshu. 'Prostitution in Colonial India.' *Mainstream Weekly*. June 2010, https://www.mainstreamweekly.net/article2142.html

20. Bhandari, Mannu, et al. *Alone Together: Selected Stories by Mannu Bhandari, Rajee Seth and Archana Varma*. Ruth Vanita, ed. New Delhi: Women Unlimited, 2013.

21. Bhaskaran, Suparna. 'The Politics of Penetration: Section 377 of the Indian Penal Code.' Ruth Vanita, ed. *Queering India Same-Sex Love and Eroticism in Indian Culture and Society.* New York: Routledge, 2002.

22. Bokhari, Afshan. 'Ars Erotica: "Visualizing" Sufism in Mughal Paintings and the Mystical Memoirs of Jahan Ara Begam.' *Marg: A Magazine of the Arts,* March 2012, http://www.marg-art.org/p/465/volume-63-number-3

23. Boswell, John. *Christianity, Social Tolerance, and Homosexuality: Gay People in Western Europe from the Beginning of the Christian Era to the Fourteenth Century.* Chicago: University of Chicago Press, 2011.

24. Boswell, John. *Same-Sex Unions in Premodern Europe.* New York: Vintage Books, 1995.

25. Breazeale, Daniel, ed. *Nietzsche: Untimely Meditations.* Trans. R. J. Hollingdale, Cambridge: Cambridge University Press, 1997.

26. Burton, Antoinette M., ed. *Gender, Sexuality and Colonial Modernities.* Oxfordshire: Routledge, 1999.

27. Buswell, Robert E., and Donald S. Lopez. *The Princeton Dictionary of Buddhism.* New Jersey: Princeton University Press, 2014.

28. Chandra, Shefali. *The Sexual Life of English: Languages of Caste and Desire in Colonial India.* New Delhi: Zubaan, 2013.

29. Chase, Karen. *Jamali-Kamali: A Tale of Passion in Mughal India.* Ahmedabad: Mapin Publishing, 2011.

30. Chatterjee, Indrani. 'When "Sexuality" Floated Free of Histories in South Asia.' *The Journal of Asian Studies,* vol. 71, no. 4, 2012, pp. 945–962.

31. Chughtai, Ismat. *A Life in Words: Memoirs.* Trans. M. Asaduddin. New Delhi: Penguin Books, 2013.

32. Chughtai, Ismat. *Lifting the Veil: Selected Writings*. Trans. M. Asaduddin. New Delhi: Penguin Books India, 2009.

33. Dalrymple, William. 'On Pilgrim Road.' *Mail and Guardian*, April 2010, https://mg.co.za/article/2010-04-07-on-pilgrim-road

34. Dalrymple, William, 'India: The Place of Sex,' *The New York Review of Books*, June 2008. http://www.nybooks.com/articles/2008/06/26/india-the-place-of-sex/

35. Das, Kamala. *My Story*. New Delhi: HarperCollins, 2009.

36. Dasgupta, Rohit K. 'Queer Sexuality: A Cultural Narrative of India's Historical Archive.' *Rupkatha Journal on Interdisciplinary Studies in Humanities*, vol. 3, no. 4, 2011, pp. 651–670.

37. Datta, Surendra Kumar. *The Desire of India*. South Carolina: Nabu Press, 2012.

38. Dehejia, Vidya. *Slaves of the Lord: The Path of the Tamil Saints*. New Delhi: Munshiram Manoharlal, 1988.

39. Dehejia, Vidya. 'An Eleventh-Century Master Sculptor: Ten Thousand Pearls Adorn a Bronze.' A.W. Mellon Lectures in the Fine Arts, National Gallery of Art, Washington DC, 2016, https://www.nga.gov/content/ngaweb/audio-video/mellon.html

40. Dehejia, Vidya. *The Body Adorned: Dissolving Boundaries between Sacred and Profane in India's Art*. New York: Columbia University Press, 2009.

41. Dehlvi, Amar, ed. *Masterpieces of Urdu Poetry*. New York: Star Publications, 2009.

42. Dehlvi, Sadia. *The Sufi Courtyard: Dargahs of Delhi*. New Delhi: HarperCollins, India Today Group, 2012.

43. Derné, Steve. *Culture in Action: Family Life, Emotion, and*

Male Dominance in Banaras, India. New York: State University of New York Press, 1995.

44. Derrida, Jacques. *Of Grammatology.* Trans. Gayatri Chakravorty Spivak. Baltimore: Johns Hopkins University Press, 1998.

45. Desai, Devangana, ed. *Erotic Sculpture of India: A Socio Cultural Study.* New Delhi: Munshiram Manoharlal Publishers, 1990.

46. Desai, Devangana, ed. *Khajuraho (Monumental Legacy Series).* New Delhi: Oxford University Press, 2010.

47. Detha, Vijayadan. *Chouboli and Other Stories.* Trans. Christi A. Merrill and Kailash Kabir. New Delhi: Katha, 2010.

48. Devi, Mahasweta. *Breast Stories.* Trans. Gayatri Chakravorty Spivak. New Delhi: Seagull, 2014.

49. Devi, Shakuntala. *Figuring: The Joy of Numbers.* New Delhi: Orient Blackswan, 1986.

50. Devi, Shakuntala. *The Book of Numbers.* New Delhi: Orient Blackswan, 2006.

51. Devi, Shakuntala. *The World of Homosexuals.* New Delhi: Vikas Publishing House, 1977.

52. Diamond, Debra, curator and ed. *Yoga: The Art of Transformation.* Washington, D.C.: Arthur M. Sackler Gallery, Smithsonian Institution, 2013, https://www.si.edu/Exhibitions/Yoga-The-Art-of-Transformation-4911

53. Doniger, Wendy, trans. *Hindu Myths: A Sourcebook Translated from the Sanskrit.* London: Penguin Classics, 2004.

54. Doniger, Wendy. 'What is the *Kamasutra* Really About? Wendy Doniger Reads the Classic Text.' Scroll.in Aug. 2015, https://scroll.in/article/746560/what-is-the-kamasutra-really-about-wendy-doniger-reads-the-classic-text

55. Doniger, Wendy. *Hindu Myths*. London: Penguin Classics, 2004.

56. Doniger, Wendy. *On Hinduism*. New Delhi: Aleph Book Company, 2013.

57. Doniger, Wendy. *Reading the Kamasutra: The Mare's Trap and Other Essays on Vatsyayana's Masterpiece*. New Delhi: Speaking Tiger, 2015.

58. Doniger, Wendy. *The Ring of Truth: Myths of Sex and Jewelry*. New Delhi: Speaking Tiger, 2017.

59. Dover, Kenneth James. *Greek Homosexuality*. Cambridge, MA: Harvard University Press, 1989.

60. Dudney, Arthur. *Delhi: Pages from a Forgotten History*. New Delhi: Hay House India, 2015.

61. Dutta, Amaresh. *Encyclopedia of Indian Literature: Devraj to Jyoti*, Volume 2. New Delhi: Sahitya Akademi, 1988.

62. Dwivedi, Sharada, and Shalini Devi Holkar. *Almond Eyes, Lotus Feet: Indian Traditions in Beauty and Health*. New York: HarperCollins, 2005.

63. Edelman, Lee. *Homographesis: Essays in Gay Literary and Cultural Theory*. London: Routledge, 1994.

64. Edelman, Lee. *No Future: Queer Theory and the Death Drive*. Durham: Duke University Press, 2007.

65. Ejaz, Manzur. 'That Laughing Son of a Weaver—Shah Hussain (1538-1599).' *The Friday Times*, September 2011, http://www.thefridaytimes.com/beta3/tft/article.php?issue=20110909&page=24

66. Enloe, Cynthia. 'Base Women' in *Bananas, Beaches and Bases: Making Feminist Sense of International Politics*, California: California University Press, 2014, pp. 125–173.

67. Ernst, Carl W. *Refractions of Islam in India: Situating Sufism and Yoga*. New Delhi: SAGE Publications India, 2016.

68. Éwanjé-Épée, Félix, and Stella Magliani-Belkacem. 'The Empire of Sexuality: An Interview with Joseph Massad.' *Jadaliyya*, March 2015, http://www.jadaliyya.com/pages/index/10461/the-empire-of-sexuality_an-interview-with-joseph-m

69. Faiz, Faiz Ahmad. *100 Poems by Faiz Ahmed Faiz*. Trans. Sarvat Rahman. New Delhi: Abhinav Publications, 2002.

70. Flaubert, Gustave. *Madame Bovary*. New Delhi: Penguin Classics, 2003.

71. Forster, E. M. *Abinger Harvest*. California: Harcourt Brace and Co., 1966.

72. Foucault, Michel. *The History of Sexuality*. Trans. Robert Hurley. London: Vintage, 1998.

73. Freud, Sigmund, and James Strachey. *On Sexuality: Three Essays on the Theory of Sexuality*. Harmondsworth: Penguin, 1977.

74. Gaborieau, Marc. *Muslim Shrines in India: Their Character, History and Significance*. Ed. Christian W. Troll. New Delhi: Oxford University Press, 2004.

75. Ghalib, Mirza Asadullah Khan. *Selections from Diwane-e-Ghalib: Selected Poetry of Mirza Asadullah Khan Ghalib*. Trans. Khwaja Tariq Mahmood. New Delhi: Star Publications, 2000.

76. Ghosh, Shohini. *Fire*. Vancouver: Arsenal Pulp Press, 2010.

77. Ghulam, Chatha Akbar. *Faith, Not Religions: A Collection of Essays*. Indiana: IUniverse, 2012.

78. Glover, William J. 'Construing Urban Space as "Public" in Colonial India: Some Notes from the Punjab.' *Journal of Punjab Studies* vol. 14, no. 2, 2007, pp. 211-24.

79. *Good Hair*. Dir. Jeff Stilson. Perf. Chris Rock, Maya Angelou. 2009.

80. Guha, Brishti. 'The Story of Shunya.' *The Indian Express*, March 2015, http://indianexpress.com/article/opinion/columns/the-story-of-shunya/

81. Hafiz. *The Nightingales are Drunk*. Trans. Dick Davies, London: Penguin Books, 2015.

82. 'Hair India.' *Al Jazeera English*, January 2014, http://www.aljazeera.com/programmes/witness/2010/01/201012712 1316920743.html

83. Harris, Jonathan Gil. *The First Firangis: Remarkable Stories of Heroes, Healers, Charlatans, Courtesans & Other Foreigners Who Became Indian*. Delhi: Aleph Book Company, 2015.

84. Hasan, Fakhra. 'From Pederasty to Paedophilia and Freudian Slips.' *The Express Tribune Blog*, May 2014, http://blogs.tribune.com.pk/story/22110/from-pederasty-to-paedophilia-and-freudian-slips/

85. Hedger-Gourlay, Fiona, Lindy Ingham, Jo Newton, Emma Tabor, and Jill Worrell. 'Lal Kot and Siri.' *Tabor*, September 2006, http://www.tabor.me.uk/places/sevencities/lalkot.pdf

86. Husain, Intizar. *The Death of Sheherzad*. Trans. Rakhshanda Jalil, New Delhi: HarperCollins 2014.

87. Hyam, Ronald. *Empire and Sexuality: The British Experience*. Manchester: Manchester University Press, 2004.

88. Jaffrey, Madhur. *Climbing the Mango Trees: A Memoir of a Childhood in India*. London: Ebury Press, 2005.

89. Jain, Kajri. *Gods in the Bazaar: The Economies of Indian Calendar Art*. Durham: Duke University Press, 2007.

90. Jalil, Rakhshanda, ed. *New Urdu Writings from India and Pakistan*. New Delhi: Tranquebar Press, 2013.

91. Jayadeva. *Love Song of the Dark Lord: Jayadeva's Gitagovinda*. Trans. Barbara Miller. New York: Columbia UP, 1977.

92. Joshi, Manohar Shyam. *The Perplexity of Hariya Hercules.* Trans. Robert A. Hueckstedt. New Delhi: Penguin India, 2009.

93. Kakar, Sudhir, and Ramin Jahanbegloo. *India Analysed.* New Delhi: Oxford University Press, 2015.

94. Kakar, Sudhir. 'A Tradition of Quiet Tolerance.' *India Today.* December 2013, http://indiatoday.intoday.in/story/a-tradition-of-quiet-tolerance/1/332156.html

95. Kakar, Sudhir. *Intimate Relations: Exploring Indian Sexuality.* New Delhi: Penguin Books India, 1989.

96. Kakar, Sudhir. *Shamans, Mystics, and Doctors: A Psychological Inquiry into India and Its Healing Traditions.* New Delhi: Oxford University Press, 2012.

97. Kakar, Sudhir, and John Munder Ross. *Tales of Love, Sex, and Danger.* Delhi: Oxford University Press, 2011.

98. Kakar, Sudhir. *The Ascetic of Desire.* London: Penguin, 1999.

99. Kakar, Sudhir. *Young Tagore: The Making of a Genius.* London: Penguin, 2014.

100. Kakoty, Juanita. 'The Saga of Jamali-Kamali.' *The Thumb Print—A Magazine from the East.* March 2013, http://www.thethumbprintmag.com/the-saga-of-jamali-kamali-mughal-india-homosexuality/

101. Kalidasa, *Kumarasambhava.* Trans. Hank Heifetz. New Delhi: Penguin Random House India, 2017

102. Kapoor, Shruti. 'Why Is Everyone Talking about Bhabhi Ji Ghar Par Hain?' *India Today*, October 2015, http://indiatoday.intoday.in/story/why-is-bhabhi-ji-ghar-par-hain-so-popular-andtv-vibhuti-narayan-mishra-tiwari-ji-angoori-bhabhi-anita-bhabhi-hawaldar-happu-singh/1/500359.html

103. Kautilya. *The Arthashastra.* Trans. L.N. Rangarajan. New Delhi: Penguin, 2010.

104. Khusrau, Amir. *In the Bazaar of Love: The Selected Poetry of Amir Khusrau*. Trans. Paul E. Losensky and Sunil Sharma. New Delhi: Penguin Books India, 2013.

105. Kodoth, Praveena. 'Courting Legitimacy or Delegitimizing Custom? Sexuality, Sambandham, and Marriage Reform in Late Nineteenth-Century Malabar.' *Modern Asian Studies*, vol. 35, no. 2, 2001, pp. 349–384.

106. Krishnaswamy, Revathi. *Effeminism: The Economy of Colonial Desire*. Michigan: University of Michigan Press, 2011.

107. Ksetrayya. *When God Is a Customer: Telugu Courtesan Songs by Ksetrayya and Others*. Ed. and Trans. A. K. Ramanujan, V.N. Rao, David Shulman. Berkeley: University of California Press, 1994.

108. Kugle, Scott. *When Sun Meets Moon: Gender, Eros, and Ecstasy in Urdu Poetry*. Chapel Hill: University of North Carolina Press, 2016.

109. Kurtz, Stanley N. *All the Mothers Are One: Hindu India and the Cultural Reshaping of Psychoanalysis*. New York: Columbia University Press, 1992.

110. Lakhnavi, Ghalib, and Abdullah Husain Bilgrami. *The Adventures of Amir Hamza: Lord of the Auspicious Planetary Conjunction*. Trans. Musharraf Ali Farooqi. New Delhi: Aleph Book Company, 2012.

111. Lal, Vinay. 'Not This, Not That: The Hijras of India and the Cultural Politics of Sexuality.' *Social Text*, no. 61, 1999, pp. 119–140.

112. Levine, Philippa. *Prostitution, Race, and Politics: Policing Venereal Disease in the British Empire*. New York: Routledge, 2003.

113. Lowry, Glenn. 'Delhi in the 16th Century', in Attilo Petruccioli, ed. *Environmental Design: Journal of the Islamic Environmental Design Research Centre*, 1984.

114. Maddy. 'The Legend of Vavar.' *Maddy's Ramblings*, December 2008, http://maddy06.blogspot.in/2008/12/legend-of-vavar. html

115. Manucci, Niccolao. *A Pepys of Mongul India, 1653-1708: 1653-1708: Being and Abridged Edition of the 'Storia do Mogor' of Niccolao Manucci*. New York: E. P. Dutton, 1913.

116. Massad, Joseph A. *Desiring Arabs*. Chicago, IL: University of Chicago Press, 2008.

117. Mathur, Saloni. *India by Design: Colonial History and Cultural Display*. New Delhi: Orient Black Swan, 2011.

118. Menen, Aubrey. 'My Grandmother and the Dirty English.' *The New Yorker*. July 1953, http://www.newyorker.com/ magazine/1953/07/04/my-grandmother-and-the-dirty-english

119. Menon, A. Sreedhara. *Social and Cultural History of Kerala*. New Delhi: Sterling, 1979.

120. Menon, Harish. 'Women in Sabarimala: Legends, Dogmas and Hypocrisies.' *National Confederation of Human Rights Organizations*, July 2006, https://goo.gl/9wc79t

121. Menon, Madhavi. *Indifference to Difference: On Queer Universalism*. Minneapolis: Minnesota University Press, 2015.

122. Menon, Nalappattu Narayana. *Rathisamrajyam*. 10th ed. Mathrubhumi, 2013.

123. Menon, Ramesh. *Siva: The Siva Purana Retold*. New Delhi: Rupa & Co., 2006.

124. Merchant, Hoshang, ed. *Yaraana: Gay Writing from South Asia*. New Delhi: Penguin Books India, 1999.

125. Mukherjee, J. 'Castration—A Means of Induction into the Hijirah Group of the Eunuch Community in India: A Critical Study of 20 Cases.' *American Journal of Forensic Medicine & Pathology*, 1980.

126. Mukherji, Anahita. 'Hijra Farsi: Secret Language Knits Community.' *The Times of India*, Oct. 2013, http://timesofindia. indiatimes.com/india/Hijra-Farsi-Secret-language-knits-community/articleshow/23618092.cms

127. Mulmi, Amish. 'Savita Bhabhi Is the New Face of Freedom.' *The New Indian Express*, June 2009, http://archive. is/20130208134100/newindianexpress.com/lifestyle/books/ article104262.ece

128. Murugan, Perumal. *One Part Woman*. Ed. Aniruddhan Vasudevan. New Delhi: Penguin Books India, 2014.

129. Nanda, Meera. *Science in Saffron: Skeptical Essays on History of Science*. Haryana: Three Essays Collective, 2016.

130. Nanda, Serena. *Neither Man nor Woman: The Hijras of India*. California: Wadsworth Publishing Co. Inc., 1999.

131. Nandy, Ashis, ed. *The Secret Politics of Our Desires: Innocence, Culpability, and Indian Popular Cinema*. Oxford: Oxford University Press, 1998.

132. Nandy, Ashis. *The Intimate Enemy: Loss and Recovery of Self under Colonialism*. New Delhi: Oxford University Press, 2015.

133. Nandy, Ashis. *The Savage Freud and Other Essays on Possible and Retrievable Selves*. London: Oxford University Press, 2000.

134. Narrain, Arvind, and Vinay Chandran, eds. *Nothing to Fix: Medicalisation of Sexual Orientation and Gender Identity*. New Delhi: SAGE Publications, Yoda Press, 2016.

135. Nasir, Hasham. 'Limitless Boundaries: Homosexuality in the History of the Subcontinent.' *Laaltain: Pakistan's First Bilingual Youth Magazine*, March 2015, http://www.laaltain. com/limitless-boundaries-homosexuality-in-the-history-of-the-subcontinent/

136. Nawaz, Mumtaz Shah. *The Heart Divided: A Novel*. New Delhi: Penguin Books India, 2004.

137. Nelson, Dean. 'First Female Indian Troops Are "Prostitutes"' *The Telegraph.* 28 September 2009, http://www.telegraph.co.uk/news/worldnews/asia/india/6239790/First-female-Indian-troops-are-prostitutes.html

138. Nilayagode, Devaki. *Antharjanam: Memoirs of a Namboodiri Woman.* Trans. Indira Menon and Radhika P. Menon. New Delhi: Oxford University Press, 2012.

139. Olivelle, Patrick. 'Celibacy in Classical Hinduism', in Carl Olson, ed. *Celibacy and Religious Traditions.* Oxford: Oxford University Press, 2007.

140. Olivelle, Patrick. *The Asrama System: The History and Hermeneutics of a Religious Institution.* Delhi: Munshiram Manoharlal Publishers, 2004.

141. Orsini, Francesca. *Before the Divide: Hindi and Urdu Literary Culture.* New Delhi: Orient BlackSwan, 2011.

142. Orsini, Francesca. *Love in South Asia: A Cultural History.* Cambridge: Cambridge University Press, 2006.

143. Osella, Filippo, and Caroline Osella. 'Migration, Money and Masculinity in Kerala.' *Journal of the Royal Anthropological Institute,* vol. 6, no. 1, 2000, pp. 117-33, http://onlinelibrary.wiley.com/doi/10.1111/1467-9655.t01-1-00007/epdf

144. Ovid, Publius. *Metamorphoses.* Ed. E.J. Kenney and A.D. Melville, Oxford: Oxford University Press, 2008.

145. Padhi, Biswajeet. 'Radio Kisan's Betel Victory.' *Inclusive Media for Change,* April 2016, http://www.im4change.org/media/radio-kisans-betel-victory-biswajit-padhi-4679214.html

146. Pande, Alka, and Lance Dane. *Indian Erotica.* New Delhi: Roli Books, 2001.

147. Pande, Alka. *Shringara: The Many Faces of Indian Beauty.* New Delhi: Rupa & Co., 2011.

148. Patel, Geeta. *Lyrical Movements, Historical Hauntings: On Gender, Colonialism, and Desire in Miraji's Urdu Poetry*. New Delhi: Manohar Publishers, 2005.

149. Patil, Vimla. 'The World's Most Romantic Leaf Is Heart-Shaped.' *E-Samskriti: The Essence of Indian Culture*. August 2011, http://www.esamskriti.com/e/Culture/Indian-Culture/The-World-colon-S-Most-Romantic-Leaf-Is-Heart~Shaped-1.aspx

150. Pattanaik, Devdutt. 'Daughters of Shiva.' *Devdutt*, December 2012, http://devdutt.com/articles/daughters-of-shiva.html

151. Pattanaik, Devdutt. 'Lustful Intentions.' *Devdutt*, March 2011, http://devdutt.com/articles/indian-mythology/lustful-intentions.html

152. Pattanaik, Devdutt. *Jaya: An Illustrated Retelling of the Mahabharata*. New Delhi: Penguin Books India, 2010.

153. Pattanaik, Devdutt. *Shikhandi and Other Tales They Don't Tell You*. New Delhi: Zubaan, 2014.

154. Pattanaik, Devdutt. *The Pregnant King*. New Delhi: Penguin Books, 2008.

155. Paul, Priya. *Maya Mahal: An Enchanted Look at Hindi Cinema through the Priya Paul Collection*. New Delhi: Priya Paul, 2013.

156. Peddana, Allasani. *The Story of Manu*. Ed. Velcheru Narayana Rao and David Shulman. Cambridge, MA: Harvard University Press, 2015.

157. Plato. *The Symposium*. Trans. Christopher Gill. London: Penguin Classics, 2004.

158. Poonam, Snigdha. 'A Tale of Two Beards: When I Went Tinder Dating in Delhi.' Scroll, September 2014, https://scroll.in/article/679611/a-tale-of-two-beards-when-i-went-tinder-dating-in-delhi

159. Prasad, Dinesh. *East of Love, West of Desire*. New Delhi: Tara Press, 2014.

160. Preston, Laurence W. 'A Right to Exist: Eunuchs and the State in Nineteenth-Century India.' *Modern Asian Studies*, vol. 21, no. 2, 1987, pp. 371–387.

161. Pritchett, Frances W. *Nets of Awareness: Urdu poetry and Its Critics*. New Delhi: Katha Books, 2004.

162. Priya. 'Operation Majnu.' *Chattpriya*, December 2005, http://chattypriya.blogspot.in/2005/12/operation-majnu.html

163. 'Public Parks and Pavements in India—Just Vestiges of the Colonial Era or Do They Mean More?' *Rhetoric2Reality: Inspiraction*, Nov. 2010, https://rhetoric2reality.wordpress.com/2010/11/14/public-parks-and-pavements-in-india-just-vestiges-of-the-colonial-era-or-do-they-mean-more/

164. Quli Khan, Dargah. *Muraqqa-e-Delhi: The Mughal Capital in Muhammad Shah's Time*. New Delhi: Deputy Publication, 1989.

165. Rahman, Tariq. *From Hindi to Urdu: A Social and Political History*. Karachi: Oxford University Press, 2011.

166. Rakesh, Mohan. *Lingering Shadows*. Trans. Jai Ratan. New Delhi: Hind Pocket Books, 1969.

167. Ramanujan, A.K. *Folktales from India: A Selection of Oral Tales from Twenty-Two Languages*. New York: Pantheon Books, 1991.

168. Ramanujan, A.K. *The Collected Essays of A.K. Ramanujan*. Ed. Vinay Dharwadker, New Delhi: Oxford University Press, 2004.

169. Ramanujan, A.K., trans. *Speaking of Śiva*. London: Penguin Classics UK, 2015.

170. Ramanujan, Attipat K., and Molly Daniels-Ramanujan. *The Oxford India Ramanujan*. New Delhi: Oxford University Press, 2005.

171. Ramanujan, A.K., 'Hanchi: A Kannada Cinderella', in A. Dundes, ed., *Cinderella: A Folklore Casebook*. New York: Garland Publishing, 1982.

172. Randathani, Hussein. 'Genesis and Growth of the Mappila Community.' *Jaihoon*. December 2005, http://www.jaihoon.com/456.htm

173. Rangacharya, Adya. *The Natyasastra: English Translation with Critical Notes*. New Delhi: Munshiram Manoharlal Publishers, 1996.

174. Rao, Velcheru Narayana, et al. *Symbols of Substance, Court and State in Nayaka Period Tamilnadu*. Delhi: Oxford University Press, 1993.

175. Reddy, Gayatri. *With Respect to Sex: Negotiating Hijra Identity in South India*. New Delhi: Yoda Press, 2006.

176. Revathi, A. *The Truth About Me: A Hijra Life Story*. Trans. V. Geetha. New Delhi: Penguin Books India, 2010.

177. Ringrose. Kathryn. 'Journal of the History of Sexuality.' *Journal of the History of Sexuality*, vol. 7, no. 3, 1997, pp. 439–442.

178. Ruhela, Satya Pal, and Ahrar Husain, eds. *Sex Education in India in the 21st Century*. Delhi: Indian Publishers Distributors, 2002.

179. Sabhlok, Sanjeev. 'Chanakya's Well Regulated System of Prostitution in Ancient India.' *Sanjeev Sabhlok's Revolutionary Blog*, December 2011, http://www.sabhlokcity.com/2011/12/chanakyas-well-regulated-system-of-prostitution-in-ancient-india/

180. Saeed, Salman. 'Sufis—Wisdom against Violence.' *The-South-Asian*, 2001, http://www.the-south-asian.com/July-Aug2006/Sufis-wisdom-against-violence-1.htm

181. Sarkar, Nilanjan. 'Forbidden Privileges and History-Writing in Medieval India.' *The Medieval History Journal*. 2013, pp. 21–62.

182. 'Savita Bhabhi.' *Indpaedia*, 2014, http://indpaedia.com/ind/index.php/Savita_Bhabhi?tag=indifash06-20

183. Sedgwick, Eve Kosofsky. *Epistemology of the Closet*. Berkeley, CA: University of California Press, 2008.

184. Sekhar, Ajay. 'Breast-tax in Kerala History: Nangeli and Mulachiparambu.' *Margins: A Blog by Ajaysekhar*. August 2012, http://ajaysekher.net/2012/08/28/nangeli-mulachiparambu-breasttax-travancore/

185. Sengupta, Somini. 'Is Public Romance a Right? The *Kama Sutra* Doesn't Say.' *The New York Times*. January 2006, http://www.nytimes.com/2006/01/04/world/asia/is-public-romance-a-right-the-kama-sutra-doesnt-say.html

186. Seth, Leila. *Talking of Justice: People's Rights in Modern India*. New Delhi: Aleph Book Company, 2014.

187. Shah, Bulleh. *Sufi Lyrics*. Trans. Christopher Shackle. Cambridge, MA: Murty Classical Library of India, Harvard University Press, 2015.

188. Shah, Waris. 'The Adventures of Hir and Ranjha, Recounted in Panjabi by Waris Shah and translated into English by Charles Frederick Usborne, 1874—1919', http://www.casas.org.uk/papers/pdfpapers/hir.pdf

189. Shaikh, Sadiyya. *Sufi Narratives of Intimacy: Ibn Arabī, Gender, and Sexuality*. Chapel Hill: University of North Carolina Press, 2012.

190. Shakespeare, William. *The Norton Shakespeare*, Stephen Greenblatt et al, eds.: New York: W.W. Norton and Co., 2004.

191. Sharar, Abdul Halim. *Lucknow: The Last Phase of an Oriental*

Culture. Trans. and ed. E.S. Harcourt and Fakhir Hussain. Delhi: Oxford University Press, 1994.

192. Sharma Ugra, Pandey Bechan. *Chocolate and Other Writings on Male Homoeroticism.* Trans. Ruth Vanita. Durham: Duke University Press, 2009.

193. Sherrow, Victoria. *For Appearance' Sake: The Historical Encyclopedia of Good Looks, Beauty, and Grooming.* Connecticut: Greenwood, 2001.

194. Shukla-Bhatt, Neelima. *Narasinha Mehta of Gujarat: A Legacy of Bhakti in Songs and Stories.* New York: Oxford University Press, 2014.

195. 'SI Goes for Same-Sex Marriage.' Tribune News Service, April 23, 2017, http://www.tribuneindia.com/news/punjab/si-goes-for-same-sex-marriage/396251.html

196. Singh, Dhiraj. 'Sex-Agenarians', *Outlook.* 31 December, 2001, https://www.outlookindia.com/magazine/story/sex-agenarians/214187

197. Singh, Khushwant, and Humra Quraishi. *On Love and Sex: Selected Writings.* New Delhi: Rupa Publications India Pvt. Ltd, 2014.

198. Sinha, Ashish. 'Gays Are Still Men of Dishonour in the Army.' *India Today,* July 2009, http://indiatoday.intoday.in/story/Gays+are+still+men+of+dishonour+in+the+Army/1/50299.html

199. Smith, Paul, trans. *Amir Khusrau: Life & Poems* Volume 1. CreateSpace Independent Publishing Platform, 2014.

200. Srinivasan, Pavithra. 'Power of Shunya.' *The Hindu,* September 2014, http://www.thehindu.com/features/kids/power-of-shunya/article6445007.ece

201. Śrīnātha, 'Śiva in the Forest of Pines,' in Velcheru Narayana

Rao and David Shulman, trans. and ed., *Classical Telugu Poetry: An Anthology*. New Delhi: Oxford University Press, 2002, 182–193.

202. Srivastava, Sanjay, ed. *Sexuality Studies*. New Delhi: Oxford University Press, 2013.

203. Stewart, Neil. 'Imperialism and the Indian Army.' *Labour Monthly*, May 1957, pp. 155–159, https://www.marxists.org/history/international/comintern/sections/britain/periodicals/labour_monthly/1947/05/1947-05-indianarmy.htm

204. Stone, Lawrence. *The Family, Sex and Marriage in England (1500-1800)*. London: Penguin, 1990.

205. 'Swami Vivekananda's Quotes on Sex.' *Swami Vivekananda's Quotes*, December 2013, http://www.swamivivekanandaquotes.org/2013/12/swami-vivekanandas-quotes-on-sex.html

206. Thadani, Giti. *Sakhiyani: Lesbian Desire in Ancient and Modern India*. London: Cassell, 1996.

207. 'The Untold Story of the Alleged Mass Rapes by the Indian Army in Kunan Poshpora.' *Youth Ki Awaaz*, Nov. 2013, https://www.youthkiawaaz.com/2013/11/untold-story-alleged-mass-rapes-indian-army-kunan-poshpora/

208. Tiwari, Nityanand. 'Homosexuality in India: Review of Literatures.' *Social Science Research Network*, 2010, https://ssrn.com/abstract=1679203

209. Tolstoy, Lev. *The Kreutzer Sonata and Other Stories*. Trans. David McDuff and Paul Foote. London: Penguin Classics, 2008.

210. Trivedi, Ira. *India in Love: Marriage and Sexuality in the 21st Century*. New Delhi: Aleph Book Company, 2014.

211. Troll, Christian W., ed. *Muslim Shrines in India: Their Character, History and Significance*. New Delhi: Oxford University Press, 1992.

212. Valmiki. *Ramayana*. Trans. Arshia Sattar. Penguin Global, 2010.

213. Vanita, Ruth, and Saleem Kidwai, eds. *Same-Sex Love in India: A Literary History*. New Delhi: Penguin Books India, 2008.

214. Vanita, Ruth. 'Sexuality.' *Brill's Encyclopedia of Hinduism*, Ed. Knut A. Jacobsen et al., 2012.

215. Vanita, Ruth. *Gender, Sex, and the City: Urdu Rekhti Poetry in India, 1780-1870*. New York: Palgrave Macmillan, 2012.

216. Vanita, Ruth. *Love's Rite: Same-sex Marriage in India and the West*. New Delhi: Penguin Books India, 2005.

217. Vanita, Ruth. *Queering India: Same-Sex Love and Eroticism in Indian Culture and Society*. New York: Routledge, 2002.

218. Vasudev, Sadhguru Jaggi. 'What Is Tantra Yoga? Definitely Orgasmic, But Not Sexual.' *The Isha Blog*, May 2013, http://isha.sadhguru.org/blog/yoga-meditation/demystifying-yoga/the-truth-about-tantra/

219. Vatsyayana. *Kamasutra*. Trans. Wendy Doniger and Sudhir Kakar, New York: Oxford University Press, 2009.

220. Vatsyayana. *Kamasutra*. Trans. A.N.D Haksar. New York: Penguin Classics, 2011.

221. Vembu, Venkatesan. 'Save Our Savita Bhabhi.' *DNA*, July 2009, http://www.dnaindia.com/analysis/column-save-our-savita-bhabhi-1270664

222. Vyasa. *Mahabharata*. Ed. Krishna Dharma. New Delhi: Torchlight Publishing, 2008.

223. Wald, Erica. *Vice in the Barracks: Medicine, the Military and the Making of Colonial India, 1780-1868*. London: Palgrave Macmillan UK, 2014.

224. Walker, Benjamin, ed. *Hindu World: An Encyclopedic Survey of Hinduism*. New Delhi: Munshiram Manoharlal, 1983.

225. Ward, Tim. *Arousing the Goddess: Sex and Love in the Buddhist Ruins of India.* Rhinebeck, NY: Monkfish Book Pub. Co., 1996.

226. Watsa, Mahinder. *It's Normal!* New Delhi: Penguin Books India, 2015.

227. White, David Gordon. 'Yoga, Brief History of an Idea', in D.G. White, ed. *Yoga in Practice*, Princeton University Press, 2011, pp. 1–23, https://press.princeton.edu/chapters/i9565.pdf

228. White, David Gordon. 'Yoga in Transformation', in Diamond, Debra, curator and ed. *Yoga: The Art of Transformation.* Washington, D.C.: Arthur M. Sackler Gallery, Smithsonian Institution, 2013, pp. 35–45.

229. Wilde, Oscar. *The Ballad of Reading Gaol and Other Poems.* London: Penguin Classics, 2010.

230. Yadava, Rajendra. *Strangers on the Roof.* Trans. Ruth Vanita. New Delhi: Penguin Books India, 2014.

231. Yesudas, R.N. *A People's Revolt in Travancore: A Backward Class Movement for Social Freedom.* Trivandrum: Manju Pub. House, Kerala Historical Society, 1975.

INDEX

CPSIA information can be obtained
at www.ICGtesting.com
Printed in the USA
FSHW022225010821
83725FS